THE SMALL BUSINESS BOOK

THE SMALL BUSINESS BOOK

SIXTH EDITION

A New Zealand Guide for the 21st Century

Leith Oliver
John English

ALLEN&UNWIN
SYDNEY•MELBOURNE•AUCKLAND•LONDON

The information contained in this book is, to the best of the authors' and the publisher's knowledge, true and correct. Every effort has been made to ensure its accuracy. Neither the authors nor the publisher accepts any liability for any loss, injury or damage caused to any person acting as a result of information in this book nor for any errors or omissions.

This edition published in 2012
First edition published in 1993

Allen & Unwin
Sydney, Melbourne, Auckland, London

83 Alexander Street
Crows Nest NSW 2065
Australia
Phone: (61 2) 8425 0100
Fax: (61 2) 9906 2218
Email: info@allenandunwin.com
Web: www.allenandunwin.com

National Library of New Zealand Cataloguing-in-Publication Data

Oliver, Leith.
The small business book : a New Zealand guide for the 21st century /
Leith Oliver and John English. 6th ed.
Previous ed.: Crows Nest, N.S.W. : Allen & Unwin, 2007.
Includes index.
ISBN 978-1-877505-12-6
1. Small business—New Zealand—Management. 2. New business
enterprises—New Zealand. I. English, John W., 1944- II. Title.
658.0220993—dc 22

ISBN 978 1 877505 12 6

Index by Sue Jarvis
Set in 11/14 pt Adobe Caslon by Midland Typesetters, Australia
Printed in Australia by Pegasus Media & Logistics

20 19 18

Contents

Part D: Operations management 267

List of figures and tables

Part A
Getting started

Part A introduces the field of small business in New Zealand. Chapter 1 examines the pros and cons of self-employment and takes you through the start-up process. Chapter 2 continues with the evaluation of business opportunities and the sources of initial ideas for a business. Chapter 3 provides information on the assistance that is available to small business in the form of advisory services and grants. Chapter 4 covers some of the legal requirements for running a business in New Zealand. Chapter 5 is a discussion of franchising in New Zealand and Chapter 6 describes the process of developing a business plan.

1 Getting on the launch pad

The purpose of this chapter is to consider the process of becoming self-employed and the early steps in starting up. We begin by identifying the pros and cons of self-employment, the personal characteristics that have been found to be associated with success, and the role of management skills and experience. Then we look at a typical sequence of events leading to a business start-up, establishing a new business and buying an existing business. The chapter concludes with a discussion about the risk of failure.

Pros and cons of self-employment

Competition is the essential ingredient in the New Zealand business environment. It encourages businesses to make efficient use of resources. People will patronise efficient businesses rather than their inefficient rivals, so the efficient firms flourish and the inefficient ones go out of business. In this way success and prosperity are earned by those firms that best serve their customers. Engaging in competition means that you must face the fact that the operation of a small business is one of the toughest ways there is to make a living. Before you make the decision to become self-employed, you need to seriously examine the advantages and disadvantages of organising and operating a small business.

Advantages

- You can be your own boss, you can be independent, and you can exercise your own talents and capabilities.
- You will have the chance to make money—maybe even a great deal of money—and you will not be dependent on a fixed wage or salary.
- You will have the opportunity to achieve a feeling of personal worth, accomplishment and recognition.
- You can develop your own ideas, products and services.
- You will be able to work at something you enjoy by doing personally satisfying work, and perhaps succeeding where others have not.
- You may achieve economic security for yourself and your family.
- You may be able to provide something of value to the community.

Disadvantages

- You can fail and lose your money as well as the money your friends or relatives may have invested in your business.
- You will have to work hard, perhaps as long as 15 hours a day for many weeks at a time, meaning that time for family and friends will be difficult to find.
- Your income may be uncertain and could fluctuate tremendously as a result of factors that you cannot control.
- You will face the unrelenting pressure of having to make decisions and solve problems that may call for expertise beyond your current capabilities.
- You will still have a boss: in fact, you will have many bosses, including customers, suppliers, government agencies and your banker.
- You may eventually hate your business in the same way that other people hate their job, and you may find it difficult to get out without incurring an unacceptable loss.

Personal characteristics and success

Small businesses are frequently in the hands of men and women who are the rebels of the business world. They have a highly developed sense of independence, a strong sense of enterprise, and often a dislike of conformity and routine. Is there something about successful small business operators that makes them different from other people?

Research studies from all over the world have attempted to identify the personal characteristics that result in a successful small business operator. While certain personal characteristics are found more frequently among successful small business operators, it is simply not possible to *predict* success based on them. Here are some of the personal characteristics that have been found to be associated with successful small business operators:

Drive and energy	Self-confidence
Long-term involvement	Persistence
Goal-setting	Sense of time
Moderate risk-taking	Dealing with failure
Using feedback	Initiative
Tolerating uncertainty	Using outside resources
Innovation	Assertiveness
Opportunity recognition	Ambition
Competitiveness	Independence
Resourcefulness	Determination
Task orientation	Optimism

If you possessed all of these characteristics, then you would most certainly be Superman or Wonder Woman. Neither Superman nor Wonder Woman, however, was a small-business operator. There is tremendous diversity in the types of small business and even greater diversity in the characteristics and motives of the people who successfully own and operate them. What really matters is a passion for what you want to do, how you feel about yourself and whether you think your personality is suited to the particular type of business you want to operate. Self-development exercise A at the end of this section will help you gain some insight into your personal characteristics and the motivating factors behind your desire for self-employment.

Management skills and experience

To become a successful small business operator you need to be able to wear many hats. A good knowledge of one or two elements of business management is simply not enough. What you need before you can realistically contemplate organising and operating your own business is well-rounded management skills together with some hands-on experience in the line of business you want to enter. To the extent that you lack these prerequisites, your chances for survival and prosperity will quickly diminish.

Management skills fall into three categories: marketing, finance, and operations. Within each category, the need for each skill varies depending on the nature of your business. Many, but not necessarily all, of the items that follow will apply to you and your business. Do you know what needs to be done? Have you had any experience in doing it? They include:

Marketing skills

Business location	Sales forecasting
Product life cycle	Competitor evaluation
Marketing research	Guarantees and service

Marketing strategy	Distribution channels
Product positioning	Packaging and presentation
Store layout	Personal selling
Pricing and discounts	Advertising and promotion
Credit terms	Merchandising

Financial skills

Profit planning	Profit and loss statements
Budgeting	Balance sheet
Cash flow management	Ratio analysis
Break-even analysis	Debtor control
Contribution analysis	Creditor control
Book-keeping	Cost control
Types of finance	Payroll
Applying for finance	Tax planning
Banking relationship	Using an accountant

Operating skills

Purchasing	Improving productivity
Stock control	Quality control
Warehousing and storage	Scheduling and workflow
Plant and equipment	Transport and freight
Recruitment and selection	Computer systems
Regulations and awards	Negotiating
Staff training	Problem-solving
Supervising	Decision-making

The best time to get your management training is *before* launching into business. A thorough preparation for self-employment is just as important as any other form of apprenticeship and you should be prepared to devote a significant amount of time to it. The best way to gain experience is to work in the type of business in which you intend to become self-employed.

If you are already in business and your management skills are weak, then you need to do something about closing the gap before it is too late. Finding the time to attend a training program may not be easy, and getting hands-on experience in another firm may not be practical. More expedient and effective alternatives may include employing people with complementary skills, taking on a partner with complementary skills, engaging outside consultants and advisers, or seeking assistance from support agencies and organisations. Chapter 3 will help you to identify sources of support.

Start-up sequence

The reasons that entice people into self-employment can vary enormously. However, most individuals typically proceed through a similar sequence of events before launching into business. Thinking about each of the steps below in relation to your situation may help you to clarify some of the issues.

Examine your motivation for going into business

Although thousands of new businesses begin each year, owning and operating a small business is not for everyone. The decision to become self-employed needs to be based on a realistic evaluation of your personal objectives, your individual talents and your personality. If you go into business without an honest evaluation of your motives, you run the risk that you will find yourself unhappy and disillusioned.

Choose a business that suits you

The type of business you choose is a highly personal matter. Factors to consider include your experience, your talents and your interests. Experience plays a big part in understanding the market and avoiding costly mistakes. If you have a particular talent, then you may want to choose a business that capitalises on it. A deep interest in a particular type of business is also important because it will help to sustain you through the long hours and hard work.

Evaluate the feasibility of your chosen business

At this point you have examined your personal motivation for going into business and you have chosen an exciting possibility. Now you are anxious to get started. A common mistake is to blindly rush into business without adequately evaluating the feasibility of the idea. You need answers to the following types of questions.

- Is there enough demand for what you want to sell? Have you done some market research or are you just guessing and hoping?
- Can the business generate enough cash to pay its own expenses and leave you with a profit? How long can you keep going if it doesn't?
- Do you have enough money to get started? If not, can you realistically expect to be able to borrow enough money?
- What is the worst thing that could happen if the business fails? Could you cope with this?

A business is financially feasible if it can produce the level of income that you require from it. One approach is to determine the amount of sales necessary to achieve the required level of income, and then investigate whether or not the business is likely to achieve that level of sales. The following steps demonstrate how to determine the required sales.

1   What are your annual living expenses?
    Say, $50 000
2   What is the gross income (before tax) that is required to leave you with $50 000?
    At 30% tax rate = $50 000 × 1.43 = $71 500
3   How much money will be invested in assets for the business?
    Say, $50 000
4   What rate of return should you get on the assets given the riskiness of small business?
    Say, 15%
5   How much return should you receive annually? Step 3 times step 4.
    $50 000 × 15% = $7500
6   What income do you require from this business? Step 2 plus step 5.
    $71 500 + $7500 = $79 000
7   For this type of business what is the average net profit as a percentage of sales? This figure can be obtained from your local small business agency, a trade association or your accountant.
    Say, 10%
8   What amount of sales are necessary to generate the level of income you require? Item 6 divided by item 7.
    $79 000 ÷ 10% = $790 000

The business will be financially feasible if it can achieve sales of $790 000 per year. Now we need to determine whether this amount of sales is likely or not. The following steps demonstrate how to investigate the sales potential.

1   How many households are in the target-market area and what are their characteristics? This information is available from Statistics New Zealand.
    Say, 5000 households
2   What is the average weekly household expenditure for this type of product or service? Consult the Statistics New Zealand *Household Expenditure Survey.*
    Say, $10.52 per week or about $547 per year
3   What is the total potential for sales of this product or service in this target market? Step 1 times step 2.
    5000 households × $547 per year = $2 735 000 per year
4   What are the actual sales for this product or service in this target market? To

determine how much of the market is currently held by competitors, consult the Statistics New Zealand *Business Activity Statistics.*
Say, $850 000 per year

5 What is the potential for sales in your business? Step 3 minus step 4.
$2 735 000 – $850 000 = $1 885 000 per year

This business requires minimum annual sales of $790 000 to be financially feasible and we have estimated potential sales of $1 885 000. These are rough estimates, but they are enough to suggest that this idea is worth exploring further.

List all your start-up requirements

There are many requirements that need to be attended to before you can actually get started. Here are some examples:

- Choosing a legal form of organisation and establishing a legal entity
- Identifying suitable premises and negotiating a lease
- Finding out what permits, licences, rules and regulations apply to your proposed business
- Locating suitable suppliers and negotiating supply agreements
- Determining what type of records you will need to keep to comply with the reporting requirements of local and national agencies, including the Inland Revenue Department
- Identifying the risks for which you are responsible and what you need to cover by insurance.

Many mistakes can be made during the start-up sequence. Here are some of the errors you should try to avoid:

- Thinking that others, such as your accountant or an advisory agency, will do your planning for you
- Entering into an informal, verbal partnership that later becomes unworkable because of misunderstandings about money, family interference or disagreements about work responsibilities
- Paying licences and other fees or entering into contracts such as a lease before being certain that there is enough money to start the business
- Discovering that everything costs more and takes longer than you expected.

Develop a business plan

A business plan contains your strategy for the development and operation of your business. It is a blueprint for making the transition from an initial idea to a successful enterprise. It is the result of meticulous research, careful deliberation and a vision about the results you expect to achieve. It represents concrete plans for creating a competitive advantage and exploiting it. A business plan identifies the characteristics of the market and the marketing strategies that will be employed. It includes plans for the facilities, staffing and procedures to operate the business together with financial forecasts that project profits and cash flow. Chapter 6 contains more information about developing a business plan.

Establishing a new business

A new business of an *existing* type is justified if either the market has expanded and is not adequately served, or the present suppliers are clearly failing to meet the needs of customers. A new business of a *new* type is justified if a new product or service exists that the public will buy. Establishing a new business is a high-risk option. There are fewer factors that you know for sure and greater uncertainty about how to begin. Errors of judgement can be costly, especially if the business is organised around an entirely new product or service. On the other hand, a new business can fill a gap in the marketplace, with exceptional rewards for the adventurous small business operator.

There are a number of advantages if you start a business from scratch. You can match the business to your own goals. It is easier to innovate when you have the flexibility to select your target market, product and service strategy, competitive strategy, location and facilities. You can design the business around the policies and procedures that you select and you can train the staff your own way. You also avoid the 'goodwill' expense of buying an existing business along with the possibility of unknown or contingent liabilities. Moreover, you will not inherit any pre-existing ill will from previous customers, suppliers, creditors or employees.

Starting a new business also has some disadvantages. It carries the highest risk of failure because there is less certainty about market demand. It takes time and energy to create an image, build patronage, work the bugs out of new systems and procedures, and reach a break-even level of sales. Meanwhile, staff need to be found, contacts developed with suppliers, and a marketing strategy implemented. There are the added risks that investment capital will be difficult to obtain, unexpected competition may emerge, and potential customers may be more difficult to attract than you anticipate. New businesses always run a significant risk that the time-lag between investment and cash flow will be too long. Starting a business from scratch requires particular attention to a number of critical start-up factors, including:

- Identifying a target market and its basic needs
- Assessing the size of the target market and its ability to sustain a profitable business
- Determining the amount and availability of start-up capital

- Devising a product strategy that matches the target market
- Devising a competitive strategy that can gain and protect a share of the market
- Finding a suitable location and physical facilities
- Selecting and training staff
- Obtaining equipment, fixtures and supplies
- Determining and meeting legal obligations
- Developing a carefully considered business plan.

Buying an existing business

Buying a going concern has the initial advantage that you will not only receive immediate income from sales to existing customers, but you will also save the time and effort needed to equip and stock the business yourself. A successful business will have a proven location, established relationships with suppliers and creditors, and existing employees. Buying a going concern as a package may turn out to be cheaper than trying to assemble all the bits and pieces yourself. It is much simpler to finance a single-purchase transaction, and a proven track record makes an existing business easier to finance. When you purchase a business, the risk of failure may be less than if you tried to start the same business from scratch.

There are also potential disadvantages in buying an existing business. Initially, you are stuck with the previous owner's bad decisions. For example, the existing stock may be unsaleable, the choice of equipment and fixtures may be outmoded, some of the staff may not be suitable, or the location may prove to be poor. You could pay too much for the business if you misjudge its value, and there could be unexpected expenses if the business turns out to be run-down. If the previous owner had a bad reputation, you are likely to inherit ill will from some customers and poor morale among staff. There are two very important parts to the process. They are valuation and negotiation.

Valuation

When you buy an existing business, the price you pay should be based on its abilty to earn a profit. The first step in assessing the profit of a business is for you and your accountant to analyse past financial statements and income-tax records. Have sales and profits been increasing or decreasing? What has been the rate of return on the owner's equity? You can use the business performance model in Chapter 7 to help you analyse the seller's financial information.

If possible, obtain an industry profile for this type of business. A comparison of the seller's figures with an industry profile will uncover any material discrepancies that need to be explained. This also helps you to discover any operating problems that may affect your decision to buy the business or how much you are willing to pay for it. Ask to see the GST returns and compare them with the sales and costs stated in the figures you have been given.

There are two basic methods used to determine the value of a business. The first method is based on expectations of future profit and return on investment. It is called the *capitalised value* method. The second method is valuing the business on the basis of the *appraised value* of the assets.

Capitalised value

Capitalised value is the amount of money that you would need to invest at a specified rate of interest in order to earn an income equal to the profit potential of the business. The interest rate used is called the *capitalisation rate*. Capitalised value is found by dividing the annual profit by the capitalisation rate.

For example, suppose you have projected that a business is capable of earning $25 000 per year after paying all of its expenses including your own salary but before interest and tax. If the investment in this business is as safe as a bank term deposit, you could use the term-deposit rate of about 5 per cent to capitalise the profits and arrive at the following value for the business.

$$\text{Capitalised value} = \frac{\$25\ 000}{5\%} = \$500\ 000$$

No small business, however, is as safe as a bank term deposit. Capitalisation rates ranging from 20 per cent to 50 per cent are more realistic. If we use a capitalisation rate of 25 per cent for this business, its capitalised value drops to $100 000.

Two factors are important in determining capitalised value. First, it is very sensitive to the capitalisation rate used. Be sure that you use a capitalisation rate that fully reflects the amount of risk involved. Second, keep in mind that you are valuing long-term profits. If there is a chance that the profits will not be sustained over the long term, then you need to increase your capitalisation rate to compensate for this risk.

Appraised value

Some small businesses are purchased on the basis of the net value of the assets to be transferred. The process consists of establishing what assets are going to be transferred and appraising their current market value. Generally, the assets to be transferred are stock, sales and office supplies, fixtures and equipment, and goodwill. If the business sells on credit, you will have to consider whether or not you want to take over the debtors—the people or firms who owe money to the business. Since none of the assets are likely to be new, you will need to take their remaining useful life into consideration when you value them. It is important to be sure that stock is saleable and debtors are collectable.

If the asking price is greater than the value of the assets, the difference is an intangible asset called *goodwill*. Goodwill represents the ability of the business to earn greater profits than if you started the same business from scratch. The value of goodwill should not be any greater than the difference between the capitalised value of the business (method one) and the value of the assets (method two). Since few small businesses that are put up for sale are genuinely producing extraordinary profits, the value of goodwill is usually not very high.

Negotiation

The aim of the negotiation process is a formal contract covering the details of the purchase. There are a number of matters over which you and the seller may have differences. For example, the seller is interested in the best price, getting paid as quickly as possible, favourable tax treatment on gains from the sale (they want the assets to be valued low and the goodwill valued high), avoiding any continuing liabilities associated with the business, and avoiding any contract terms that are not in their interests. You, on the other hand, will be looking for the lowest price, extended payment terms, a favourable tax basis for resale and depreciation (you want the assets to be valued high and the goodwill valued low), and warranties that will give you extra protection. Depending on your relative negotiating positions, the final contract for purchase may reflect either compromise by both of you or capitulation by one of you.

The central negotiating issue is usually price. What is actually paid for a business can be quite different from what it is worth. In other words, price and value are not the same thing. The price paid reflects the negotiating positions of the parties. Is the seller's desire to sell stronger than your desire to buy? This might be true if the seller is selling because of age, health or financial reasons, and the value you receive may be greater than the price you pay. On the other hand, if you are unable to raise enough money to purchase the business, the seller may offer to accept deferred payment if you will agree to a higher price. In this case, you are paying a price that is greater than the value of the business in order to get vendor finance.

When you find the right business, try not to fall in love at first sight. An emotional decision may cost you dearly. Make sure you know exactly what the vendor is selling before you make an offer. Decide what the business is worth to you and be cold-blooded about negotiating the best price. Go back for a second look and a third look before you make an offer, then be patient and let your offer lie on the table until the vendor shows a willingness to negotiate.

Have your solicitor check to ensure there are no mortgages, back taxes, or other creditor claims against the assets you are buying. It is not usually a good idea to assume any of the seller's liabilities. Occasionally, however, these can represent a source of finance for you. If you do assume any of the seller's liabilities, their value must be subtracted from the asking price to arrive at the net price for the business.

A number of new problems will emerge when you ask your solicitor to exchange contracts. At this point, you and the seller will probably have reached agreement on price, assumption of liabilities, and terms of payment. To protect your interests, however, your solicitor will advise you to include a number of other matters in the contract.

Questions to consider include:

- What if the seller's financial statements turn out to be inaccurate or false?
- What if the seller has undisclosed liabilities that have not been taken into account in arriving at the price?
- What if some of the assets that you are purchasing do not actually belong to the seller?
- What if substantial changes occur to the business between the exchange of contracts and settlement?
- What if the seller decides to open a competing business next door?

These questions reflect the uncertainty of your position as a buyer. It is important to get the protection you need formally written into the contract.

Risk of failure

Small business failures involve a mixture of forced receiverships, voluntary closures or transfer of ownership. Only a small proportion of failed businesses end in receivership. The vast majority simply fail to measure up to the owner's expectations and are either sold or closed.

Receivership generally results from a lack of cash flow. A serious shortfall in cash flow prevents the business from paying its bills on time. Eventually, the creditors are forced to take action in order to protect the debts owed to them. The business is closed, the assets are liquidated, and the proceeds are used to satisfy some of the debts.

Small businesses that do not meet the owner's profit expectations are not failures from a legal point of view but they have still failed to survive. These businesses lack the degree of success that justifies their continued operation. They are weak businesses that could become outright failures if the owners do not cut their losses and abandon them. A number of research studies have revealed that many of these businesses falter because the owner's motives are misguided. Here are some examples.

- A desire to be one's own boss—some individuals do not succeed because they underestimate the commitment that a small business requires and the impact this commitment will have on their lifestyle.
- A desire for financial independence—some aspiring small business operators do not realise that along with the opportunity for financial independence goes the risk of losing everything they own.
- A dislike of working with others—if an individual does not work well with others, then it is going to affect how they get on with their customers, employees and suppliers.

- A disdain for bureaucracy and paperwork—with increasing regulation, paperwork has become a significant and unavoidable part of the life of every small business operator.
- A desire for creative freedom—everybody wants to be able to do their own thing. However, the 'thing' needs to be a product or service that appeals to a large enough market to enable the business to succeed.

There are a number of other reasons why small businesses may eventually fall short of the owner's expectations and are abandoned. Here are some examples.

- Some businesses do not succeed because the owner relies on the advice of family and friends. The advice is generally offered with the best of intentions but it can be coloured by a close personal relationship. Someone close to you does not want to tell you that your product is not up to scratch, your service is inferior or your prices are too high. Family and friends are not likely to offer the kind of hard-nosed business advice that you need.
- Some businesses do not succeed because the small business operator gets worn out. To run your own business you need to be energetic and a self-starter. Over half of small business operators work more than 60 hours per week. You need to make a serious commitment to hard work and long hours in order to give your business a good chance for success.
- Some businesses do not succeed because they exert too much pressure on the owner's family. There is a conflict between what is best for the family and what is best for the business. The two most sensitive issues are time and money. There is never enough of either. In order to give both the business and the family the best opportunity to prosper, a small business operator needs to strike a mature balance between conflicting pressures.
- Some businesses do not succeed because the owner is not fully aware of the nature of the marketplace. The owner may overestimate the number of potential customers or underestimate the size and strength of the competition. Even when a good market exists, it is necessary to understand it thoroughly in order to target customers effectively.
- Some businesses do not succeed because the owner does not appreciate the importance of timely and accurate financial information. Financial information is the scorecard that tells a small business operator how well they are doing. This information is important for every business, but it is critical for a new business.

The risk of failure is real and the evidence tells us that it is greatest during the first year of operation. We also know that there are many reasons for small business failures.

However, it is clear that the vast majority of early failures are caused by issues relating to the small business operator's personal circumstances and lack of business ability rather than by external factors. There is also an element of luck, which means that success may elude you no matter how carefully you do your homework.

You should carefully consider the consequences of failure before you decide to become self-employed. If you fail, you will lose some money, maybe even all of your money, if you do not take some precautions before you start. You may feel bad for a while because your self-esteem may be damaged. There may even be some lingering ill will on the part of former partners, suppliers, employees or customers. The independent small business operator is respected for what he or she is attempting to do: the person who tries and fails is not finished. People learn from their mistakes and make a go of it the next time around. If you honestly want to go into business and you are doing it with realistic expectations, then do it now!

2 Discovering business opportunities

There are several myths about the ways in which the initial idea for a new business unfolds. One myth is that there is some procedure by which you can reliably search for and discover all the good business ideas. It simply doesn't happen that way. Good ideas tend to emerge unexpectedly or you stumble upon them inadvertently. What is important is that you are able to recognise a good idea when you see it. Another myth is that a good idea will ensure success. However, there have been thousands of businesses based on good ideas that went broke. New ventures take a great deal of time and much effort to succeed. A good idea needs to be supported by a thoroughly researched feasibility study followed by a carefully developed business strategy before it stands a reasonable chance of becoming a successful business operation.

One popular myth is that you must discover a unique idea, or come up with a new invention involving some enormous leap of the imagination. However, there is simply no correlation between commercial success and the creative or technological brilliance on which an idea is based. In fact, the vast majority of new business ideas are no more than excellent copies of other successful operations.

A business opportunity is not a guarantee of success but it does represent a likely prospect for creating a successful business. In this chapter, the ways in which change creates new business opportunities is investigated and different types of business opportunities are examined.

How change creates opportunities

Change is nothing new and we adapt to it daily without much thought. If we stop to consider the changes taking place around us we will discover clues about emerging demand for new products and services. In the absence of change, existing businesses do well because they have proven products and services, smooth operations, established business models and loyal customers. When conditions change, however, confusion and disruption create gaps in the marketplace that open up new business opportunities. Change produces an environment that is actually loaded in favour of new players because they tend to be more flexible and adaptive than existing businesses. Keeping abreast of these changes means gaining some perspective about shifts in demographic, lifestyle, social, technological, political, regulatory and economic trends. The objective is to recognise how changes in these trends manifest themselves as new business opportunities.

Demographic trends

Demographic trends are used to answer questions about the population. For example, are the number of households in a particular area increasing or decreasing? Is the population mix getting older or younger? Is household income rising or falling? Statistics New Zealand and other agencies report demographic information for population size, age distribution, geographic distribution, family structure, employment, race and ethnicity, education, health and welfare, literacy and spending patterns. These trends are closely linked to consumer purchasing behaviour. The number of people in each age group is reflected in different spending patterns including the tremendous influence children have over adult spending decisions. Gender demographics reveal the preferences between men and women and have been used to uncover opportunities in clothing, soft drinks, non-prescription medications, toiletries, magazines and even cigarettes. Race and ethnicity demographics are used to discover opportunities in food, music, clothing and cosmetics. Population and income levels across geographic areas are used to measure market density and to anticipate changes in spending power and the desire for certain lifestyles.

Marital status and the presence and ages of children, a characteristic called the family life cycle, are used to reveal opportunities in housing, appliances, food and beverages, automobiles and recreational products. There has been a decline in the traditional family partly due to fewer marriages, higher divorce rates and couples having fewer children. There are now more one- or two-person households than ever before. The birth rate is declining in the 15–29 year age group and rising in the 30–39 year age group. The number of one-parent families is also rising. These demographic trends are reflected in shifting family spending patterns.

The post-World War II 'baby boom' and the progression of this generation through their lives has been an abundant source of business opportunities. As they approach retirement, the baby boomers bring with them a strong desire to live well past the age of their parents and maintain a healthy lifestyle in the process. Life expectancy has been increasing at about 2.5 years per decade and the over-50 population will more than double during the next 35 years. Seniors control nearly half of discretionary spending, so the combination of demographics and dollars suggests that many business opportunities will emerge in areas like home services, health services, travel, recreation and retirement counselling. At the other end of the age spectrum are New Zealanders aged six to thirteen. They represent increasing spending power because of the trend towards older parents with higher disposable incomes and smaller families with increased spending per child. They have sophisticated tastes, they are avid consumers, they are heavily influenced by the media and they are technologically savvy.

Lifestyle trends

Thanks to globalisation and rising incomes, consumerism plays a big part in the lifestyle of many people. New Zealanders who want a way of life that relies on consumer goods and services will continue to generate new business opportunities. Lifestyle is closely aligned with consumers' motives for making purchases such as appearance, convenience, affiliation, status, safety or health.

One consequence of the modern world is that most of us feel pressed for time so we substitute products and services to compensate for lack of time. Nearly one-third of lunches are eaten on the run fuelled by the fast-food industry. Speed dating is having a major impact on the dating scene. More and more people are condensing a holiday into a weekend or short trip resulting in more spontaneous travel for shorter periods. Convenience is also an increasingly important feature of the goods and services we consume and the ways in which we buy them. Personal shoppers, home-cleaning services and dog walkers are examples of the trend towards convenience. Many consumers are willing to pay extra for convenience in order to save time for other pursuits. Understanding the effect of time compression on lifestyle is one of the keys to unlocking new business opportunities.

Another interesting trend is consumers' loss of trust in food authorities who keep changing the 'facts' about nutrition. We can all read the labels now but we no longer trust what we read. We do not want eating to be a stressful or difficult task. We want to buy food we know is 'authentic'. Authentic means not made in a laboratory, it means safe, it means reliable and it means trustworthy. One symptom of this trend is consumers willing to pay a premium for organic produce simply to get peace of mind. Another consequence is consumers seeking more information about the origin of their food, such as where it was grown and how was it handled.

The 1990s saw a huge change in lifestyle emphasising physical fitness and healthy living. Since that time, many people have been taking responsibility for their own health by challenging the traditional authority of the doctor and seeking more information and other options. The trend toward bottled water is also driven by increased concern for health and wellbeing. However, now it has taken on symbolic values as well so we have water bars, recipes for rainwater, regional waters, branded waters and spas based on pure-water locations.

New trends in shopping are emerging. The weekly shopping trip is on the decline as more people shop every day. More men are becoming grocery shoppers. Why are they taking a greater interest in food? Is it because more men are living alone or is it a result of more women in the workforce with less time for shopping? At the same time, more women are becoming interested in renovation and shop at hardware stores. Why is this happening? What do they want? How could these trends translate into new business opportunities?

Social trends

New business opportunities emerge from changes in our society. These include changes in value systems, accepted norms of behaviour, approaches to sexuality, religion and spirituality, pursuit of wealth and possessions, and shifting aspirations, fears, desires and anxieties. For example, how many parents no longer allow their children to ride a bicycle without supervision because they have a nagging fear of potential dangers lurking outside the home? This trend may not be good for sales of children's bikes, but the upside is new business opportunities for supervised play groups, structured extracurricular activities and organised sports events.

Consumer interest in 'green' or environmentally friendly products has become pervasive. Together with growing environmental awareness is a shift towards non-material experiences that affect the ways in which consumers spend their money. Rather than focusing solely on price and quality, many buyers consider ethical, religious and other beliefs in their spending decisions. For example, the use of sweatshop labour affects spending decisions for some consumers when they buy clothing and footwear. Similarly, some consumers will only buy fair-trade coffee.

Women continue to gain social, political and economic power propelled by changing values and social attitudes. These changes have been accelerated by more women entering higher education and the growth in the number of couples who are both in paid employment. Another reason for the increasing economic power of women is the decline in the manufacturing sector and the rise of service industries. The qualities most often attributed to women are also those associated with the skills needed to succeed in customer-focused and service-oriented businesses. These changes have also led to opportunities for products and services that are 'feminised' or that assist women to balance the demands of career and family.

Migration into New Zealand and migration between different regions in New Zealand shows no sign of slowing. The movement to coastal areas for a sea change and to country areas for a tree change is driving urbanisation in smaller communities. With shifting population comes increased demand for services and cultural change in regional areas. This is altering the lives of those who are relocating as well as the character of the regions that receive them. Migration affects language, social values, food, entertainment, housing and other spending patterns resulting in new business opportunities.

Technological trends

Technology is rapidly and comprehensively changing the world in which we live. Blogs, podcasting, YouTube, Myspace, Facebook and Twitter have created a whole new realm in which we can interact with each other. Social networks and data democracy based on user-generated content mean we are living more of our lives online and out of the reach of the institutional gatekeepers and bureaucrats. The evidence suggests that New Zealanders are early adopters of technology and willing to try products and services that are new. For example, the internet is now the most important booking tool for air travel, accommodation, hire cars, tour operators, cruise ships, travel centres and motoring clubs. New businesses such as Wotif have taken advantage of these technology trends.

One reason for the burgeoning role of technology is that the cost of technology has dropped dramatically compared with disposable income. New technology has created powerful opportunities in home-based electronic leisure activities such as interactive television, online gaming services and home theatres. It is getting easier to install, easier to use and wireless devices will infiltrate every aspect of our lives as more products roll out with access anywhere, anyplace and any time. A new form of online business called a 'mash-up' illustrates the business opportunities available on the internet. A mash-up uses online services and tools to combine data from several sources to create a new business. They are relatively easy to start and require fewer resources than traditional technology start-ups. For example, data from online real-estate advertising has been combined with Google Maps to create a new type of real-estate marketing service.

The traditional media began to lose its grip on the New Zealand public when we started to use the internet. Many New Zealanders now read newspapers and magazines less frequently and watch less television. These changes have important consequences for advertising. As we turn our backs on traditional media, the internet and mobile phones have emerged as important new marketing channels. Even word-of-mouth recommendations are turbo-charged by the social networks spawned in these media. These are not only new business opportunities but also new ways of pursuing existing business. For example, retail businesses capture our mobile phone number and email address to inform us about new stock arrivals, special offers and sales. Consulting and related services are benefiting from new opportunities in education and training, transport, health and medical services, and systems and hardware upgrades. Other technology opportunities are found in network management, firewall security systems, e-commerce applications, website development, Voice over Internet Protocol (VoIP) applications and business process outsourcing.

Political and regulatory trends

The role of politics in business can be pervasive. A single vote or a budget speech in Parliament can change an entire industry. Regulations stem from government as well as a number of government-sanctioned authorities. Examples of political and regulatory trends include industrial relations reform, welfare reform, deregulation of the financial sector, changes to superannuation legislation and reforms in telecommunications.

There is growing political acceptance that global warming is resulting in climate change accompanied by an increased interest in environmental sustainability. With increased environmental consciousness has come legislation that created new opportunities for renewable energy, environmental technology and building products.

Another trend over recent years has been for government to gradually withdraw from the direct provision of a range of services. This results in opportunities for new businesses to take over where government left off. There is a profit to be made by providing needed services in areas like ancillary healthcare, respite services, day care centres, learning centres and transportation services. For example, the government prefers to house aged people in their own homes for as long as possible. Rising government funding of aged care pays for personal and nursing care for older people and creates new business opportunities for the providers.

Over the past two decades the world has been transformed by the growth of free trade, the advent of the internet and the deregulation of financial markets. Now small business operators can think and act globally, with more access to information, goods and services than at any time in history. Globalisation is affecting domestic politics, international relations, business activities and consumer behaviour. It is opening up many new business opportunities for speciality and high-value products in niche markets.

Economic trends

Economic trends are commonly tracked and reported in the mainstream media including business investment, unemployment statistics, changes in consumer confidence and retail spending. Other measures of economic activity include average wages, inflation, interest rates, building approvals, productivity and the value of the New Zealand dollar. When the economy is expanding new business opportunities are more likely to emerge. When the economy is contracting business opportunities tend to dry up as well. Consumer confidence is the key that triggers decisions to take a holiday, buy a car or renovate the house. If the economy is healthy and interest rates are low, consumers will feel confident about their future and are more likely to open their wallets. Economic trends outside New Zealand are also important. Asian countries are strengthening their economic clout and boosting their participation in world trade. Whether measured by GDP growth, new technology or new goods and services, there are huge changes occurring in places like Bangalore, Shanghai and Bangkok with enormous implications for new business opportunities in New Zealand for importing and exporting.

Business opportunity grid

The business opportunity grid represents four different approaches to identifying new business opportunities. It distinguishes between *recognising* opportunities for existing products and services as opposed to *creating* opportunities with new products and services. It also distinguishes between *contested* markets in which there are already competitors as opposed to *uncontested* markets in which there are no current competitors.

Figure 2.1: Business opportunity grid

	Contested market	Uncontested market
Opportunity recognition	Parallel opportunities	Market opportunities
Opportunity creation	Product/service opportunities	Radical opportunities

Opportunities in contested markets consist of entering an existing market space, exploiting existing demand and beating the competition by using either a differentiation strategy or a low-cost strategy. Opportunities in uncontested markets consist of creating a new market space and creating new demand and capturing it before potential competitors can get a foothold. Each approach in the business opportunity grid represents a different proposition in terms of the nature of the opportunity, the risks involved and the business model you might adopt.

- Parallel opportunities consist of recognising the potential for existing products or services to be sold into an already contested market in competition with one or more

existing businesses. A new hairdressing salon in an area that already has a salon is a parallel opportunity.
- Market opportunities consist of recognising the potential for existing products or services to be sold into a new uncontested market in which no competitors are currently operating. A new domestic application for an existing industrial product is a new market opportunity.
- Product/service opportunities consist of creating a new or modified product or service aimed at an existing contested market. Organic and environmentally friendly versions of well-known products are new product opportunities.
- Radical opportunities consist of creating an entirely new product or service aimed at a completely new uncontested market. Nanny software aimed at protecting children from inappropriate internet content is a new product providing a solution to a new problem.

Parallel opportunities

The biggest myth of all is that successful businesses come from new ideas that never existed before. In fact, the majority of new business opportunities consist of competing in parallel with other businesses by selling similar products and services to the same sorts of customers. You might be able to capture existing customers by offering a product in a different size, changing the distribution system to improve delivery, finding other product uses or offering bulk discounts. You might be able to attract customers away from competitors by differentiating your product or service, changing the promotional strategy or offering price concessions. These are the most straightforward types of business opportunities because the number of known factors is greatest. Parallel opportunities, however, also run the greatest risk of being exposed to severe competition from the other businesses who sell the same services or products to the same customers.

Parallel start-ups make sense when existing firms are unable to meet demand or when you realise that you can offer better value to customers. In some cases, existing businesses have had it too good for too long and have grown complacent. In other cases, existing operators with poor quality, high prices or poor service allow you to gain a foothold because you are more competent and determined. There are plenty of parallel opportunities in the services sector. Every doctor, accountant or lawyer who enters private practice is pursuing a parallel opportunity. The same is true for other service businesses such as house painters, hairdressers and gardening services. Parallel opportunities in the services sector are easy to exploit when the capital required is low and specialist know-how is not too important. New entrants usually compete with lower prices and longer hours and gradually shift toward greater dependability and closer customer relationships. The key to parallel opportunities is to position your business in a way that easily distinguishes it from the others. Let's look at some examples of parallel business opportunities.

Buying an existing business

When you buy an existing business, you get what someone else has put together. You are buying the location, premises, equipment, stock, customers, staff and goodwill that have been established by the seller. That can make it much easier to get started or you could be buying a big mistake if the seller's original decision to start the business was wrong. You should be particularly concerned with the ability of a business to continue to earn profits. If you choose to buy one that is not doing so well, then you need to be sure that you have the knowledge and skills to turn it around. To find businesses for sale look for newspaper advertisements, commercial real-estate agents and people in the trade. You can also talk with your accountant and solicitor to see if they know of any businesses for sale. Keep an eye out for owners who may want to retire or sell for other reasons like loss of interest, partnership disagreements, divorce or bad health.

Copying another business

Copying another business makes sense if the market has expanded and is not adequately served or if the existing operators are clearly failing to meet the needs of customers. There are a number of advantages to starting a new business over buying an existing one. You can choose your own target market, select the right mix of products and services, design your own competitive strategy and decide on your own location and facilities. Copying an existing business also has some disadvantages. It takes time to build patronage and work the bugs out of new systems. All the while the bills have to be paid and it could be some time before you reach a break-even level of sales. There is also the added risk that unexpected competition may emerge from existing operators trying to protect their market share or that potential customers may be more difficult to attract than you anticipate.

Alternatively, look for a successful product or service to copy. What do you see that is currently doing well with continuing prospects for the future? Are there potential customers that would be prepared to buy something similar from you? Can you identify the key factors responsible for the success of the product or service and can you reproduce them? What are the worst features and can you improve on them? Are you able to deliver the same thing for a lower cost? Make sure you do not infringe anyone's patent, copyright or licence. Ask potential customers if they would buy the product or service if you offered it.

Filling a shortage

Shortages occur when a product or service is not available or when demand significantly outstrips supply. Are you aware of any supply shortages? Can you provide a product or service that will fill the gap? Have any potential customers indicated there is a genuine shortage and they would be prepared to buy from you? You can search for shortages by asking distributors, agents and retailers what they have trouble obtaining. Similarly, ask which products and services take the longest to get delivered. Listen to potential customers when they complain about products or services they cannot conveniently source. You can also look for supply shortages caused by businesses closing down or changing their priorities by reading the business news and trade publications, and investigating businesses that are in receivership. It is important to understand the causes of a shortage to ensure that you don't get caught in the same way. Having alternative suppliers in other countries may enable you to overcome a seasonal shortage or more efficient distribution channels may enable you to solve supplier issues.

Reintroducing a product or service

It is not uncommon for a good product or service to fail because of shortcomings in marketing, production methods, logistics or some other reason. If you can identify the problem and eliminate it, then the potential may exist to successfully reintroduce a product or service that has disappeared. Do you know of any interesting products or services that are no longer available? Do they have the potential to become successful with changes in the marketing mix, management methods, new investment or a different business strategy? What kind of changes would it take and can you do it? Are there potential customers who have indicated they would be buyers? Ask around if anyone knows about any worthwhile products or services that are no longer available and why they think they were discontinued. Similarly, look at business failures and ask the same questions. Some ideas could have been ahead of their time and might be successful now if they are reintroduced. Sometimes, you can rediscover ideas by looking through old magazines and catalogues. Ask potential customers what they were previously able to buy that they would like to be able to buy again. Make sure you test the idea thoroughly because some products will have failed for very good reasons and no amount of effort will resurrect them.

Assembling a product

There are parallel opportunities in which you can save someone time, effort or money by setting up an assembly operation. An example is assembling furniture for people who are willing and happy to pay for the convenience of not having to deal with a 'flat pack'. What could you assemble that would save someone time, money or effort? Is there a market for it? Look for products in which the assembly process is cumbersome and expensive or the parts come from different locations and you are centrally located to become a convenient assembly point. Also look for products that are sold unassembled but the average person is not willing or able to put them together.

Subcontracting

A subcontractor supplies a product or service that is used by another business as part of a larger offering. With the rise in outsourcing, subcontracting for services is now common for many businesses from complex technical support to routine activities such as parcel delivery and rubbish disposal. Sometimes there is an opportunity to become a secondary supplier when a large company does not want to rely on a single source of supply. What could you supply to other businesses as part of their product or service? Contact purchasing agents in large businesses and ask them about their supply needs. What items are hard to locate, too expensive, or have unreliable supply or delivery? Check the newspapers for 'request for tender' advertisements and 'expression of interest' advertisements from organisations looking for subcontractors. Get on the mailing lists of government purchasing agencies that are required to advertise for tenders. Look through trade journals for information about supply problems in particular industries. Your goal is to identify a product or service that you can supply to other businesses as part of their overall offering.

Replacing imports

Replacing imports means producing a product or service in New Zealand that is currently being imported. We are surrounded by all sorts of imported products that could be produced locally. Do you know of an imported item that you could produce locally? Can you match its quality at the same price? Can you get a cost advantage by eliminating shipping costs or tariffs? To find out what is imported into New Zealand subscribe to import publications and importers' catalogues. Contact purchasing agents and ask them what they are importing. Examine the products where you shop to find out where they are made. What are your areas of expertise and how do they match up with the import replacement opportunities you have discovered? Talk to potential customers and ask them if they would be prepared to switch to a locally made item.

Exploiting abandoned markets

Exploiting abandoned markets means entering a market that has been left behind by another business. This sometimes happens because they do not want to handle smaller orders any longer, or they may be at the leading edge of technology and no longer want to service older equipment or stock the same range of products. Other businesses may be expanding into new markets and find themselves unable to properly service their existing customers. One example of a business opportunity arising from an abandoned market is a repair service for appliances that are no longer produced. What industries or companies have made big changes as a result of new technology, new products or new ways of doing business? Have any of these changes resulted in some customers being abandoned? Are there enough of them that would continue to buy the product or service if you offered it? Make sure you know why the market was abandoned because there may have been some very good reasons to pull out.

Becoming an agent or distributor

Agents and distributors sell the products and services of other businesses. Some businesses do not have the resources to develop and manage their own distribution channels and they look for other organisations that can fulfil this role. Other businesses simply prefer to concentrate on what they do best and outsource distribution. An agent contracts with a producer to sell their products or services for a fee or a commission. A distributor buys the producer's products or services and resells them directly to consumers or wholesales them to other businesses. What types of products or services could you sell as an agent or a distributor? What producers can you find that need the services of an agent or a distributor in your area? Have any retailers or consumers indicated the need for a product or service that you can distribute?

Can you identify a product or service that you believe you can sell directly to consumers or wholesale to other businesses? Ask the producer of this product or service if they need someone to handle direct sales or wholesale sales. Look for new businesses that have not established their own marketing department and need marketing services. Look for producers who cannot afford to market to rural areas or specialised niche markets. Look for a producer who only wants to handle large orders but the product requires distribution in small lots. Find a group of customers or retailers who have to wait too long for delivery and will buy from you if you carry stock for immediate delivery. Look for advertisements for agents and distributors under *Business Opportunities* in the classified section of the newspaper.

Market opportunities

Market opportunities consist of selling existing products or services to new customers. They may be in new geographical areas or they may be new customers that can be serviced by new distribution channels, new merchandising methods, or other advertising media. Since there is already some experience with existing products or services, new market opportunities usually involve only medium risk. Let's look at some examples of market opportunities.

Imitating other businesses

When you see a successful business concept in another place, consider the possibility of imitating the same idea in your own market. What businesses have you seen in your travels that might work well for you? Have you seen any successful products or services that are not available where you live? Keep your eyes open for products or services in other locations that you can expand into your area. Talk with purchasing agents and people who have seen business opportunities that you could introduce into your area. Buy a few overseas newspapers and read through the advertising and the stories about local businesses. Check out the local Yellow Pages when you travel and visit some of the businesses that look interesting.

Buying a franchise

Franchising has been responsible for the spectacular growth in new market opportunities. The franchisor not only provides the product, service and trade mark, but also the entire business format consisting of a marketing plan and support, operating methods and manuals, training, quality control and ongoing back-up services. In the retail sector, examples include auto parts, apparel, paint and hardware, electrical appliances and fast food. Franchising can also be found in such diverse service industries as motels, income tax services, business and professional services, and real-estate agencies. Keep a sharp eye out for successful franchise operations in other locations that are likely to be successful in your area. Talk to some of the franchisees and ask them what they think about the franchise system they operate. Chapter 5 contains a detailed description of franchising and how it works.

Importing and exporting

Importing is a source of new market opportunities in New Zealand. An importer brings products and services into New Zealand from other countries for resale to wholesalers or directly to customers. Many foreign producers are looking for local agents or distributors. The embassies of foreign countries are an excellent source of information about agency and distribution opportunities. Another source of information is the World Trade Centers Association website at www.wtca.org.

Exporting is a source of new market opportunities in other countries. Most New Zealand exporters concentrate their efforts on the countries that make up the APEC region, the United States and the European Union. Do you have contacts in other countries that may become distributors? Do you know of any New Zealand producers who need help to export their products and services?

Importing and exporting are highly specialised activities. You need to be aware of your legal obligations in both the country of origin and the destination including quarantine laws, tariffs, quotas, duties and other restrictions. Chapter 14 contains important information about export marketing and regulations on importing can be found at www.business.govt.nz.

Special-interest groups

Adapting or tailoring a product or service to meet the needs of a special-interest group can uncover a new market opportunity. A special-interest group's needs may relate to their physical characteristics such as having mobility restrictions or being left-handed, their lifestyle such as occupation or leisure pursuits, their ethnicity such as food or language, or a variety of other reasons. Can you find a group of people with special needs that are not being met by the marketplace? What unique group can you serve with specialised products and services?

Good sources of information can be found in newspapers, magazines and research reports produced for special-interest groups. Analyse the special needs of a group by studying the unique characteristics of the people involved and asking what they look for and what they have difficulty buying. Look for products and services that are either not offered to a special-interest group or are not very well adapted to their needs. Look at other special-interest groups for similar ideas about products or services that you can adapt for your target group. Talk to members of your target group and ask them what they need and if they would buy from you.

Packaging

Packaging, repackaging or unpackaging products can be the basis for a business opportunity. For example, commodities sold in bulk may be repackaged into smaller units for individual consumers. Food sold in family-sized packaging may find a new market as single serves aimed at one-person households. Regulations affecting air travellers have created a new market for mini packs of hair care and skin care products in clear containers. Alternatively, look for products that are individually packaged in small units and consider packaging them in larger units to lower the price such as house lots of energy-efficient light bulbs.

Some items can be repackaged in order to make them more attractive, more convenient, reusable or easier to store such as resealable packaging to extend shelf life. Other examples include bottling cleanskin wines under custom labels for restaurants or putting washing powder in dispenser packs that deliver a measured quantity and prevent waste. Look for products that are poorly packaged and think about how they could be improved. Look for products that are sold without packaging and design a package that would increase sales. Look for two or more products that people generally buy or use at the same time and consider packaging them together as a single unit. Consider how unpacking or repacking might be able to address environmental concerns. Ask potential customers what they think about your packaging ideas. What products do you think could be packaged, repackaged or unpackaged to make them more marketable? What new markets could you open up by changing the packaging for an existing product?

Digital marketing

The internet is a tremendous source of new market opportunities. If your prospective customers already buy products or get information via the internet then you can be there as well. An internet site gives you access to markets all over the world. Sometimes the internet is more cost-effective than other marketing tools. For example, a commercial artist can put their portfolio on a website and direct potential clients to it without incurring the expense of sending out an entire portfolio every time they bid for a job.

The role of a website in creating new market opportunities can vary. Some businesses have a website that is designed simply to create a marketing presence as part of an overall advertising and promotion strategy. Other businesses have a website that goes one step further by offering an online catalogue and product specifications and contact details for handling orders and customer inquiries. A complete website goes beyond general marketing and customer support to online ordering and credit card approval while the customer is online. Fully featured websites are also capable of tracking a customer's preferences and transaction history as part of a strategy for cross promotion and on-selling. Chapter 13 explains digital marketing in detail.

Product and service opportunities

Product or service opportunities consist of developing, acquiring or producing a new product or service for an existing target market. These may be genuine new products and services or only modest improvements. To the extent that you have little previous experience with a particular product or service, the risks become greater. Product and service opportunities that are totally new are very rare indeed. Instead, look for products and services that are already working in the marketplace which you can improve or expand by:

- Improving quality or service
- Broadening or narrowing the range of products or services offered
- Improving usability, performance or safety
- Changing the delivery method, packaging or unit size
- Adding new features, accessories or extensions
- Introducing simplification or convenience
- Simplifying repair, maintenance, replacement or cleaning
- Increasing mobility, access, portability or disposability
- Changing colour, material or shape
- Making them larger/smaller, lighter/heavier or faster/slower.

If you spend a little time observing customers to see how a product or service is being used it may reveal opportunities for complementary services or products that can be bundled with the existing ones. Similarly, a product that is bought for its functional benefits can be transformed into a product that is sold for its aesthetic qualities in the way that budget watches were transformed from simple timepieces into fashion accessories. Let's look at some examples of product and service business opportunities.

Take advantage of switching

When customers switch from one product or service to another, additional new business opportunities may also be created. For example, the switch from fixed telephone handsets to mobile phones has created a flood of add-on services and accessories such as personalised ring tones, phone covers and thousands of 'apps'. Can you think of any recent consumer switches? Can you take advantage of changes in customer buying habits as a result of switching from one product or service to another? Have potential customers expressed a need that is based on a market switch? You might be able to discover changes in consumer buying habits by looking at market-research reports and trade-association studies. You can also look for fads that are turning into permanent changes or new products that are rapidly growing in popularity. Think about changes in your own buying habits. If you think a switch has definitely occurred, look for related products or services that will complement it.

Piggybacking on growth

Growth in a product or service occurs when more people become customers. Piggybacking on growth consists of offering additional related products or services. For example, there is a long-term trend toward personal fitness and health. Businesses offering fitness-monitoring equipment, health foods and apparel designed for specific activities such as yoga are piggybacking on this trend. What current trends can you identify? What products or services could you provide that fit into these trends? Have any potential customers indicated a desire to buy these products or services?

You can look for growth trends by surfing the internet and reading books, magazines and research reports on social and economic trends. Run a Google search for 'trend spotters' and see what you get. Where are the growth trends in overseas markets that you can translate into your market area? Make a list of growth trends and consider how your skills, knowledge and experience could be applied to related opportunities that fit into these trends. Talk with potential customers and ask them if they would purchase such a product or service.

Adding value

You add value when you buy an existing product or service and then add materials, components, processing or services to resell a more valuable product or service. There are a number of ways to add value including putting a product through another process, combining a product with other products, offering a product as part of a package of services such as installation and maintenance, or increasing the level of service. Can you identify an existing product or service that would benefit from an additional process, more material or increased service? It may be a product or service that does not work properly or it may be unsuitable for some other reason. Locate the new elements and develop a method of adding them. Ask the target customers if they would purchase the product or service with these changes.

Improving a product or service

Improving an existing product or service can take place in different ways such as improving quality, reducing the cost, reducing the price to the end user or improving durability. Other improvements might include making it bigger, smaller or more convenient, for example easier to clean. Improving a product or service is different from adding value. When you improve a product, you not only use the idea from the existing product, but you improve on it to create a new product. An example is the design of ergonomic tools for the building trade that help to prevent repetitive strain injuries. Select a product or service that interests you and analyse its strengths and weaknesses. Can you identify ways in which it can be improved? How would you make these improvements? How would it make the product or service more marketable? Can you actually produce a better product or service? Is there a market for it?

Sometimes a product can be improved by substituting the material with which it is made to alter its characteristics such as making it lighter, stronger, more flexible or cheaper to make. For example, substituting plastic for metal in producing fishing lures made them less expensive and more versatile. Products with new characteristics may appeal to a different target market. Can you think of any products that could be made with different materials? Can you think of any inferior products that could be improved with better materials? Examine existing products to determine if they might appeal to a different market by substituting materials. Alternatively, consider materials that you have in good supply and think about the sorts of products that might benefit from using these materials. Look for production processes that suffer because the materials used are too expensive or prone to big price fluctuations, difficult to use, unsafe, in short supply or wasted. Look for substitute materials that eliminate these problems.

Making new combinations

Sometimes it is possible to combine existing products and services to create a new business opportunity. One example is combining a beauty salon with a medical centre in order to offer an expanded range of beauty and cosmetic treatment services. Another example is combining the skills of several tradespeople to offer a comprehensive home maintenance and repair service. The objective is to combine products, services, people, businesses and assets to create a new combination of products or services that is more powerful than its separate parts. What combinations can you envisage? Which ones suit your skills and experience? Start with a business concept, idea, product or service that interests you. Ask yourself what could be combined with it to create something significantly better. Look for consumer groups with compatible needs that could be served by combining existing products or services. Make a list of different types of businesses from the Yellow Pages and play with various combinations. Ask potential customers what types of combinations they would like to see.

Information services

One of the consequences of living in a modern world is the amount of information people are expected to process and manage. In a survey by Reuters, 49 per cent felt they were unable to keep up with the flow of information, 43 per cent were having trouble making important decisions because of information overload, 38 per cent said they wasted valuable time trying to locate important information and 33 per cent suffered from stress-related health problems brought on by too much information. Managing information for other people is a huge opportunity for new businesses. Can you offer a consulting or information service providing advice, services or information in a subject area you know well? Do you have experience, knowledge or skills that you can sell to others? Do you know of potential clients that need your expertise?

Look for information-service ideas in business newspapers and trade magazines, company reports and by talking directly with potential clients. Other ideas may come from the popular press, radio and television shows and community activities. The key is to identify up-to-date sources of information to which you can add value by offering a service. Examples for business customers include information about production problems, business planning, marketing strategies, staffing issues, computer services, financial management, training, political lobbying and public relations. Consumer examples include information about things like navigating building and renovating planning-approval processes, interior decorating, personal budgeting, major appliance purchases, landscaping or career planning.

Radical opportunities

A radical opportunity consists of a new product or service that is targeted at an uncontested market. It is radical because the idea is novel and it has the potential to upset the way in which established products and services have previously operated. These are typically new inventions that take a long time to develop and are costly to bring to market. The risks are extremely high but if you get it right so are the rewards. Radical opportunities are a combination of foresight and chance. They depend on an ability to see where an opportunity might fit into a future market environment. Some radical opportunities are *pushed* by technological developments but the majority are *pulled* into existence by a market that is seeking them. Let's look at some examples of radical business opportunities.

Inventing a new product or service

Inventing a new product or service can be the basis for an excellent business opportunity. What products or services are needed but don't exist? What customer needs could be met by a new invention? Are you familiar with any processes that you could improve by inventing a new procedure, product or service? Do you already have an idea that you could develop into an invention? Is there a market for it?

First, concentrate on products or services with which you are familiar and try to think of ideas for significant improvements. Can you think of ways to make an existing product or service more efficient by saving time, effort or money? What products and services are people asking for but do not exist? Examine the products and services that you use and look for the potential to add something, subtract something, change something or combine them with something else. Look through magazines and research reports devoted to consumer topics and search through the Intellectual Property Office New Zealand (IPONZ) website at www.iponz.govt.nz and the Google Patent Search website at www.google.com/patents to see what has already been registered. IPONZ can also provide you with information about how to apply for a patent over your own invention. Once a patent is granted, you have an exclusive right to produce and sell it including the right to sell a licence to someone else who wants to produce and sell it.

Buying a licence

The flip side of selling patent rights is to buy a licence to produce and market an invention patented by someone else. Is there an interesting patent for a product or service with genuine market potential that has never been produced, or has it been produced but not successfully exploited? Some patents are available under licence and there are many old patents that have expired and can be produced without a licence. A licence may be exclusive and unrestricted or it may only grant rights for a particular geographic area, a particular market or a limited period of time. Buying a licence requires specialised professional financial and legal advice.

Do a search of the Intellectual Property Office New Zealand and Google Patent Search websites to see what you can find. Look through magazines and trade journals for articles about new product ideas and attend trade shows that feature products and services that interest you. You may also want to approach companies that hold patents on products they are not currently producing, as well as venture-capital organisations that know about potential opportunities. Even very old patents that were ahead of their time may represent ideas that are marketable today.

Transferring an idea

Sometimes you can take an idea that was developed for a particular purpose and transfer it into an unrelated field. Many of the ideas that were developed for NASA's space program have been transferred into commercial products for industrial and domestic applications. For example, there are medical products developed for humans that have been adapted for use in veterinary practice. What successful ideas or concepts can you identify that might be transferred into another type of business, market or activity? Make a list of successful ideas that you can imagine applied in a different setting. Alternatively, look for problems in one line of business and try to identify potential solutions from other types of businesses. Ask potential customers if they would buy a product or service resulting from the transferred idea.

Special situations

Demand for a product or service may arise spontaneously as a result of a special situation. Examples include the goods and services that were suddenly in demand as a result of the Y2K fears in the late 1990s and, more recently, the focus on climate change and global warming is driving changes in products such as energy-efficient light bulbs. What current situations might spawn a new business opportunity? What goods and services could you provide to address a market created by these situations? Pay attention to what you see and hear in the media and look for sudden changes in society, the economy, legislation, politics, the environment and business activity that leave people in unfamiliar circumstances.

3 Assistance that is available

Small business operators have generally depended on their own judgement and initiative to succeed. Yet analysis of business closures continues to point towards a lack of management information and a lack of skill and experience to use it. A significant proportion of closures could be avoided, especially in the early life of a small business, if small business operators recognised the limits of their own experience, skills and resources, and turned to the sources of counsel, information and assistance that are theirs for the asking. To take advantage of outside sources of information and assistance, you need to know where to look. The purpose of this chapter is to point you in the right direction.

Think about your own needs. Do you need information? For example, you may need to know how many potential customers there are in your target market. Or you may wonder if your advertising budget is above or below the average for your line of business. Do you need advice? There are usually several ways to solve a problem. People who understand problems like yours are the ones to see for advice. Perhaps what you are really looking for is guidance or counselling? Sometimes a problem is difficult to identify or to isolate. In this case you may need a specialist to examine the problem at first hand, assist you to identify its cause and recommend a solution.

Government programs

There are all sorts of national and local government programs for small business operators. It is a waste of time, however, to try to keep tabs on all of the government programs as they ebb and flow with the political and economic tide. The secret to getting the most benefit from government programs is to use the information services they have put in place to help you find the right program and the right person to contact. The key information source is the New Zealand government business website www.business. govt.nz or phone their Biz business information line on 0800 424 946. Here are some other programs that may help.

New Zealand Trade and Enterprise (NZTE)

NZTE offers a wide range of services and programs including training programs, market information and funding assistance. NZTE also facilitates networking and partnering opportunities for qualifying companies. The services cover the following areas of business support.

- Services for businesses starting up and at an early stage of development.
- Services for businesses seeking to grow and internationalise, including new exporters, high-growth businesses and other exporters.
- Investment services for investors seeking existing and start-up New Zealand-based ventures with excellent future potential.
- Business partnerships: supporting companies working together in export networks and regional and national clusters to achieve higher growth.
- Regional development: working with and funding regions to grow by encouraging them to focus on their regional advantages.
- Industrial Capability Network: providing access to government markets through a low-cost, one-port-of-call service.
- Fostering an enterprise culture: encouraging New Zealanders to have a positive attitude towards business success.

NZTE can be contacted via their website at www.nzte.govt.nz or phone the Enterprise Hotline from within New Zealand on 0800 555 888.

TechNZ

TechNZ is run by the Ministry of Science and Innovation. The scheme helps businesses develop and adopt new technology. Current programs offered by TechNZ provide funds and information for research and development (R&D) projects and access to technology experts and consultants. Information services are available at the Ministry of Science and Innovation (MSI) or visiting the website at www.msi.govt.nz.

Economic Development Agencies of New Zealand (EDANZ)

EDAs are supported by funding from national and local government, and local industry. The centres provide a variety of advisory services and access to government programs including business skills training, business facilitation, mentoring and specialist-topic seminars on business subjects. The website is at www.edanz.org.nz or phone (04) 978 1291.

Government departments

Many government departments have a direct involvement with business or an indirect link through crown entities. The most significant of these are listed below, with a brief outline of what they offer to small businesses.

Statistics New Zealand

Statistics New Zealand provides three types of services that will be of interest to small business owners: catalogue services (e.g. books and reports), electronic database services and research bureau services.

Catalogue services include reports such as the Household Economic Survey which provides data on the average weekly expenditure by households on a wide range of products and services. The Census of Populations and Dwellings provides data on the demographic profile in each geographic area. Business Demographic Statistics and the Annual Enterprise Survey provide data on businesses categorised by geographic location, industry type, persons employed and aggregated financial performance.

Electronic databases include a table-building facility that can interrogate large amounts of statistical data and produce reports online. The information is provided at a detailed geographic level to show demographic and business data within towns and city suburbs. This enables a business owner to specifically identify ideal business locations or design highly targeted marketing strategies.

Statistics New Zealand also provides customised searches of its databases to provide you with specific information. For this service contact the Information Consulting staff at Statistics New Zealand in the nearest main centre. They will advise you what can be provided and give you a quote for what it will cost. The website www.stats.govt.nz also provides information and special reports.

Inland Revenue Department (IRD)

The IRD provides books and advisory services for small business. The service aims to provide support and tax education for new businesses and organisations to help them meet their tax obligations. Most IRD offices also have a Maori Community Officer who can assist Maori individuals with their business's tax obligations. *Smart Business IR320* is an introductory guide for businesses dealing with business tax for the first time. Many IRD transactions and services are available online or through their automated telephone service. The website is at www.ird.govt.nz or phone 0800 377 774.

Work and Income

Work and Income is a service of the Ministry of Social Development. It provides a combination of income support and employment services for the unemployed. Part of the service is to provide business training and support to the unemployed and people without business skills who are interested in self-employment. The *'Be Your Own Boss'* program focuses on testing the viability of specific business ideas by training people in basic market research and business plan writing skills.

The *Enterprise Allowance Subsidy* aims to help job seekers to become self-sufficient by setting up a small business. It provides some financial assistance during start-up that is linked to attendance at a business training course at an approved provider location and the development of a business plan. The website is at www.workandincome.govt.nz or phone 0800 559 009.

Ministry of Agriculture and Forestry (MAF)

Although not strictly a business advisory service, the Ministry of Agriculture and Forestry works to create an environment that enables private land-based enterprises to conduct their businesses profitably and sustainably. MAF provides policy advice to government but also provides technical advice and a database of agricultural and forestry publications. The website is at www.maf.govt.nz.

Local government programs

Councils and other local agencies also play a role in stimulating business and industrial development. Local councils sometimes pool their resources by forming regional development authorities that attract firms into an industrial estate by offering demographic information and management advice.

Local governments also administer a variety of regulations covering land-use zoning, building codes, health regulations and fire restrictions. These regulations can represent a minefield for some small business operators, but you can avoid most of the hassles if you approach local government administrators in advance and tell them exactly what it is you want to do. Local government websites can be found at www.localcouncils.govt.nz.

Advisory services for Maori business

Maori Business Facilitation Service (MBFS)

This business mentoring service was set up by Te Puni Kokiri to provide advice, guidance and facilitation services essential to developing a new or existing business. The Maori Women's Development Fund provides loans to Maori women to help start or expand their own business. Applicants are required to complete an application form, present a comprehensive business plan and provide evidence of having undertaken some form of business education. Applicants have to prove, through research, that the business has a viable place within the relevant industry. Contact details for the MBFS are at the website www.tpk.govt.nz or phone 0800 949 997.

Te Putea Whanake Business Development Grant

If you are a Maori organisation or individual needing help to get a business started, the Poutama Trust can help with funding from Te Putea Whanake. Application forms, terms and conditions are available at the website www.poutama.co.nz or phone 0800 476 882.

Business incubators

A business incubator is designed to help small business start-ups by reducing costs through shared facilities and providing an accessible, low-cost consultancy network for advice on finance, marketing, product development and business strategies. The average stay in an incubator is around 18 to 24 months, after which time the business has usually established itself and is able to move on to bigger and better things. Information on incubators in New Zealand is available from the NZTE website at www.nzte.govt.nz, or from Incubators New Zealand at www.incubators.org.nz.

The ICEHOUSE

A prominent incubator in New Zealand is the ICEHOUSE. This incubator has been developed by the University of Auckland Business School in partnership with seven major corporate organisations from banking, technology, communications, legal and accounting fields. The ICEHOUSE is recognised as a world-class incubator because its partnerships and networks of advisers and mentors extend internationally, and because the wide range of support activities reach from market validation, to managing innovation and technology, angel investment and help with sourcing other funds, as well as networking and continuous coaching in general business planning and management.

The ICEHOUSE also run development programs for existing medium-sized businesses ($5–100 million sales) to help them overcome constraints that have caused their growth to plateau. These programs, offered only to owners and their senior managers, are delivered in three-day residential blocks that are scheduled monthly over several months. The objectives of the program are to expand the vision, capability and confidence in the small and medium enterprise (SME) sector to enable transitional development and continuing growth of both the business and the owner. The website is at www.theicehouse.co.nz.

Education and training

There are hundreds of small business education and training programs throughout New Zealand. They include informal discussion groups, one-day workshops, part-time courses and formal full-time diploma courses. Many programs can be undertaken through home study. The government business information website (www.business.govt.nz) and the Economic Development Agencies site (www.edanz.org.nz) will direct you to small business programs in your local area. If you are a new starter, you may want to look for a basic course that covers all the important aspects of small business management. If you are already in business, you may prefer to look for short seminars on topics that currently concern you, or enquire about more ambitious programs such as the ICEHOUSE owner-manager program. There are many providers of small business education and training and you can check the list at the end of this chapter for useful sources of assistance and advice.

Publications and databases

There is published material on practically every aspect of small business management. A website at www.searchnz.co.nz provides links to New Zealand organisations and a search on 'small business publications' brings up many links to other sites, including government departments that usually have 'Publications' on their site maps. Specific searches in GoogleNZ will also bring up a wealth of information on small business in New Zealand. Other important resources are your local library and university. Some specific directories and databases include:

- The *Universal Business Directory* business information website at www.ubd.co.nz is a searchable database of over 208 000 New Zealand businesses.
- Directory information services supply business lists and data services. One such service is available at www.cd-rom-directories.com which gives access to data on over 297 000 New Zealand businesses and also to other international databases.
- The New Zealand Yellow Pages Business Search CD-Rom allows targeted generation of mail-out lists using data on more than 100 000 businesses. Further information is available at www.datamarket.co.nz.

Libraries

Libraries hold a vast store of information useful to business. The task of finding a particular item is sometimes daunting, but librarians can provide the assistance you need. They have special references and computer search facilities that can be used to locate the materials you need. Even if your library does not hold a particular item, there are arrangements between libraries that enable your local library to obtain it for you. You can get access to the National Library, municipal libraries, educational-institution libraries and government-department libraries. Libraries hold more than books. They also have journals, magazines, newspapers, technical indexes, maps and charts, films, video tapes, audio tapes, directories, material on microfiche and microfilm, and catalogues.

Trade associations

Trade associations consist of people who are engaged in the same or similar types of business. These organisations tend to be the best source of industry-specific information and assistance. There are many professional and trade associations in New Zealand.

To locate a trade association for your type of business, check the Yellow Pages of your local telephone directory under 'Associations—Professional' and 'Associations—Trade &/Or Industry', do a Google search on 'trade associations' or see the list of major trade associations at the end of this chapter. When you find the trade association for your type of business, join it and take advantage of all the information and assistance that it provides. Most trade associations hold regular meetings where you can meet others in the trade to discuss matters of common concern. There are a number of services that you may be able to obtain from your trade association. Here are some examples:

- Information and publications
- Computer software and systems
- Inter-firm comparisons and industry profiles
- Advice and/or advocacy on industrial relations matters
- Advice on legislation and government regulations
- Taxation advice
- Insurance packages and insurance advice
- Joint advertising and promotion of industry products
- Liaison service between the industry and government
- Publicity and public relations
- Technical and economic research
- Seminars, lectures, workshops and conferences
- Referrals to specialist consultants.

Chambers of commerce

There is a Chamber of Commerce in most communities. To find the nearest go to www.newzealandchambers.co.nz. It is not only important to participate in the activities of your local Chamber of Commerce; it is equally important to know what services are available. Here are some examples of what you can expect:

Legal advice

Financial advice

Small business advice

Economic and taxation advice

Industrial relations advice

Import–export information

Tariff advice

Overseas trade missions.

Reference library and database

Legislation advice

Government representation

Education and training

Business information

Networking functions and briefings

Chamber publications

Professional advisers

One way to create a solid management team without having to take on partners or employees is to carefully select and cultivate professional advisers. Initially, they will consist of your accountant and your solicitor. Later, you will probably find the need for specialist advice in other areas such as insurance, real estate or advertising. The key to getting the most benefit from professional advisers is learning to manage them. Make sure they know what you expect of them and if they do not deliver the goods, sack them! At the same time, do not forget that good advice costs money. Be prepared to pay for the best advice you can get. Poor advice will cost more in lost profits than any fees you pay out.

Your accountant

Finding an accountant is easy—just look in the telephone directory, or Google 'account-ants' including a location. Finding an accountant with whom you can work effectively may take a little digging. Ask your friends, business associates or trade association to recommend an accountant. Your solicitor and your bank manager may also be able to recommend someone. Experience has shown that most small business operators only use their accountant for the preparation of tax returns and statutory reports. Accountants are notoriously backward about telling their clients about the full range of services they can provide, which generally includes:

Taxation advice

Planning and budgeting

Preparing loan applications

Investment advice

Financial statements

Information systems

Auditing

Computer facilities

Book-keeping

Payroll

Purchase/sale of a business

Statutory reports and returns

Cash flow analysis   Superannuation planning
Cost analysis   Estate planning.

Some accountants do not offer the full range of accounting services and a few do not take the trouble to provide simplified accounting reports that can be easily understood. Let your accountant know exactly what you want. If necessary, keep changing your accountant until you find one that does the job to your satisfaction. When you do find the right accountant, make maximum use of this major source of information and assistance. Be sure to see an accountant *before* you start or buy a business. Meet with your accountant personally and as frequently as you require. You can save time and money if you prepare for these meetings by drawing up a list of the matters on which you need advice.

Your solicitor

Finding a good solicitor will also require some digging. Ask for referrals from a number of sources and make a note if the same name keeps cropping up. Remember that it is important for your solicitor and your accountant to work together, so ask for a recommendation from your accountant. A good solicitor anticipates your legal needs. They cannot do this effectively, however, unless you take them into your confidence and keep them informed of any matters with legal implications. Some solicitors understand the needs of small business clients better than others. If your solicitor does not do the job to your satisfaction, look for a new solicitor who will. A solicitor should be able to provide you with a full range of legal services and advice including:

Registration procedures   Leases
Forms of business structure   Partnership agreements
Contracts   Employment agreements
Conveyancing   Warranties
Trade marks and patents   Litigation
Effects of legislation   Winding-up
Liabilities and insurance.

Your bank manager

Banks offer small business operators a range of financial services. Your bank manager can also advise you on some business and financial topics. For these reasons, you need to establish a personal relationship with your bank manager. Small business operators frequently fail to keep their bank manager informed about the progress and prospects of their business until they need a loan. Remember, when you go to the bank for a loan, you are asking the bank manager to invest someone else's money in your business. A bank manager who knows little or nothing about you or your business may not be inclined to give you a loan. At the very least, you will not get any money until your loan application has undergone prolonged investigation and consideration. If, however, you have regularly kept your bank manager informed about your affairs, then they will be in a better position to meet your needs for finance and advice.

Consultants

The time may come when you run into a tough problem that you cannot handle yourself. This may be an occasion when you need to call in a consultant. Consultants can help with a variety of matters:

Management	Marketing
recruiting	advertising
training	packaging
industrial relations	distribution
compensation	location
motivation.	point-of-sale.

Production	Finance
methods	computer systems
layout	feasibility studies
standards	financing proposals
quality control	expansion
costs.	buy-outs.

A consultant may be an individual, a consulting firm, or a division of a larger organisation. Weigh the costs against the benefits. Most consultants can provide you with a firm estimate of their fees and expenses before they accept an assignment. A consultant needs an accurate *brief* that describes the nature of the work to be done. Take the consultant into your confidence by having a frank and open discussion about the problem.

You can expect the consultant to give you either a letter or a formal contract incorporating their terms of reference. Make sure that your solicitor reviews it before you sign anything. Ensure that the consultant understands that the work for you is confidential and they should give you regular reports on their progress. At the completion of the assignment, the consultant should provide you with a comprehensive report and discuss the details with you.

Locating a consultant may pose some difficulties if you have never used one before. Start by checking with your local BIZinfo agency. Your accountant, solicitor and bank manager may also be able to help you. Do not forget other sources of referrals such as business associates, suppliers, your trade association and the Yellow Pages. Be sure that the consultant you choose is a specialist in the field, dedicated to the problem at hand, and only retained for as long as it takes to complete the assignment. Obtain references from past clients and check them before you commit yourself.

Inter-firm comparisons

Inter-firm comparisons and industry profiles are reports that tell you what sort of results are being achieved by firms like your own. By measuring your performance against these practical yardsticks, you can determine your strengths and weaknesses in order to improve the performance of your business. You can also use this information to do a feasibility study if you are looking at entering the industry. It is helpful if you analyse inter-firm comparison information in conjunction with your professional advisers.

The two principal sources of inter-firm comparison and industry-profile reports are the University of Waikato Management Research Centre and Dun & Bradstreet, an international firm specialising in credit-reporting services. Other sources are trade associations and Statistics New Zealand. Your professional advisers and the government's business advice service at www.business.govt.nz can help you to locate inter-firm comparison information for your business.

Business in the Community

Business in the Community is a mentoring scheme that aims to make available, free of charge, the skills and experience of people who have proven themselves successful in business. The mentor program matches mentors with businesses requiring assistance. Any business that has been operating for more than six months and has fewer than 25 employees can call on the services of a mentor to help overcome operating difficulties or assist in realising growth opportunities. To contact your nearest office or obtain more information go to www.businessmentors.org.nz. or phone 0800 209 209.

Suppliers

Suppliers can help you by sharing some of their expertise. Ask your suppliers what information and assistance they can offer. Here are some things to ask about.

Product information:
- Which products are growing in demand?
- Where is demand decreasing?
- What new products are in the pipeline?
- Will any product lines be discontinued?

Industry and economic forecasts:
- What are the prospects for the industry?

- Are changes in consumer spending, inflation or credit availability going to affect the industry?
- Is the industry vulnerable to substitute products, government rules or consumer action?
- Will there be any technological change?

Market and customer information:
- Will changes in customer age, income or location affect your business?
- What does the customer value most: price, quality, service, credit or warranty?
- Do customers have alternative sources of supply?
- What is the target market's buying power?

Competitor information:
- Who does the vendor supply beside yourself?
- Who are the vendor's largest customers?
- How broad (or narrow) a product line do others carry?
- Where do competitors add value?

Direct assistance:
- Point-of-sale material
- Promotional discounts
- In-store displays
- Brochures
- Advertising copy
- Demonstrations
- Technical advice
- Co-operative advertising.

List of contacts for business assistance, education and information

Field	Organisation	Website
Business Incubators	AUT Business Innovation Centre, Auckland	www.bic.aut.ac.nz/
	powerHouse, Canterbury	www.cii.co.nz
	Creative HQ, Wellington	www.creativehq.co.nz
	Dunedin Fashion Incubator	www.dfi.co.nz
	ecentre, Massey	www.ecentre.org.nz
	Soda Inc, Hamilton	www.sodainc.com
	Bio Commerce Centre, Massey	www.thebcc.co.nz

Field	Organisation	Website
	The ICEHOUSE, Auckland	www.theicehouse.co.nz
	Upstart, Dunedin	www.upstart.org.nz
	WaikatoLink Limited	www.waikatolink.co.nz
Central Government Information, Support and Funding	Community Grants, Department of Internal Affairs	www.cdgo.govt.nz
	Department of Conservation	www.doc.govt.nz
	Department of Internal Affairs	www.dia.govt.nz
	Energy Efficiency and Conservation Authority	www.eeca.govt.nz
	Ministry of Science and Innovation	www.msi.govt.nz
	Ministry of Agriculture and Forestry	www.maf.govt.nz
	Ministry of Economic Development	www.med.govt.nz
	Ministry for the Environment	www.mfe.govt.nz
	Ministry of Fisheries	www.fish.govt.nz
	New Zealand Trade and Enterprise	www.nzte.govt.nz
	Statistics New Zealand	www.stats.govt.nz
	Te Puni Kokiri	www.tpk.govt.nz
Chambers of Commerce	New Zealand Chambers of Commerce	www.newzealandchambers.co.nz
Institute of Management	New Zealand Institute of Management	www.nzim.co.nz
Legislation		
ACC	Accident Compensation Corporation	www.acc.co.nz
Companies	New Zealand Companies Office	www.business.govt.nz/companies
Consumer Protection	The Commerce Commission	www.comcom.govt.nz
Employment	Department of Labour	www.dol.govt.nz
Taxation	Inland Revenue Department	www.ird.govt.nz
Local Government		
Economic Development Agencies	Economic Development Association of New Zealand (EDANZ)	www.edanz.org.nz

Field	Organisation	Website
Local Councils	There are 78 local government councils in New Zealand. They can all be contacted via the list on the 'local councils' web page. Links on this page give the home page for each one with phone numbers, email addresses and details of any economic development projects.	www.localcouncils.govt.nz
Small Business Publications	*Exporter*	www.peoplemediagroup.co.nz/ print/exporter
	Franchise NZ	www.franchise.co.nz
	Her Business	www.herbusinessmagazine.com
	idealog	www.idealog.co.nz
	In Business	www.in-business.co.nz
	New Zealand Management	www.management.co.nz
	New Zealand Marketing	www.marketingmag.co.nz
	NZBusiness	www.nzbusiness.co.nz
	Peak (Aoraki Region)	www.peakmagazine.co.nz
	Scope (Waikato Region)	www.scopemagazine.co.nz
	Start-Up	www.techday.co.nz/start-up/
	Tourism Business	www.tourismbusinessmag.co.nz
	Unlimited	www.unlimited.co.nz
Tertiary Education Institutions		
Universities and Institutes of Technology and Polytechnics	There are seven universities and 19 institutes of technology and polytechnics in New Zealand offering a range of certificate, diploma and degree courses in business. They are listed on the accompanying national library web page. Links on this page give the home page for each one containing contact and course details.	www.webdirectory.natlib.govt.nz

Field	Organisation	Website
Trade Associations		
Franchising	Franchise Association of New Zealand	www.franchiseassociation.org.nz
Hospitality	Hospitality Association of New Zealand	www.hanz.org.nz
Manufacturing	Employers and Manufacturers Association	www.ema.co.nz
Retail	New Zealand Retailers Association	www.retail.org.nz
Tourism	Tourism Industry Association New Zealand	www.tianz.org.nz
Trades		
Building	Master Builders Federation	www.masterbuilder.org.nz
Boatbuilding	Marine Industry Association of New Zealand	www.nzmarine.com
Electrical	Electrical Contractors Association of New Zealand	www.ecanz.org.nz
Motor Trade	Motor Trade Association	www.mta.org.nz
Painting	New Zealand Master Painters Association	www.masterpainters.co.nz
Plumbing	Master Plumbers, Gasfitters and Drainlayers New Zealand	www.masterplumbers.org.nz
Venture Capital	ICE Angels	www.theicehouse.co.nz
	New Zealand Private Equity and Venture Capital Association	www.nzvca.co.nz

4 Legal requirements

In this chapter you will realise that you will not be your own boss in the way you had anticipated. You are about to discover an army of bureaucrats and public servants who have the authority to tell you how you may run your business.

Most of the laws and regulations exist to protect the public and to provide for an orderly business environment. If you are going to be successful at small business, then you need to learn to deal with the legal and regulatory issues. The alternative to spending your own time on these matters is to engage specialists (principally your accountant, solicitor and insurance broker) who know how to do it for you. The purpose of this chapter is to point out some of the legal obligations that you will face and how to meet them.

Legal forms of organisation

One of the important decisions you need to make is whether to set up your business as a sole trader, a partnership, a company or a trust. When you do select a legal form, the decision is never really final. Not only will your business grow and change in its needs and prospects, but your financial and tax situations will change and perhaps new owners will come into the business. Let's look at the most common options.

Sole trader

The sole trader is the easiest and simplest legal form in which a business can be organised. Because of its simplicity, it is also the least expensive. The proprietor is the sole owner of the business and has complete control over it. As sole owner, the proprietor is personally liable for business debts and is responsible for negligent acts and other wrongs committed by employees within the scope of the enterprise's activities. There is no legal distinction between the owner and the business. A sole proprietorship is automatically terminated by the death or incapacity of the owner. Here are the main advantages and disadvantages:

Advantages	Disadvantages
Ease of formation	Unlimited personal liability
Low start-up costs	Narrow management base
More freedom from regulation	Lack of continuity
Owner is in direct control	Difficulty in raising capital.
All profits go to the owner	
Maximum privacy	
Easy-to-change legal structure.	

Partnership

In a partnership business is conducted by two or more people who have the status and authority of owners or principals. The *Partnership Act 1908* defines 'partnership' as 'the relationship which subsists between persons carrying on a business in common with a view to profit'. Most partnerships are based on an agreement or contract among the co-owners. Without question, a carefully prepared written agreement spelling out the rights and duties of the partners is highly recommended. Nevertheless, a formal contract is not essential and a partnership can be created by two or more people conducting business together for profit. In the absence of a formal partnership agreement the rules governing partnerships specified in the Partnership Act will apply.

When partners do enter into a written agreement defining their relations and specifying how profits and losses are to be divided, it is a purely private agreement. There is no requirement that a partnership agreement be filed with a public agency. The partners are free to include almost any details they may wish. Most partnership agreements include the following provisions:

- Names and addresses of the partners
- Nature and purpose of the business
- Name of the partnership business
- Date at which the partnership may end
- Capital to be contributed by each partner
- How profits and losses are to be shared
- Arrangements for salaries and/or draws
- Managerial roles of each partner
- How the books of account are to be kept
- Location and signatories for bank accounts
- Any limitations upon the authority of a partner
- Provisions for the death, bankruptcy or retirement of a partner
- Provisions for the admission of new partners
- Provisions for how disputes among partners are to be settled
- Provisions for the dissolution of the partnership.

Although people often think of a partnership as separate and apart from the persons who are the partners, and although it is treated that way for accounting purposes, the law does not regard the partnership itself as a legal entity. Legally it is simply two or more individuals. The assets of the business are viewed as belonging to the partners, and they are personally responsible for its debts. Members of a partnership have equal rights in the firm's management and in the conduct of its business unless otherwise agreed. People dealing with the firm are not affected by agreements among the partners that limit the authority of some partners, at least if the outsiders do not know of these agreements.

Each partner is an agent of the firm and of the partners. Therefore, even a partner who is not particularly experienced or skilled in business affairs has the power to enter into contracts or other transactions that will be binding on the other partners. Under partnership law partners are both 'jointly *and* severally' liable, meaning that each partner is individually liable for the whole of the partnership debts. These drawbacks explain the limited use of partnerships in business. Here are the main advantages and disadvantages:

Advantages	Disadvantages
Ease of formation	Unlimited personal liability
Low start-up costs	Lack of continuity

More sources of capital	Divided authority
Broader management base	Friction between partners
Privacy of affairs	Limitations on size
Limited outside regulation	Less flexibility in transferring
Easy-to-change legal structure.	ownership interest.

Limited partnerships

A *limited partnership* is a variation of a general partnership. The *Limited Partnerships Act 2008* enables registration of limited partnerships and overseas limited partnerships. It permits people who want to contribute capital to an enterprise to avoid the unlimited liability of general partners by becoming limited partners in a firm. A limited partnership provides a list of activities that the limited partners can be involved in while not participating in the management of the Limited Partnership (safe-harbour activities). Limited partners are only at risk for the money that they have invested in the partnership and any other obligations that they have agreed to accept.

Limited liability company

A company is an association of individuals that has a separate legal personality. In other words, it is recognised in law as having an existence separate and apart from the individuals (shareholders) who own it. The company holds property, enters into contracts, transfers property and conducts legal matters in a capacity separate and distinct from its shareholders. The separateness of the company is also recognised for tax purposes.

The requirements for forming and operating a company are set down in the *Companies Act 1993*, which provides for the regulation of companies. All companies must be registered with the Companies Office by providing prescribed information about the company in a standard format. Your solicitor or accountant will help you to form your company and have it registered.

Advantages of a company

- The liability of the shareholders on business obligations, and therefore their risk, is limited to the amount they pay for their shares.
- The management of the enterprise can be centralised in a board of directors, thereby permitting selection of experts as managers of the business, whether or not they are shareholders.
- The enterprise has a continuous existence, which means that it is not dissolved by the death, insanity or withdrawal of an owner.
- An interest in the business, represented by shares, can be bought or sold, thus permitting an owner to withdraw from the company without jeopardising its continuity.

- Capital can usually be attracted in larger amounts and more readily than in a proprietorship or partnership.

Disadvantages of a company
- It involves closer regulation by government and the courts.
- It is more expensive to organise and maintain.
- Management may be restricted by the registered constitution of the company.
- Extra reporting requirements necessitate more record-keeping.
- There is less privacy regarding financial and other affairs.
- Directors' duties impose a heavy responsibility.

A limited liability company is usually formed to obtain the advantage of limited liability for individuals who might otherwise conduct business as a sole trader or a partnership. The shareholders' liability is limited to the amount of their shareholding. So if you set your company up with 1000 one-dollar shares then your liability is limited to $1000 and if you pay that into the company's account so that your shares are 'paid up' then your obligations are covered. A company only need have one director and one shareholder, who can be the same individual, and Section 26 of the Act provides that a company may, but does not have to, have a constitution. If the proposed company chooses not to have a constitution then the provisions of the 1993 Act govern its rules of operation.

The duties of a company director are complex and you should be aware of the personal responsibilities that you face. Any breach of your duties may lead to a civil suit against you by your own company, by the company's shareholders, or by creditors and any other persons with whom your company has dealt. Breaches of the Companies Act can also bring penalties by the courts.

Section 135 of the Act relates to 'reckless trading' and specifies that a director must not allow the company to trade in a manner likely to create a substantial risk or serious loss to the company's creditors. When linked to the provisions of the 'solvency test' in Section 4, this means the directors are legally responsible for trading solvency—ensuring that the company can pay its debts when they fall due in the normal course of business, and the balance-sheet test of solvency—the total value of the company's assets must always be greater than the total value of its liabilities. Failure to satisfy the solvency test represents 'reckless trading' by the director(s) and makes them personally liable to the creditors.

Trusts
Some small businesses are organised as discretionary trusts or family trading trusts. A trust is not a legal entity. It simply holds property in trust for the beneficiaries.

The trustee administers the trust in accordance with the trust deed, which may give the trustee wide discretionary powers over the distribution of trust income and capital. You should seek advice from your solicitor regarding the issues surrounding the formation of a trust in your case. Here are the main advantages and disadvantages:

Advantages	Disadvantages
Flexibility	Costly to set up and run
Continuity can be preserved	More complicated to administer
Limited liability possible	Limited life of trust deed
Minimises taxation	Trustee subject to *Trustee Act 1956*
More privacy than a company.	Powers restricted to trust deed.

Registering a business name

It is good practice to pick a name for your business which is distinctive and links in some way with your product or service. Family names are usually avoided because they lack advertising power and to protect the family name in the event of any legal action involving the business.

You can register a business name only if you intend to operate your business as a company. You cannot use approval from the Registrar of Companies for a business name and then not proceed to constitute a company using that name.

If your business is not a registered company you can call it anything you like but you have no legal ownership of such a name. Another business could challenge you under the *Fair Trading Act 1986* if your name was similar to theirs and likewise you could use the Act to challenge a name that resembled your own. The *Companies Act 1993* makes the formation of a company a straightforward procedure and our advice would be to form your business as a company and hence gain protection of your business name.

It is possible for businesses that are not registered companies to gain some name protection by registering a trade mark associated with their business name. New Zealand does maintain a Trade Marks Register and company names should not be similar to a registered or pending trade mark. If you need more information about registering a trade mark, contact the Patents Office in Wellington or your solicitor.

Establishing a shop or factory

When you establish a shop or a factory you need to register it under a variety of central and local government jurisdictions. These requirements vary from district to district and involve a number of different government departments. This is one of the more frustrating experiences in store for the small business operator, and one that will require a great deal of patience. You can save yourself a lot of confusion by first determining exactly which regulations apply to your business. Shops and factories are subject to regulations including:

Health regulations	Occupational safety and health
Trading hours	Fire precautions
Weights and measures	Water supply and sewage disposal
Description of goods	Electrical connections
Boilers	Gas connections
Discharge of waste	Scaffolding
Lifts and cranes	Storage and use of dangerous goods.

While many of the regulations are enforced through government departments, you also need to pay particular attention to local-government zoning and building regulations. Local councils are required to prepare planning schemes for the orderly and balanced development of their areas. The effect of this is to create 'zones' for specific purposes, such as residential, industrial or commercial use. In addition, councils also control the construction and use of buildings in conformity with the district plan. When you have located potential new premises, you need to ensure that you conform to the local council's planning scheme. Here is what you need to do:

- Make an application to the council for a certificate indicating the uses to which the property may be put.
- Make an appointment to discuss your proposal with the council's planning staff. Any change in the use of a building or land will require an application to the council for its consent. If there are no building works, you can begin trading within the limits and subject to the conditions specified by the council in its consent.
- If any alterations or additions or new building works are proposed, then a building application will also be required. It is wise to discuss the council's building requirements in advance with both the building inspector and the health inspector.
- Approval may also be required for any form of outdoor advertising, including signage.

Licences and permits

Certain types of businesses require one or more licences and/or permits before you can begin trading. This is often a perplexing problem for the new starter because licences can be required by a variety of central- and local-government authorities. Here are some of the businesses for which special licences and/or permits may be required:

Advertising agency	Delicatessen
Air services	Driving instructor

Appraiser or assessor	Electrician
Auctioneer	Employment agency
Auditor	Firearms dealer
Barber or hairdresser	Fisherman
Broadcasting	Street vendor
Broker or agent	Importer
Butcher	Kennels
Chemist	Liquor seller
Medical specialist	Livestock dealer
Milk vendor	Second-hand goods dealer
Motor mechanic	Sawmiller
Motor-vehicle dealer	Solicitor
Pawnbroker or money lender	Stockbroker
Petroleum products	Tax agent
Plumber	Taxi or hire car
Produce dealer	Tow truck operator
Restaurant	Travel agent.

Accident Compensation Corporation (ACC)

This universal scheme to compensate and help to rehabilitate those who are injured in New Zealand in accidents, whether work-related or non-work related, is unique to New Zealand. The cost of non-work related accidents is covered by the earner's premium, which is collected via the PAYE scheme and the annual tax returns of the self-employed. To meet the cost of accidents in the workplace, all employers (including self-employers) must also pay an employer's premium. In general terms, this levy is expressed as an amount per $100 of earnings paid in the previous financial year. The rate varies from industry to industry to reflect the frequency and seriousness of accidents in each industry. The ACC scheme is a form of insurance that enables compensation to be paid to those who suffer an injury in New Zealand. There are however many other risks for which a small business owner needs protection. You can find out more at the ACC website at www.acc.co.nz.

Insurance

Insurance provides financial protection against losses such as fire, theft, burglary, accidents to employees on the job and injury to the public. You pay a premium, for a guarantee that you will be compensated for a specified loss if it occurs. Insurance policies tend to be written in legal language and you should ask your insurance broker for a Plain English policy. The common types of business insurance are listed as follows but an insurance broker can advise you on your particular needs.

Public liability insurance

In conducting a business, you are subject to the laws governing negligence to customers, and anyone else with whom you do business or who is affected by your actions in business. There are several types of risks that can be covered by public liability insurance including:

- Injuries to others while on your premises
- Injuries to others from the use of motor vehicles or equipment from your premises
- Damage to other people's property
- Injury or damage as a result of the purchaser's use of your product or service.

Failure to recognise the dangers of not carrying public liability insurance can be one of the most serious errors you can make. One judgement against you could easily wipe out all of your assets. Most of the risks can be covered under a general public liability insurance policy, sometimes referred to as a public risk or comprehensive liability policy. Some risks are excluded from general public liability policies and need to be covered separately. These include third-party motor vehicle insurance and product liability insurance.

Fire and property insurance

Fire and property insurance provides cover for your business against losses stemming from destruction of real property, such as buildings, and personal property, such as machines, furniture, fittings and goods. The term *fire insurance* has a much wider meaning than simply insuring property against damage by fire or lightning. Other risks that can be covered in a fire policy include damage caused by:

Aircraft   Water
Explosions   Flood
Storm and tempest   Earthquake
Riots, strikes and vandalism   Electric current (fusion)
Impact by vehicles, horses or cattle.

The *glass* in your business premises can be covered, including damage to shopfronts, display cases and mirrors. It will also cover the structural repairs and temporary shutters needed for glass replacement.

If you are running a business from home, be aware that home and contents policies do not normally cover business losses.

Fidelity insurance

Fidelity insurance is important to any small business that must trust employees to handle significant amounts of cash. The policy indemnifies you against loss through embezzlement or fraudulent misappropriation of money by an employee. The policy can be written to cover an individual person, a particular individual or group of employees, such as the accounts clerks, or it can be a blanket policy covering all of your employees.

Burglary insurance

Burglary insurance should be carried on that portion of your contents that can be easily removed and constitutes a significant potential loss. It is not usually worth the high premiums to cover all of your contents for their full value. Burglary insurance not only covers stolen property but it also covers damage done by burglars to premises and contents arising from forcible entry.

Transit insurance

Transit insurance covers financial loss incurred in the movement of goods. It can cover all transit risks, or it can cover only nominated risks. The cost of transit insurance can vary significantly according to the scope of the cover. Transport companies will arrange to insure the goods that they carry for a premium over and above their cartage charges.

Business continuation insurance

When your business is shut down as a result of a serious fire or flood, you may be protected for loss of property, but not for the loss of operating revenue to pay the bills while you rebuild. Similarly, if a partner or a key employee dies, you may not be able to keep operating without their skills.

Loss of profits insurance

Sometimes called 'consequential loss insurance', this is usually an addition to your fire insurance policy. It will reimburse you for part of the lost profit and a proportion of the fixed costs of your business while you are out of action. It will never cover the full amount of the loss. It is one way, however, of making sure that you have the funds to stay in business when you are temporarily unable to trade.

Partnership insurance

Partnership insurance provides immediate cash to keep a partnership business intact in the event of the death of one of the partners. Since the death of a partner legally ends the partnership, the proceeds of this insurance can be used by the surviving partners to buy the deceased partner's interest from their estate to form a new partnership.

Key person insurance

This is the same as partnership insurance except that the beneficiary is the business entity itself. This is usually considered only when the loss of a key person may put the survival of the firm in jeopardy. It is designed to cover the extra expenses that a key person's death would cause, such as the cost of finding and recruiting a replacement, training costs and lost sales to important customers.

Taxation

Taxation is complicated and it is not an area for do-it-yourselfers. Taxation affects practically every phase of business and trying to keep up with the ever-changing legislation and legal precedents is tiresome. Tax evasion is illegal but tax avoidance is not. In order to minimise your tax burden and ease the administrative nightmare, you should engage a taxation consultant who is familiar with your industry. In most cases, this will be your accountant.

If you want to learn more about the tax system, the Inland Revenue Department publishes an introductory guide for businesses and non-profit organisations called *IR320 Smart Business*. This guide is available from the IRD offices or you can download it from the IRD website www.ird.gov.nz.

The IRD has powerful legal rights of investigation and enforcement and you should take care to comply with all the taxation requirements. Here are a few basic obligations and your accountant can advise you about how to comply with them.

Apply for an IRD number

Different forms of business have different requirements when applying for an IRD number. If you operate as a sole trader, you use your personal IRD number for your business. If you don't have a personal IRD number, fill in an IR595 to apply for one.

Partnerships, companies and trusts need their own IRD numbers. To apply for a partnership number use an IR596 with a copy of the names and personal IRD numbers of each of the partners. For companies, use an IR596 with a copy of the company's certificate of incorporation. If you need an IRD number for a trust, use an IR596 with a copy of the trust deed.

Register for goods and services tax (GST)

If your annual sales are expected to be over $60 000 you are obliged to register your business for GST purposes. When you are registered for GST you must account for GST on everything you sell at a rate of 15%, but you can claim back the GST that you pay on your business costs. You can register online at www.ird.govt.nz or by completing the GST registration form IR360.

Keep records

You must keep records to be able to calculate your income and expenses and to confirm your accounts. If you're registered for GST your records must be clear enough to work out your GST liability. For business income records, you must keep:

- Books of account, such as cashbook, journals and ledgers
- Receipts and invoices
- Bank statements, cheque butts and deposit slips
- Worksheets showing tax-return calculations
- Any other necessary documents to confirm account entries.

Produce annual accounts and file annual tax returns

To assess your tax liability you need to produce annual accounts at 31 March each year. The annual accounts include the final profit and loss statement and balance sheet. If you want a balance date other than 31 March you must apply in writing to the IRD. For 31 March balance dates the tax returns are due on 7 July.

Pay your taxes on time

The IRD is not a patient creditor and will automatically add penalties to overdue amounts. Different taxes are due at various times throughout the year, as set out below.

Goods and services tax (GST)

GST is not a tax on your business income. It is collected from your customers and paid to the IRD less any GST that you have paid to your suppliers. Once you are registered, the IRD will send you the return forms in time for you to complete and return them by the due date, along with your payment. There are certain goods and services that are either exempt from GST or are zero-rated (e.g. exported goods, financial services, bank charges, wages and salaries).

The standard period for making GST payments is two-monthly, although you can pay monthly if you wish. If your annual sales are under $500 000 you are allowed to pay six-monthly. In any case, once you have established the tax period the due date is the last working day of the month after the end of the taxable period. Penalties and interest are charged on any late payments of GST.

If you are registered for GST you must issue a tax invoice for any supplies you make to another GST-registered person. A copy must be kept of all invoices you give to your customers. This will confirm the entries you make in your deposit book and cashbook.

Pay as your earn (PAYE)

Tax deducted from employees' wages and salaries (PAYE tax) is due to be transferred to the IRD on the 20th of the month following the month that tax was deducted.

Income tax

There are four income tax dates in each year. Income tax is due in three provisional part payments for the current year (7 July, 7 November and 7 March), and any residual from the previous year is due on 7 February. At the end of your accounting year you will produce a set of accounts to work out how much profit (or loss) your business has made. To do this you add up the income the business earned over the year and subtract all the allowable expenses.

If you have a 31 March balance date, you must send your tax return to Inland Revenue by 7 July. If you have a different balance date, you must send your return to the Inland Revenue by three months and seven days after your balance date.

Fringe benefit tax (FBT)

Fringe benefit tax due on any benefits given to employees on top of their salary and wages (e.g. use of motor vehicles or discounted goods or services) is due (including interest) annually on 31 May. If you want to avoid the interest component you can pay quarterly on 20 July, 20 October, 20 January, and 31 May.

Claiming expenses

All businesses incur expenses in generating taxable income. Most of these expenses can be deducted from your sales and income to arrive at net profit on which income tax is calculated. Examples of deductible expenses include:

- Rent paid on business premises
- Repairs and maintenance on business items
- Stationery and supplies for the business
- Purchases of raw materials or trading stock
- Any fringe benefit tax that's been paid
- Electricity and telephone costs
- Business vehicle and transport costs
- Interest on money borrowed for the business
- Interest on underpayments of tax
- Gross wages paid to employees
- Employer superannuation contributions
- Insurance of business assets or premises
- Premiums paid for accident insurance
- ACC levies paid to Inland Revenue
- Professional fees
- 50% of business entertainment costs
- Depreciation of asset values.

Some business expenses can't be claimed as an income-tax deduction. Examples of non-deductible expenses are:

- The cost of plant and machinery
- Legal fees incurred in setting up a business
- Loan principal repayments
- Improvements to equipment (apart from repairs and maintenance).

If you are a sole trader or in a partnership and you use your own vehicle in the business, you can claim the running costs for income tax. If you use the vehicle strictly for business only, you can claim the full running costs. If you use it to travel from home to work, or any personal travel, you'll need to separate the running costs of your vehicle between business and private use. To do this, you must keep a logbook for at least three months every three years to work out the business share of the running costs.

If you run a business from home you can claim a portion of the household expenses such as rates, insurance, power, maintenance, mortgage interest and depreciation (if you own the house). You must keep invoices for these expenses. You can only claim the expenses that relate to the area set aside for business. Calculate the work area as a percentage of the total floor area of the house, then apply this percentage to the total house expenses. You can claim 50 per cent of your telephone rental if there is one line into your home, but if you have both a domestic and commercial line you can only claim the commercial line.

Depreciation allows for the wear and tear on a fixed asset. You can claim depreciation on fixed assets used in your business that have a useful lifespan of more than 12 months. However, not all fixed assets can be depreciated—land is a common example. You'll have to keep a fixed-asset register to show assets you are depreciating. This should show the depreciation claimed and adjusted tax value of each asset. The adjusted tax value is the asset's cost price, less all the depreciation calculated since purchase using either a straight-line or diminishing-value method. The depreciation rates for various assets are set by Inland Revenue, and are based on the cost and useful life of the asset being depreciated.

Tax and cash flow

In your first year, you will have to wait until a set of accounts has been produced for the year before you can determine your income-tax liability. That amount will be due on 7 February in the following year. After your annual tax liability has been established by your first tax return, you will have to pay provisional tax from the second year onwards. Provisional tax is not a separate tax but a way of paying your income tax as the income is received through the year. With provisional tax, you pay instalments of income tax throughout the year, based on what you expect your tax bill based on projected income to be. The amount of provisional tax you pay through the year is then deducted from your tax bill at the end of the tax year. This payment schedule creates a potential cash-flow problem in the second year of business because you have to pay two years' tax in one year—the three provisional payments for year two, plus the full tax from year one.

Employment legislation

The *Employment Relations Act 2000* has 'good faith' as its central principle. Employers, employees and unions must deal with each other honestly and openly. The Act is designed to:

- Promote good employment relations and mutual respect and confidence between employers, employees and unions
- Set the environment for individual and collective employment relationships
- Set out requirements for the negotiation and content of collective and individual employment agreements
- Provide prompt and flexible options for resolving problems in employment relationships.

Here are the employer's obligations set out in the Act.

Offering employment

Several laws cover how a job can be offered. The *Human Rights Act 1993* applies to job advertisements, application forms, interviews and job offers. In most cases, jobs must be open to anyone, whatever their colour, race, ethnic or national origins, disability, gender (including pregnancy or childbirth status), marital or family status, age, religious or ethical belief, political opinion, employment status or sexual orientation. Generally, none of these reasons should be the basis for offering different terms and conditions or fringe benefits to different applicants. The Human Rights Commission deals with complaints under the Human Rights Act.

It is an offence against the Fair Trading Act to act in a misleading or deceptive way in advertising or offering employment. For instance, an employer must not make misleading statements about the type of work, work conditions, rates of pay or promotion prospects.

Employment agreements

Individual or collective employment agreements govern the terms of employment and it is in your interests to establish a good procedure for ensuring that a written contract is set up for every employee who joins your staff. Your lawyer or the Employment Relations Service can help you with the requirements for the content and structure of an employment contract.

Minimum wage

By law, employers must pay at least the minimum wage—even if an employee is paid by commission or by piece rate. The minimum wage applies to all workers aged 16 years or older, including home-based workers, casuals, temporary and part-time workers.

From April 2010 the adult minimum wage was set at $12.75 an hour. That's $102 for an eight-hour day, and $510 for a 40-hour week.

The 'new entrants' minimum wage and the training minimum wage are $10.20 an hour. That's $81.60 for an eight-hour day, and $408 for a 40-hour week.

You can contact the Department of Labour's Employment Relations Infoline (0800 209 020) to check whether these rates are still current.

Equal pay

An employer cannot pay men and women different pay rates for doing the same or substantially similar work if the only difference is their sex (*Equal Pay Act 1972*). In addition, the Human Rights Act prohibits discriminatory pay rates or employment conditions. Under the Employment Relations Act employers may not discriminate on those same grounds or on the grounds that a person has been involved in union activities.

Wages and time records

Employers must keep wages and time records for each employee, for six years. Employees and their representatives have the right to see these. These records must include the following information.

- The employee's name
- The employee's age if under 20
- The employee's postal address
- The kind of work on which the employee is usually employed
- Whether the person is employed under a collective or individual employment agreement
- If employed under a collective agreement, the title and expiry date of the contract and the employee's classification under it
- Where necessary to calculate the employee's pay, the hours between which the employee is employed each day and the days on which they are employed during each pay period
- The wages paid to the employee each pay period and the method of calculation
- Details of employment-related education leave taken by the employee.

Holidays

The *Holidays Act 2003* gives all employees rights to paid annual leave, whether they are full-time, part-time, fixed-term, temporary or casual workers, adults or young employees. Employees are not lawfully able to agree to give up these rights.

Under the Holidays Act all employees are entitled to a minimum of four weeks annual holidays after the first year of employment. This is a minimum entitlement and there is nothing preventing the parties negotiating better terms.

In addition every employee is entitled to no fewer than 11 public holidays each year, which should be paid holidays for the employee when they fall on days of the week on which the employee would normally work. Public holidays are in addition to paid annual leave days. Unless the employment agreement provides for other days, or the employee and employer concerned agree to other days, the 11 public holidays are:

- Christmas Day
- Boxing Day
- New Year's Day
- 2 January (or another day in its place)
- Waitangi Day (not Mondayised in NZ)
- Good Friday
- Easter Monday
- Anzac Day (not Mondayised in NZ)
- Queen's Birthday
- Labour Day
- Anniversary Day for the Province.

Sickness and bereavement leave

By law, after working for the same employer for six months, an employee has the right to five days' paid special leave for each subsequent 12-month period. Special leave can be used by an employee for sick leave or domestic leave to care for a sick spouse, dependent child or parent or spouse of the employee.

The Holidays Act provides for up to three days' paid bereavement leave on the death of an immediate family member. This can be taken at any time and for any purpose genuinely relating to the death. 'Immediate family members' are the employee's spouse, parent, child, sibling, grandparent, grandchild or the spouse's parent. Where there is a multiple bereavement, the employee is entitled to three days' bereavement leave in respect of each death.

Leave for Defence Force volunteers

Employees who do full-time voluntary training in the armed forces for periods adding up to three months or less have their jobs protected by the *Volunteers Employment Protection Act 1973*. Part-time training is also covered if it adds up to no more than three weeks in each year from 1 April to 31 March, based on the employee's normal working week.

Parental leave

Under the *Parental Leave and Employment Protection Act 1987*, unpaid parental leave is available to employees and self-employed women who are having a child. It is also available to employees and self-employed people who are adopting a child under six years of age. To apply for parental leave under the Act, the employee must have worked at least 10 hours a week for 12 months before the expected date of birth or adoption for the same employer or essentially the same employer. The maximum level of payment is currently $458.82 a week before tax.

If self-employed people meet the eligibility criteria, they are entitled to paid parental leave for 14 weeks. This payment is funded by the government and applications for paid leave are made to the Inland Revenue Department.

The rules regarding the entitlements for employees and their partners are complex. Further advice and assistance is available from the Employment Relations Service Infoline on 0800 209 020 and on the website at www.ers.dol.govt.nz.

Fair Trading Act

The *Fair Trading Act 1986* prohibits misleading and deceptive conduct, false representations, and unfair practices in trade. This affects your advertising and promotion and anything said to consumers during the act of selling products or services. The Act is administered by the Commerce Commission, but civil action may be taken by the Commerce Commission or any other person—including your trade rivals!

The Act must be treated with care because of its non-specific nature. Section 9 prohibits deceptive conduct or conduct that is *likely* to deceive; i.e. deception does not have to have occurred for an offence to be committed. Proof of individual deception or damage is not required. Engaging in deceptive conduct includes *omissions to act*—so failing to tell consumers the full truth about a product or service also constitutes a breach of the Act. Interpretation of the word 'likely' by the courts has been that if a significant proportion of the public, *including the gullible and poorly educated*, would be misled or deceived by your conduct then deceptive conduct has occurred.

The enforcement of the Fair Trading Act is by way of criminal and civil penalties with fines of up to $60 000 for individuals (you and your staff), and up to $200 000 for companies. The courts may also issue restraining injunctions, orders to disclose information or publish corrective advertisements, and other orders that void or vary contracts, order refunds and returns, award the payment of damages, or order the supply of certain goods or services to consumers. For more information go the Commerce Commission at www.comcom.govt.nz.

Consumer Guarantees Act

The *Consumer Guarantees Act 1993* encompasses standards for the quality of goods and services supplied to consumers, and applies to manufacturers, distributors, retailers, financiers and agents.

For products the Act creates an obligation on suppliers to guarantee ownership or title of goods, and that goods are of acceptable quality and fit for the purpose they were designed for. In addition the Act forces suppliers to deliver goods that match with samples or demonstrations. Manufacturers of products are compelled to provide repair services and spare parts for the products they make. Where price is not settled before products have been supplied, the eventual price requested by a supplier must be reasonable. For services there are four generic guarantees. Services must:

- Be performed with reasonable care and skill (section 28)
- Be fit for the purpose and achieve expected results (section 29)
- Be completed in a reasonable time where the time is not settled (section 30)
- Be reasonably priced where the price is not settled (section 31).

Section 18 defines the rules for settlement by the parties in the following manner. If the failure can be remedied, the supplier may choose to remedy, cure or replace the product or service, or make a full refund of money to the consumer. If the consumer suffers an unreasonable delay by the supplier in remedying the failure, the consumer may seek a remedy elsewhere and recover the cost. The consumer also has the power to reject replacement goods in favour of a refund. A breach of the Consumer Guarantees Act can be a breach of the Fair Trading Act. If so, penalties under the Fair Trading Act may apply.

Intellectual property rights

Patents, trade marks, designs, and copyrights (see below) are collectively known as intellectual property. The purpose of intellectual property rights is to protect the entitlement of inventors and developers to realise a commercial benefit from their work. There are two things to remember about intellectual property. The first is to ensure that you avoid infringing the intellectual property rights of others. The second is to protect the intellectual property rights to which you may be entitled.

Intellectual property law is complex, and it is in your interest to seek specialist legal advice. The Intellectual Property Office of New Zealand (IPONZ) is the government agency responsible for the granting and registration of intellectual property rights. IPONZ is a business unit of the Ministry of Economic Development (MED) and their website is www.iponz.govt.nz. The IPONZ administers the *Patents Act 1953*, the *Trade Marks Act 2002*, the *Designs Act 1953* and the *Plant Variety Rights Act 1987*. The Office manages the examination and registration or grant of intellectual property rights and maintains the registers of these rights and interests.

Patents

A patent is a right granted for any device, substance, method or process that is new, inventive and useful. A New Zealand standard patent is legally enforceable and gives the owner the exclusive right to commercially exploit the invention in New Zealand for a period of 20 years. You must make an application to IPONZ for a patent and your application will be examined to ensure that it meets all of the legal requirements before it is granted. Registering a patent in New Zealand does not give you international protection. Most countries have similar patent systems and New Zealand is party to a number of international agreements that can reduce the complexity of applying overseas.

Keep in mind that if you demonstrate, sell or discuss your invention in public before you file your patent application, you will not be granted a patent. You can talk to employees, business partners, or advisers about your invention, but only on a confidential basis. Get a signed confidentiality agreement before you disclose any information.

You can choose between filing a complete specification or a provisional specification that contains only a broad description of the invention. A provisional specification is not examined, so IPONZ does not conduct a search for similar inventions or give an opinion on the content of the application. This option gives you a further 12 months (extendable to 15 months upon request) before you need to file a complete specification. There are benefits to starting the application process in this way:

- You gain up to a maximum of 15 months to work on the development, financing and marketing of your invention.
- You do not need to publicly disclose the full or specific details of your invention.
- You establish a priority date that can help protect the invention from being patented by others.
- You gain an application number that you can use on the products you manufacture along with the words 'patent pending'.
- You can reveal your invention to interested parties to gauge how successful it may be before proceeding further.
- You avoid the larger cost of continuing your application until you can decide if you will proceed to file a complete specification.

Trade marks

A trade mark is a letter, number, word, phrase, sound, smell, colour, shape, logo, picture, aspect of packaging, or any combination of these things that identifies a product or service and distinguishes it from similar products and services. The owner of a trade mark has exclusive rights to control the use of their trade mark for the goods and services for which it is registered. You do not have to register a trade mark to use it. However, protecting an unregistered trade mark is a difficult legal process. Initial registration is for a period of 10 years, and as long as you keep using the trade mark you can renew the registration for further periods.

In special cases where a trade mark is, or appears to be, a derivative of a Maori sign, the application will be forwarded to the Maori Trade Marks Advisory Committee. The Committee will advise IPONZ whether the mark is likely to be offensive to Maori.

Designs

A design refers to the appearance of industrial or commercial articles in terms of features such as shape, configuration, pattern or ornamentation. Design registration is used to protect the new or original visual appearance of manufactured products. It does not apply to designs that are essentially artistic works that are covered by copyright laws. The full term of a design registration is 15 years. A design is initially registered for five years and then renewal fees are charged at five and ten years from the application date.

Copyright

A copyright provides protection for original material in literary, artistic, dramatic or musical works, films, broadcasts, multimedia and computer programs. Once a work is created, copyright is automatically recognised under the law. Copyright does not last forever. The New Zealand time limit will depend on the original work involved and when it was either created, published, performed and—in the case of product designs—commercialised. IPONZ provides the following guide on time limits.

Copyright work	New Zealand time limit
Literary, dramatic, musical and artistic works	50 years beyond the death of the author
Publisher's copyright (typographical layout of a published edition)	25 years from publication
Sound recordings and film	50 years from the year in which the work was made
Communication works including repeats	50 years from the initial broadcast or transmission
Plant variety right (PVR)	20 years for non-woody plants
	23 years for woody plants from the date rights are granted

Plant variety rights (PVR)

A plant variety right for a new plant variety gives you the exclusive right to produce for sale and sell propagating material of the variety. In the case of vegetatively propagated fruit, ornamental and vegetable varieties, plant variety rights give you the additional exclusive commercial right to propagate the protected variety for the commercial production of fruit, flowers or other products of the variety. A PVR holder may license others to produce for sale and to sell propagating material of the protected variety. Rights holders can, in this way, collect royalties from the commercialisation of their protected varieties.

5 Franchising

Franchising is changing the way in which many New Zealand small businesses are organised and operated. Franchising is a method of getting into business for yourself but not by yourself. It may appeal to you if you have been unable to find a suitable business idea or if you consider the risks of independent self-employment too great. The main advantage of franchising is that you have the expertise of a franchising organisation behind you. The main drawback is that you will not achieve the independence that one usually expects from self-employment. The purpose of this chapter is to explain how franchising works, its advantages and disadvantages, and how you can decide if it is right for you.

What is a franchise?

There is no universally accepted definition of the term franchise, which is used to describe a number of different types of arrangements across many different industries. Franchising is basically a marketing technique. It consists of a continuing relationship between a parent company (called the franchisor) and an individual operator (called the franchisee) in which the franchisor's knowledge, market position and operating techniques are made available to the franchisee. In other words, a franchise is a prepackaged business that you can operate under an agreement with a franchisor. There are many examples of businesses in which franchising operates including:

Accommodation	Printing
Automotive	Real estate
Building products	Recreation and leisure
Business services	Retail books
Cleaning and maintenance	Retail clothing
Convenience stores	Retail gifts
Crafts	Retail general
Education	Retail household
Financial services	Retail sports, gymnasiums and sports training
Food	Security services
Hire or rental	Trade services
Household services	Travel services
Industrial services	Video stores
Personal services.	

A franchise agreement is a legal contract between the franchisor and the franchisee. The franchisor sells the right to use a trade mark, trade name and business format to a franchisee. Sometimes the franchisee also agrees to buy equipment and/or supplies from the franchisor. There are many types of franchise arrangements, but most can be grouped into product and trade name franchises or business format franchises.

Product and trade name franchises

Product and trade name franchises refer to a distribution system in which the franchisee is licensed to sell products manufactured by the franchisor. In some cases the franchisee is licensed to do the manufacturing as well. This group includes car dealerships, petrol stations, manufacturing franchises and many wholesale distributors.

A manufacturing franchisee buys a licence to produce and sell a product. Patents, moulds, equipment and production methods are supplied by the franchisor. Examples of this type of franchise are soft drink bottlers and photo finishers. A wholesale distributor is franchised to sell a manufacturer's product to retailers. In some cases they sell only to the manufacturer's retail franchisees, such as a beer distributor.

Business format franchises

Business format franchises are broader in scope than product or trade name franchises. This is the group that has been responsible for the spectacular growth in franchising. The franchisor provides not only the product, service and trade mark but also the entire business format, consisting of a marketing plan and support, operating methods and manuals, training, quality control, and ongoing back-up services. Business format franchises generally consist of retail stores, service businesses and food service operations.

The franchisee buys the company name, the standardised operating system, and sometimes a distinctive vehicle, shop-front or building design. The best-known category of franchising is the fast-food restaurant. It is the distinctive, easily recognisable operation with a limited menu and a takeaway service. The format of a fast-food restaurant lends itself to franchising formulas.

The Franchise Association of New Zealand

The Franchise Association of New Zealand (FANZ) is the industry umbrella organisation. It has evolved from the Franchise Association of Australia and New Zealand into the current independent New Zealand organisation. It concerns itself with lobbying government, ethics in franchising, member education, industry development and the promotion of franchising. FANZ's membership includes not only franchisors and franchisees but also others with an interest in franchising such as solicitors, accountants, banks and industry consultants.

Members of the Franchise Association of New Zealand must abide by the rules of the association which include the Franchising Code of Practice. It also provides that a prospective franchisee is entitled to a seven-day cooling-off period after signing the franchise agreement as well as specifying standards of conduct and providing for the resolution of any disputes between a franchisor and a franchisee through mediation. For more information their website is at www.franchiseassociation.org.nz.

In 2003, a survey by the Franchise Association of New Zealand and sponsored by the National Bank found 350 active franchise systems in New Zealand. Industry turnover for 2010 is estimated at $14 billion being produced from 14 000 operating units that employ over 100 000 people.

An earlier study found the most prevalent types of franchises in New Zealand are non-food retailing, personal or other services, retail food and construction or trade services. Overall, 51 per cent of franchise systems are involved in services of one kind or another, 36 per cent are associated with retailing and only 13 per cent are in manufacturing.

The survival rate of new franchisee businesses over the first five years was a consistent 75–80 per cent across all industries. This compares with a variety of statistics that show the survival rates for small business in general can be as low as 50 per cent in the first three years. Not only are the survival prospects better in franchised businesses but the returns are healthy as well. The average return on a franchisee's investment is 30–35 per cent.

The lower business risk and healthy returns are reflected in the availability of finance. Results from the 2003 survey showed approximately 23 per cent of the franchise systems provided finance to franchisees at start-up. All of the respondents said that finance was available: 33 per cent said it was 'easy' to obtain, and 15 per cent said it was 'difficult' to obtain.

Advantages of being a franchisee

There are a number of potential advantages that a franchise arrangement may offer you over independent self-employment. These advantages are the reasons why some people prefer to be franchisees.

Reduced risk of failure

Research studies suggest that franchisees operating small businesses have a better survival rate than non-franchised small businesses. Franchising cannot save someone from incompetence, but it does act as a safety net for individuals who are otherwise capable but need some assistance in getting started. In particular, business format franchising reduces the scope for making the types of mistakes that lead to business closure because it represents a total business system that has already proven itself.

Overcoming limited experience

Another appeal of franchising is that it enables people with limited experience to become self-employed. You can take advantage of the franchisor's knowledge and experience that you would otherwise have to build up over a long time through trial and error. By having access to the managerial resources of a franchisor, you are able to reduce the uncertainty associated with establishing a new business.

Proven market position

As a franchisee you get a developed business concept with proven products and services. Your business has instant pulling power. To develop this pulling power on your own might take years of promotion and considerable expense. You get the benefit of regional and national advertising and promotion, ongoing market research, and the goodwill of the franchisor's name, product and service.

Access to training and assistance

The franchisor provides you with training and management assistance. You can expect to be trained in the mechanics of the franchisor's business and guided in its day-to-day operation until you are proficient at the job. Management consulting services and quality-control monitoring are often provided by the franchisor on a continuing basis.

Buying power

You should be able to benefit from the franchisor's centralised bulk purchasing of products, equipment, supplies, advertising materials and other business needs.

Location and layout

You can expect to get competently designed facilities, floor layout plans, displays and fixtures. The franchisor has usually developed highly efficient facilities based on their experience with many franchisees and they can help you to avoid functionally or aesthetically poor facilities. The franchisor can also help you to maximise customer traffic with location analysis and site-selection assistance.

Financial assistance

The franchisor may give you financial assistance by making it possible for you to start out with less than the full amount of the up-front costs. Financial assistance can be provided in the form of trade credit, low-interest loans or loan guarantees. With the name of a well-known successful franchisor behind you, your ability to negotiate with financial institutions will be strengthened.

Disadvantages of being a franchisee

A franchise also has some potential disadvantages that you do not face when you are independently self-employed. Some of these disadvantages are avoidable—others are not.

Franchisor failure

When you establish an independent small business most of the risk is in how you operate it. When you become a franchisee most of the risk is in your choice of franchisor. While franchising has a better record of survival than independent small businesses there have been, and there will continue to be, failures. Not every franchise system is the same. Not every product or service will succeed. Not every franchisor has the business and financial acumen to be successful.

Franchisee failures

A franchisee is not only vulnerable to the mistakes of the franchisor, but also to the mistakes of other franchisees. The failure of just one franchisee can do tremendous harm to the image of an entire franchise system. A few poorly managed outlets reflect on all of the others. If this discourages new franchisees from taking up outlets, then the long-term effect is to weaken the franchisor. If the franchisor becomes too weak, then it will not be able to provide the kind of support that underpins the whole franchise concept. This interdependence is the strength of franchising when it works, but it is a source of vulnerability when it does not.

Loss of independence

You will have to conform to standardised operations. You cannot make all the rules. Contrary to the 'be your own boss' lures in franchise advertisements, you will not truly be your own boss. Your business will be known by the name of the franchise, not by your own name. You will have to follow prescribed procedures, and you may have to handle products or services that are not popular or profitable in your particular outlet.

Contractual disadvantages

The franchise contract may be written to the advantage of the franchisor. Clauses in some franchise contracts may call for unreasonably high sales quotas or mandatory working hours. Most franchise agreements have expiry dates and there may be no guarantee of renewal. Even if renewal is guaranteed, the terms may not be favourable. Contracts also specify conditions for the cancellation or termination of the franchise by the franchisor, and restrictions on the franchisee selling their franchise or otherwise recovering their investment.

Competitive restrictions

You may not have the freedom to meet local competition in the ways you think are most appropriate. Under a franchise arrangement you will be restricted in the way you establish selling prices, introduce new products or services, or drop unprofitable ones. Even though the franchise system has worked elsewhere, there is no guarantee that it will work for you.

Increased cost

It could be more costly to become a franchisee than to set up your own business. In addition to the normal start-up costs, you will also have to pay an up-front franchise fee plus continuing royalty fees of between 5% and 10% of gross sales (not just out of profits). You may also find yourself paying management fees and advertising levies. You may even be required to buy merchandise, supplies or equipment from the franchisor that you can get cheaper elsewhere. The big question, of course, is whether all of these extra costs can be justified in terms of higher profits and lower risk as a franchisee.

Franchise fees

Fees charged in franchising range from the initial premium paid to gain entry through to a variety of ongoing levies and fees for services provided by the franchisor to the franchisee.

Premium

The premium paid by the franchisee on the grant of the franchise is in effect the price of entry into a system with an established reputation and accrued goodwill. It obviously incorporates a profit component to the franchisor, but it also represents payment for an array of initial services, training, operations manual, site selection, shop design, fit-out and opening assistance. Where there is no established reputation and goodwill, either because the system is new, or because it is a young and geographically isolated system expanding into a new area, the franchisee would expect to pay an appropriately discounted premium. The franchisee fee must represent a true business value for the investment being made by the franchisee and should be related to either actual or reliable future profitability of the business.

Royalties

Royalties are generally paid monthly as a percentage of sales. Part of the royalty represents profit to the franchisor but it should also reflect the cost of providing a package of continuing services and assistance to the franchisee. The strength of the relationship depends to a large extent on the quality of the continuing services. Royalties tend to range from 3 per cent to 10 per cent of gross sales. A survey of New Zealand franchises reported an average of 6 per cent in royalties.

Advertising levy

An advertising levy is generally paid monthly as a percentage of sales. A significant advantage of franchising is in the existing goodwill and reputation, which is largely generated with advertising opportunities not available to individual entrepreneurs. Although the franchisor derives no direct profit, these funds should be exclusively dedicated to advertising. The franchisor also benefits from the goodwill and reputation that will accrue to the system. In many systems the advertising levies are held in a separate account so that the operation of the advertising funds is transparent to the franchisees.

Other fees

The franchisor may of course receive other income streams through the provision of initial equipment packages, the provision of goods and services, or the leasing or subleasing of sites. A renewal fee is sometimes charged by the franchisor before granting a new contract to an existing franchisee. Similarly, a transfer fee may be charged to an existing franchisee who wants to transfer ownership to another person.

In all cases, however, the fee structure of the franchise system must make sense for both the franchisor and the franchisee. The franchisor must recover the cost of developing the franchise and receive a premium payment for the intellectual property represented in the brand and the system itself. If the franchisor tries to recover these costs too quickly with high up-front premiums and heavy royalties, then the franchisees may struggle to be profitable and the overall system will suffer. Franchisees may default on payments, disputes will increase, some franchisees may fold and new franchises will be hard to sell. The aim is to strike a working balance that gives proper returns to the franchisor in the medium or longer term, while leaving the franchisee with franchise fees that are sustainable.

Evaluating a franchise system

The price you pay for a franchise must be justified in terms of the quality of the system and the people behind it. To avoid investing in a poor quality franchise system, you need to investigate a number of elements.

The disclosure document

All franchisors registered under the FANZ Code of Practice are required to provide a prospective franchisee with a prescribed disclosure document. Although this is not a legal requirement, a franchisor's refusal to do so should immediately raise questions in your mind about their integrity. A disclosure document should contain all the information an intending franchisee needs to make an informed evaluation of the franchisor and their operation. The disclosure document prescribed by the FANZ Code of Practice requires the following information:

- The name and registered office of the franchisor and whether they are a member of the any other relevant trade or industry association
- The names, job descriptions and qualifications of the franchisor's directors, executive officers and principals
- A detailed resumé of the business experience of the franchisor (and any related entities) and its directors, secretary, executive officers and principals
- A viability statement with key financial information in respect of the franchisor
- Details of any materially relevant debt, criminal, civil or administrative proceedings or bankruptcies or insolvencies (past or pending) concerning the franchisor (and any related entities) or any of its directors, executive officers or principals
- A summary of the main particulars and features of the franchise
- A tabulated list of the components making up the franchise purchase, such as the franchise fee, stock, fixtures and fittings, and working capital
- Details of any financial requirements by the franchisor of the franchisee, such as a specific amount of non-borrowed capital towards the franchise purchase price

- The number of existing franchises and company or principals' outlets
- A list of existing franchisees (including the address and phone number of each and the year they commenced business) for referee purposes
- The number of franchises terminated or not renewed over the past year
- Details of any current unresolved litigation with existing or former franchisees
- Projections of business performance should be qualified by statements that explain the basis/assumptions upon which the representations are made, and a clear warning to prospective purchasers of the franchise that there is no guarantee of achieving the same results, and that the projections should not be relied on as a guarantee
- A clear statement indicating whether or not the projections include depreciation, any salaries or wages for the franchisee and the cost of servicing loans
- A statement as to whether the territory or site to be franchised has been subject to any trading activity, particularly a previous franchise, and if so, the history and details, including the circumstances, of any cessation of the franchise
- A requirement to have the contract explained to you by an experienced solicitor and to have independent accountancy and financial advice on the franchise proposition
- A Director's Certificate stating that the franchisor is solvent.

The aim of the disclosure document is to make the whole situation transparent for the buyer. It is important, however, to remember that the disclosure document is not the franchise agreement. You and your solicitor need to read and understand everything contained in both the disclosure document and the franchise agreement itself before you sign the franchise agreement.

The franchise organisation

In addition to the disclosure document, you need to find out everything you can about the franchise organisation. You want to be sure they are reputable, financially strong and very good at what they do. There are a number of sources of information and advice about franchisors including:

- The franchisor
- Existing franchisees
- The Franchise Association of New Zealand
- Retail traders' associations
- *Franchise New Zealand* magazine
- Newspaper and magazine articles
- Business opportunity shows and franchise exhibitions
- Franchise departments of leading banks
- Franchise specialists in some accounting firms

- Franchise specialists in some legal firms
- Specialist franchise consulting firms
- New Zealand Securities Commission
- The Consumers' Institute
- The Commerce Commission
- The Companies Office
- Chambers of Commerce
- Credit bureaus such as Dun & Bradstreet.

Product or service

Exactly what products or services does the franchise offer? Who are the customers that buy these products or services? Are the products or services popular and reputable? To get answers to these questions, talk to people who are familiar with the product or service and then check it out for yourself.

What assurances does the franchisor offer you regarding their ability to keep you consistently supplied with the product at reasonable prices? Ask where they produce or buy the products that they sell to you. Be very wary of a product or service that is seasonal in terms of supply or demand.

Distribution system

Is the franchise exclusive or non-exclusive? In some cases the franchisor retains the right to sell direct in the franchise territory, or they may retain the right to sell more than one franchise in a given territory. There is nothing wrong with a non-exclusive franchise, provided you are aware of the situation before you buy the franchise. The obvious disadvantage of a non-exclusive franchise is a smaller sales potential.

You will also want to know what kind of advertising and promotional material is available to support your local franchise outlet. The franchisor should supply you with packaged programs, which may include advertising copy, radio scripts, television commercials, direct-mail copy, point-of-sale material and sample publicity releases. The opening of your franchise outlet is news, and the franchisor should provide plans and materials for your grand opening.

Warning signs

The vast majority of franchisor organisations are reputable and honest. Unfortunately, there are a few operators who make misleading claims when they are promoting themselves to prospective franchisees. The following warning signs may help you to avoid them:

- An advertisement for a job vacancy that turns out to be a franchise
- Offers to sell you manufacturing equipment with 'guaranteed' buyers for the goods produced

- Offers that depend upon advertising that will not take place until after all the participants have signed up
- Offers that are vague about exactly how the system will operate
- Operators who take no interest in your previous business experience
- Operators who claim that their scheme has been cleared or approved by a public agency
- Operators who are not offering a true franchise package but rather a name and an idea
- Operators who are selling you the right to recruit sub-distributors as opposed to the right to sell products
- Advertisements giving only a post office box number for a reply
- Promises of getting rich quick with little work
- Refusal to show you audited financial statements
- High-pressure tactics to get your signature on a contract.

Sales of franchises are subject to the consumer protection provisions of the Fair Trading Act. False and misleading representations concerning the viability of a business activity are prohibited.

Evaluating a franchise agreement

It is essential that you have a written franchise agreement. It constitutes the legal relationship between you and the franchisor. Make sure that every aspect of the franchise agreement is spelled out in detail. Have your solicitor, your accountant and an independent, specialist franchise adviser review the terms and conditions of the agreement and explain them to you. Do not depend upon people who represent the franchisor for advice, and don't sign an agreement unless you are completely satisfied that it represents a viable working relationship with the franchisor. Things to check are listed below.

Undertakings

A franchise agreement is usually drawn up by the franchisor's solicitors after negotiations have taken place. It should embody all of the promises, and undertakings, that you have made to each other. What rights does the franchisor grant to the franchisee? What obligations does the franchisor undertake to fulfil? What obligations does the agreement impose upon the franchisee? Be sure that the undertakings in the contract are what you agreed to during the negotiations.

Franchise fees

All fees payable must be clearly set out. What is the premium? What are the royalties and what level is the advertising levy? Are there any other fees or levies?

Site

If your franchise requires office space or the construction or lease of a building, the exact role of the franchisor in getting your business started should be spelled out in the franchise agreement. Is the site evaluation cost included in the establishment fee or is it extra? What about the costs to construct and fit out the building? If you are leasing, be sure that the term of the lease corresponds to the term of the franchise agreement.

Expiry

Some franchisors grant franchises in perpetuity but the usual term is for five years. The majority of expiring contracts are renewed. Unless provided for in the agreement, however, the franchisor is not legally required to do so. A prospective franchisee should ask for a perpetual renewal option that remains in force so long as you fulfil your obligations according to the agreement. Renewal should not involve further franchise fees, but you may want to have some means for reviewing the royalty or advertising levy.

If a franchise expires, the franchisor can either resell it or operate it as a franchisor-owned outlet. Under these circumstances, the agreement should provide a formula by which the franchisor can buy back the franchise and its assets.

Termination

Most franchise agreements provide for termination if the franchisee does not fulfil their obligations. Be sure that the franchisor cannot terminate the agreement unless it is for a specific reason, which must be stated in writing. See that there is a grace period in which you can remedy any problem and prevent the termination. Also make sure that the agreement sets out both parties' rights and obligations if termination occurs.

Assignment

Under what circumstances can you assign or sell the franchise to another party? You will not be free to sell the franchise without some sort of consent from the franchisor. Try to minimise the extent to which the franchisor can prevent you from selling your franchise if you wish to do so.

Financial forecasts

Ask the franchisor to provide you with a written forecast of income and expenses that reflects an average outlet in normal circumstances. Have your accountant review it with you and indicate whether all reasonable risks have been disclosed. Also, compare the forecast with the results of two or three current franchisees and ask them to comment on the forecasts. If the franchisor does not supply a valid forecast of income and expenses in writing, or cannot give reasonable answers to your questions about the forecasts, consider these as strong reasons not to enter into the franchise agreement.

Does the forecast meet your personal goals? Will it enable you to earn a salary that compensates you for the hours and responsibility you will have to accept? Will the salary support your family satisfactorily? In addition to a salary, does the forecast show an adequate return on your cash investment in the franchise? Would you be better off by investing your money elsewhere with less risk? Are you satisfied that a franchise operation is a better proposition for you than setting up your own independent small business?

Emerging trends

The growth in franchising has established it as a viable marketing concept. It is clear that more firms are using it as a way to expand, and thousands of small business operators are using it to gain access to managerial expertise. If this remarkable growth continues, franchising could become the dominant form of small business operation in the future.

The business environment has changed significantly over the last few years and these changes are having a continuing affect on franchising as they create new market opportunities and new competitive threats. The largest of these is the way technology and the internet have changed the range of business models and ways of doing business. Direct selling on the internet has cut into the sales of many traditional retail and service businesses including those in franchised systems. Territory or sales area agreements in franchising are challenged by the internet's disregard for geographic boundaries. At the same time there are increasing opportunities for the development of web-based franchises. This means that to be competitive into the future, franchise systems increasingly need to invest in technologically smart systems. This not only means internet selling but also a wider range of technology sophistication in areas such as supply-chain management, customer relations management, internal reporting, benchmarking and decision-support systems.

Other changes in the demographic and natural environments also create many opportunities for developments in franchising. These include increasing demand for products and services related to the natural environment, retirement and old-age care, and health products including diet systems, fitness products and other healthcare services.

The effect of globalisation is also creating changing franchise situations as New Zealand franchises expand into overseas markets and as international operations spread into New Zealand. Exporting a franchise system is well suited to the New Zealand situation because it is far less constrained by distance and transport costs or any duties or other trade tariffs that might affect other product exporters.

As franchise systems grow to become major economic units, there is a trend towards more investment, merger and acquisition activity as growth-oriented franchise owners drive towards market-share dominance and economies of scale. Although the interest of regulators is aroused by the increasing economic influence of these larger systems, the industry in New Zealand is expected to remain self-regulating through the activities of the Franchise Association of New Zealand and their Code of Practice.

In summary, the world of franchising is proving to be adaptable and resilient in the face of rapidly changing business and consumer environments. Franchises that are proactive to the opportunities of change continue to find competitive advantage and growth from applying proven business systems and good business practice to new products, new services and new markets.

6 Developing a business plan

There are three types of business plans: marketing plans, operating plans and financial plans. Marketing plans are all about identifying and satisfying market segments and their needs, and creating a strong competitive advantage (see page 90). Operating plans build from the requirements of the marketing plan and are concerned with day-to-day processes, procedures, workflow and efficiency (see page 92). Financial plans represent the dollar quantification of the marketing and operating plans (see page 92). They are used for budgeting and to support applications for finance. Sometimes one type of planning can dominate your thinking, but the most effective business plan is the result of an integrated approach that encompasses all three.

Most of the books about business planning are designed for cash-hungry start-up situations in which a 100-page document is needed to prise money out of a tight-fisted venture-capital organisation. That kind of business plan is simply irrelevant for the vast majority of small businesses. The purpose of this chapter is to explain why planning is important, dispel some of the myths about planning, describe a set of guidelines for writing a business plan and present an example.

Why planning is important

Planning helps you to work smarter rather than harder. It keeps you future-oriented and motivates you to achieve the results you want. Moreover, the process of completing a business plan enables you to determine what commitment you are prepared to make to the business. Planning significantly increases your chances of survival and prosperity by focusing your attention on the following areas in which small business operators sometimes get lost.

- Realism: It is easy to become excessively optimistic about a new idea. Planning helps to prevent you from viewing the future in ways that the facts do not support.
- The need for outside advice: Planning enables you to recognise problems that call for outside sources of information and assistance.
- Recognising change: The nature of markets and consumer needs change rapidly. Planning cannot predict change, but it helps you to recognise it and to construct your business strategy accordingly.
- Balancing growth: Small businesses tend to grow either too fast for their capital base or too slowly to maintain cash flow. Planning helps you achieve smooth growth and avoid unexpected crises.
- Results orientation: A detailed business plan enables you to monitor your results against a set of goals and performance standards.
- Obtaining finance: When someone puts money into your business they want to know what to expect. A business plan not only enables you to plan your capital needs in advance, but also provides the information that financiers need to evaluate your application for finance.

Myths and reality of planning

The first myth is that a business plan is some sort of guarantee of success. The reality is that no matter how well you plan there is a risk of failure. However, the chances of survival increase with the frequency and quality of planning. A focused marketing plan makes a big impact on sales volume, and operational planning affects how those sales are converted into profits. When you get these two right, the financial plan is a simple extension.

A second myth is that small businesses cannot afford the time and expense of a formal planning process. It is true that many small firms fail to plan, but research suggests that a significant proportion of small firms do plan and that the proportion of firms that engage in planning increases as they become larger.

A third myth is that planning is basically the same process for all firms, whether they are large or small. The reality is that planning in small firms needs to be different in the following ways:

- Stick to a short planning period of two or three years.
- Do your planning in conjunction with external advisers.
- Write it down, but don't make it long or complicated.
- Integrate your marketing and operational planning with specific goals for each functional area of the business.
- If you are already in business, go for a flexible rolling plan that you review and update quarterly or half-yearly.
- If you are looking at a new venture, keep in mind that a realistic business plan might save you from yourself by persuading you to abandon a bad idea while your mistakes are still on paper.

A fourth myth is that you don't need to do the business plan yourself because you can pay someone else to do it for you. The reality is that the business plan is a reflection of *your* vision and *your* aspirations. You can ask your accountant for advice and you can engage a consultant for specialised expertise, but you cannot expect them to make a strong personal commitment to planning your business. If you do not do the business plan yourself, then it is not really your plan. If it is not your plan, then how can you be sure it will work? There are some excellent software packages that provide templates to assist you to write a business plan.

Writing a business plan

The preparation of a business plan represents a unique opportunity to think through all the aspects of organising and operating a small business. It provides you with the means for examining the consequences of different strategies and determining what resources are necessary to launch or expand your business. Your business plan also provides the information needed by others to evaluate your venture if you need to seek outside financing. The following guidelines are applicable to a wide range of businesses, however, common sense should be used in applying the guidelines to your own circumstances.

The introduction

This is the first part of the business plan and its job is to give an overview of the business and the people who run it including the following.

The objectives

It should state the objectives of the plan or proposal as simply as possible. Is it an operating guide, a loan request or a proposal for equity funding? If the plan is to be used as a financing proposal, the introduction should specify who is asking for finance, how much money is required, the purposes for which the funds will be used, and how the funds will benefit the business.

The industry

Indicate the present status and prospects for the industry in which the business will operate. Discuss any new products, new markets and customers, and any other national, regional or economic trends that could have an impact on the business.

The business

Briefly describe what type of business you are in or intend to enter. Indicate its name, how it is organised (proprietorship, partnership, company), and its main activities (retailing, service, manufacturing, wholesaling or some combination). Identify the status of the business (start-up, expansion, or purchase of an existing operation). Describe its location and facilities. Be sure to include anything of importance that you may have learned from trade suppliers, banks or other business people.

Management

If your business plan is to be used as a financing proposal, this section is particularly important. Venture capitalists and lenders invest as much in people as they do in business propositions. For this reason, you need to demonstrate the capacity of your management team and its advisers. Outline the personal history of the principals and show what work experience they bring to the business. State their duties and responsibilities and indicate the salaries they expect to draw from the business. Be sure to list advisers such as your solicitor, accountant and banker.

The product or service

Describe what you are going to sell. Indicate the primary use for your product or service, as well as any important secondary uses. Emphasise those factors that make your product or service unique or superior to that which is already on the market. Discuss any opportunities for the expansion of your product line or the development of related products or services or if the product, process or service requires any design or development before it is ready to be placed on the market.

Marketing plans

The purpose of this section is to demonstrate that your business can achieve the sales indicated in your financial forecast. This section is the most difficult to prepare, but it is the key section in any business plan. There are four basic steps in determining the nature and size of your market. Here they are:

Step 1: Identify your customer profile

Who are, or will be, your customers? You can classify customers into groups with common characteristics such as age, sex or geographical location. What are their basic buying motives with regard to price, quality, service, convenience or perhaps necessity?

Step 2: Determine the size of the market

How many potential customers exist within your trading area? How much should they be spending on your product or service? Can this market be expanded? Why?

Step 3: Assess the competition

Who are your nearest competitors? What have you learned about their operations? Explain why you think you can capture a share of their business or keep them from capturing a share of yours. What is their share of the market?

Step 4: Estimate your sales

Based on the previous three steps, estimate the sales that you expect over the next three years. Be careful—make sure that your estimates line up with the facts. This information is critical to your financial forecast.

Your marketing strategy needs to follow from the assessment of the market. It should identify your target market, show how you are going to satisfy that market, indicate your pricing policy, and explain your tactics for advertising and promotion. Do not forget to keep track of your marketing costs because they go into the financial forecast. Here are the strategies you will need to consider.

Product/Service strategy

What are the specific characteristics of your product or service and what are the special or unique features that will help to create success in the marketplace? Include any diagrams, photographs or other examples that will give the reader a better idea of the product or service. List the back-up service or guarantees that you will offer.

Price strategy

What price are you going to put on your products or services and how do these compare with market rates? What discounts will you offer to retailers or agents and how will you use other price discounts to induce bulk buying or fast payment?

Place strategy

What are the characteristics of your physical place of business, including geographic location, size, image, style, parking, visibility and proximity to main roads and main markets?

Positioning strategy

What is an ideal market position for your business and how do you plan to establish it in the minds and perceptions of customers?

Promotion strategy

What are your plans for promoting your products or services? What advertising media will you use? What is the calendar of promotional events and what is the value of the promotional budget?

Operating plans

The operations section of the business plan shows how you intend to get it all done! It defines the plant and the people, the processes and procedures. Here are the things you will need to consider.

Operational priorities

In which operational fields will you seek to be excellent? Will you compete on cost, quality, flexibility or delivery? How will you achieve excellence?

Plant and machinery

What types of machinery and capacities are needed to produce the sales volume outlined in the marketing plan and what level of investment is needed? What functions do your premises need to fulfil? Consider space, facilities and other necessary features.

Staff

Identify your staffing needs now and over the next three years. What skills are required and are the people you need available? Will they be permanent or casual, full-time or part-time? What will be the costs?

Processes and procedures

Describe the processes you will use to produce or handle your product including any special technologies or proprietary systems. What are the routines and cycles in the production of products or services?

Financial plans

This section should represent your best estimates of future performance. If the business already exists, show its current financial position before proceeding to the forecasts. If your business plan is also a financing proposal, you need to insert a statement showing how the funds will be used.

The financial plan is concerned with profitability and liquidity. Profitability forecasts are based on the sales estimates in your market analysis and the expenses related to achieving those sales. They are documented in the form of forecast profit and loss statements. Liquidity refers to the need for sufficient cash to pay your bills as they become due. Liquidity forecasts are based on projected cash receipts and disbursements and are documented in the form of forecast cash flow statements. Financial forecasts should be shown monthly for the first year and quarterly for the succeeding two years. Here are the things you will need to include.

Set-up
The financial plan should include details of the set-up costs for a new business or expansion costs for a new development.

Funding
Once the set-up costs have been identified, the amounts and sources of borrowed funding need to identified.

Costing, pricing and break-even
The business plan should show how you have calculated your product costs and charge-out rates. The costs are then related to the prices established in the marketing plan and presented in a break-even calculation.

Forecast cash flow
Provide monthly cash flow forecasts for the first three years.

Forecast profit/loss
Provide quarterly profit and loss forecasts for the first three years.

Forecast balance sheet
Provide the opening balance sheet and forecasts of the closing balance sheets for the first three years.

Supporting exhibits
When the business plan is used to seek finance, you should include copies of documentary evidence to substantiate your claims. Here are some examples of supporting exhibits:

- Detailed resumés of the principals
- Credit information
- Quotations or estimates
- Leases or buy/sell agreements
- Legal documents
- Census or demographic data.

There are many publications available on how to write a business plan. You will also find more examples and information about business plans on the following websites:

- www.business.govt.nz to find out about government support for business start-up and growth. The site provides guides and templates for developing business plans.
- www.edanz.org.nz is the site for the Economic Development Agencies in New Zealand. Member sites have resources to assist you to write your business plan.
- www.incubators.org.nz is the site for Incubators New Zealand. Do a search there for 'business plans'.
- www.businessplanarchive.org is the site for a partnership between the US Library of Congress and several other organisations. The Archive collects business plans from the dot-com era so that future generations will be able to learn from them.
- Do a Google search for 'business plans' for a wealth of information and examples.

Small business life cycle

Your business will change as it grows and you will find it necessary to adapt your business plan as a result. The small business life cycle consists of a number of phases, each with a different set of goals and requiring a different management role. Figure 6.1 represents the four phases of the small business life cycle.

Phase 1: Start-up

The start-up phase is characterised by tremendous uncertainty. You may lack confidence and your decisions may be impulsive, erratic and inconsistent. The newborn business will almost certainly face a cash crisis caused by the huge cash drain that usually occurs early in its life. A large proportion of closures occur during the start-up phase. The main goal is to survive and stay in business.

The successful small business operator needs to be a good initiator, innovator and organiser during the start-up phase. An idea has to be transformed into reality.

Figure 6.1 Small business life cycle

Phase	Start-up	Take-off	Harvest	Renewal
Goal	Survival	Sales	Profits	Revival
Role	Initiator	Developer	Administrator	Succession
	Innovator	Implementer	Manager	Reorganiser
	Organiser	Delegator	Leader	Revitaliser
Typical crises	Confidence	Cash flow	Leadership	Inertia
	Cash flow	Delegation	Complacency	Succession

That means generating enough innovative inspiration and persuasiveness to appeal to both your banker and customers while you work toward creating a strong competitive advantage.

Phase 2: Take-off

The take-off phase is characterised by a sharp increase in sales volume. The dominant goal is to capitalise on your competitive advantage. You make a heavy investment in more resources to support the increased sales volume. The additional investment aggravates any lingering cash flow problems left over from the start-up phase. After an agonising period of losses, the business finally turns the corner and shows a modest profit.

Now the business is too big for one person to handle. Overwork and stress start to take a heavy toll. A delegation crisis will occur unless you make the transition from being just an owner to an owner/manager. It is time to develop and implement management policies that will guide your staff in your absence. During the take-off phase, the successful small business manager learns how to delegate responsibility while exercising sufficient control to ensure that the business keeps on the right track.

Phase 3: Harvest

Eventually the rapid growth in sales volume begins to stabilise and the business enters the harvest phase. This can be a prolonged part of the small business life cycle when the dominant goal is to make profits. Internal matters such as cost control and efficiency occupy more of your time. Your competitive advantage is entrenched and the business settles into a more predictable routine. You become more distant from the day-to-day operations and tend to get things done through supervisors. In this phase of the small business life cycle the successful small business operator learns to become an effective administrator, manager and leader.

The inevitable growth of administrative detail and paperwork may eventually sap your enthusiasm, and prolonged prosperity may cause you to lose sight of the fact that in order to continue harvesting one also needs to be sowing the seeds for future crops. Complacency leads to a void in leadership, and you find your competitive advantage endangered.

Phase 4: Renewal

The renewal phase begins with the recognition that the firm's competitive advantage has eroded. It often coincides with the original owner wanting to withdraw from the business. There is resistance to changing the way things have operated in the past. Faced with deadening inertia, the business is in danger of withering away. Unless the owner gets a new burst of enthusiasm or finds a successor, the business may close.

In this phase of the small business life cycle, the successful small business operator will be a reorganiser and revitaliser. The objective is to breathe new life into the business by reasserting its competitiveness and recapturing its ability to harvest.

Shifting the strategic gears

It is obviously important to learn how to construct an effective business strategy, but it is equally important to recognise when to change the strategy. It is like shifting gears in your car. First you make an assessment of your competitive advantage, then you determine your place in the small business life cycle model. You always need two strategies; one that capitalises on the forces that are naturally at work, and a second that acts as a safety net if the first strategy does not succeed. Figure 6.2 represents eight types of business strategy. Each is not only associated with a particular phase of the small business life cycle but also is dependent on the strength of the firm's competitive advantage.

Figure 6.2 Business strategies

Phase	Strong competitive advantage	Weak competitive advantage
Start-up	Entry strategies	Exit strategies
Take-off	Growth strategies	Concentration strategies
Harvest	Profit strategies	Contraction strategies
Renewal	Turnaround strategies	Liquidation strategies

Phase 1: Start-up

Entry strategies are designed to get into business. They may be aimed at a new business of a new kind or a new business of an existing kind. The avenues for entry include starting from scratch, buying an existing business or perhaps buying a franchise. Effective entry strategies rely on a strong competitive advantage.

Exit strategies are designed to get out of the business during the start-up phase if the competitive advantage is too weak to be effective. They consist largely of minimising the losses associated with discontinuing operations. Inasmuch as the firm does not usually have significant assets to liquidate, the focus is on how to handle the existing obligations and how to avoid any further liabilities that may arise from winding up.

Phase 2: Take-off

Growth strategies are designed to significantly and permanently increase the level of sales. The rapid increase in sales means the firm needs to invest in a larger asset base and more specialised staff in order to support greater sales volume. Growth strategies include sophisticated refinements to the firm's competitive advantage in order to meet competition that is attracted by the firm's success.

Concentration strategies are designed for recovery when a growth strategy prematurely expires because rivals have damaged the firm's competitive advantage. The objective is to refocus the firm's assets on a slightly different target market in order to improve short-run cash flow and long-run profits. It usually means selling off some of the firm's assets and concentrating new investment in those areas where the firm has its greatest competencies and advantage.

Phase 3: Harvest

Profit strategies are designed to make the best use of the firm's competitive advantage and existing resources to produce large profits and positive cash flows. The focus shifts from acquiring new customers and new assets to exploiting connections with existing customers and efficiently utilising existing assets. The ultimate profit strategy is the eventual sale of the business as a going concern for a price that reflects its strong competitive advantage and long-term profitability.

Contraction strategies are designed to reduce the investment in the firm while maintaining its profitability. Contraction strategies are called for when the firm's asset base is too large for the sales and profits it generates. Contraction strategies improve the firm's return on investment when profits are static, by selectively selling surplus assets and taking the cash out of the business.

Phase 4: Renewal

Turnaround strategies are designed to reverse the declining fortunes of a business on the premise that it is worth saving. Turnaround strategies are usually based on revenue-increasing measures or cost-reducing measures depending on which measures will have the greatest and most expedient effect on the firm's cash flows.

Liquidation strategies are the result of a decision to abandon a business. They are designed to generate as mush cash flow as possible while methodically withdrawing from the business. Liquidation strategies work best when the firm can control the situation. They consist of liquidating the firm's assets and winding it up, or attempting to sell the firm as a potential turnaround opportunity for a new owner.

Strategic thinking and imagineering

The previous sections have discussed generic strategies. The business environment is continuously shifting with new opportunities and threats regularly affecting the future development of the business. This means that business owners need to develop the skill of thinking in the future as well as managing the present. A useful practice is to create a forecast of your business environment in five years from the present, and then visualise an ideal state for your business in that future environment. Your forecast will have to predict likely changes in the legal, economic, demographic, social and technical environments. The visualisation of your ideal future business needs to include the following:

- Size in terms of revenue, employees, and market share
- The products and services it sells and the markets it serves
- The internal systems, technology and operational details
- The people skills and competencies
- The financial performance in terms of profit, cash flow and returns.

The process of 'imagineering' consists of imagining yourself standing in this future time zone and ideal business state, and looking back at the current business. The 'back from the future' view will starkly reveal what has to change before you can realise the vision. These changes become the critical issues of your strategic thinking and planning for the future, and they will drive goals, tactics and budgets aimed at achieving your vision.

SWOT analysis

No discussion on business planning would be complete without reference to SWOT analysis. A SWOT analysis looks at strengths, weaknesses, opportunities and threats. It is a good way to assess the current competitive situation of a business and it may be included in the marketing section of a business plan. The analysis allows you to evaluate strategies that will match the strengths of the business to the opportunities in the marketplace while isolating, minimising or eliminating weaknesses and threats. There are standard factors that are outlined in Figure 6.3 (see page 99). However, a SWOT analysis for your particular business should also capture unique aspects relative to your business and its environment. There are a variety of ways to rate and analyse the factors. A simple approach is illustrated here.

The SWOT process starts with a list of all the strengths and weaknesses of opportunities and threats to a business. Each factor is weighted for importance: from 1 for low to 10 for high. In the next column, rate your current ability or weakness relative to each factor: 1 for low to 10 for high. The third column is the product of the first two (obtained by multiplying the numbers) resulting in a weighted score for each factor.

In Figure 6.3, weaknesses rate higher than the strengths by 350 to 274, and threats rate higher than opportunities by 241 to 160. This is a good reflection of reality for many small businesses operating in highly competitive environments with low resources and a shortage of management skills. In the 'Resulting strategy' column, the SWOT analysis points toward strategies that match strengths to market opportunities, overcome weaknesses and protect you against threats.

Figure 6.3 SWOT analysis

Internal factors (1 low–10 high)	Importance	My ability to capitalise	Weighted score	Resulting strategy
Strengths				
Motivation	10	9	90	Focus strengths on
Passion	8	9	72	customer needs and market
Flexibility	6	7	42	opportunities.
Personal service	10	7	70	
			274	

	Importance	My degree of weakness	Weighted score	Resulting strategy
Weaknesses				Upgrade training and
Skills	10	(8)	(80)	qualifications. Build systems
Resources	8	(10)	(80)	and integrate them internally
Cash flow	9	(10)	(90)	and externally.
Lack of systems	10	(10)	(100)	Build a strong relationship
			(350)	with the bank.
Total internal rating			**(76)**	

External factors (1 low–10 high)	Importance	My ability to capitalise	Weighted score	Resulting strategy
Opportunities				Focus personal strengths
Niche markets	8	7	56	on service quality and
E-commerce	10	2	20	fast response to changing
Service	10	7	70	customer needs.
Changing markets	7	2	14	Focus systems development
			160	on e-commerce
				opportunities.

	Importance	My degree of weakness	Weighted score	Resulting strategy
Threats				
Intense competition	10	(6)	(60)	Focus on quality and
Substitutes	5	(9)	(45)	uniqueness. Build working
Supplier power	7	(7)	(49)	associations and skill
Buyer power	5	(3)	(15)	networks with others.
New entrants	8	(9)	(72)	
			(241)	
Total external rating			**(81)**	

Example of a business plan

Mobile Entertainment Gaming Advertising Ltd (MEGA)

Acknowledgement: This plan has been adapted from a draft copy kindly supplied by Runfeng Lin of Phone Media Group Ltd. The company name and names of the directors have been changed for privacy reasons.

Introduction

MEGA is a start-up company working in the social media/Web 2.0 environment. These environments provide for the sharing of video, gaming and picture content on the web and through mobile phones. The market for these activities is growing very rapidly, especially in the Asia–Pacific region. Global statistics show the volume of use is doubling every seven months and there are some examples of phenomenal growth rates

However the majority of this traffic is peer-to-peer (P2P) file sharing of non-monetised video. The MEGA business model, by contrast, is based on motivating large amounts of user-provided content in the form of videos, games and pictures, that then provide a vehicle for advertising messages in the form of short clips attached to each content file. The advertising provides a revenue stream for MEGA that can be shared with the suppliers of content.

The MEGA service offers a group of unique advantages to users and advertisers. World advertising statistics show a rapidly increasing use of online media for advertising and the MEGA platform allows advertisers access to this new form of highly targeted marketing. The MEGA system allows advertisers to optimise their advertising spend by an auctioned 'cost per view' structure and by giving advertisers connection to a self-defined target market at self-decided prime time.

A further feature for advertisers is that the system includes an advertisement response management system (RMS) that allows a deeper connection to be made with people who respond to the advertisement and this creates a potential for on-selling an extended range of products and services.

For content providers and users it allows integration between web and mobile platforms, and can reward content providers with systems for generating revenue from their content.

Downstream cash flows and profitability forecasts are high but start-up costs are also high. Initial software development costs are high along with the sales and marketing costs associated with building market awareness and funding national and international market entry strategies. The MEGA shareholders are therefore looking for an equity partner that can help fund the early stage development.

This business plan provides the operational detail that supports the business model and the marketing objectives.

100

Company Description

MEGA Ltd is a limited liability company with two director/shareholders—Chae Wuwei (50 per cent) and Lu Shiwei (50 per cent). Both directors have tertiary qualifications in business management, computer science and software development, and have seven years of commercial experience in corporate software development, and information technology management. The current paid up capital of the business is $200 000 but the directors forecast the company will take three years to reach profitable trading and the company will therefore need $650 000 of start-up capital to cover software development costs and pre-sales marketing. The directors are seeking an equity partner (angel investor) investment of $450 000 to bring the start-up capital up to the required $650 000.

The goal for the company is to launch a business in the social media and mobile market that incorporates the sharing and selling of video content, games and photos through the integration of web and mobile-phone technologies. The name of this business is MEGA and the plan is to generate revenues from advertising that can be attached to social media content and also from commissions on gaming content that is sold through the MEGA site.

The initial objective is to capture market share in New Zealand and then to move into Australia, Singapore, Hong Kong and Taiwan. However funding is required to continue the software development of the product, and to fund market development activities that are required to enter and promote within these markets.

The social media and mobile markets have very high growth projections according to market research done by Universal McCann and Morgan Stanley. The use of mobile-phone technology that is linked to the web enables users to be connected at a level that has not been available in the past.

The primary users of the service will be those people interested in sharing and downloading video or gaming products onto their PCs and mobile phones. A second significant group will be amateur developers who want to set up their own distribution system to sell or promote their work at low or almost no cost. The demographics of this group are young people who depend on broadband and mobile-phone technologies to maintain and build social connection with their contemporaries.

The two directors have a strong potential to give their company competitive advantage in this market based on the following attributes:

1. They are part of, and understand, the target market—its demand factors, and the features and benefits that represent customer satisfaction. This has particular relevance in the Asian markets.
2. They both have tertiary qualifications and industry experience in the necessary technical fields.

3. They have developed a leveraged business model in terms of web-based connectivity and revenue streams between users, suppliers and advertisers.
4. They have established an exclusive relationship for the use of a proprietary response management system (RMS) that enhances the benefits to advertisers who engage in advertising contracts with MEGA.

The Product/Service

For the end user the business enables people to watch, share and upload/download videos, photos and images, and mobile games. All content on the site is free to view, download and send directly as a MMS (PXT) message to any mobile phone in the world.

Initially users can create a sub-domain and choose to allow or not allow advertisers to place advertisements on their content. This sub-domain will have unlimited space and hold only the users' content. If users create saleable content they can generate income from their sub-domain. However, after the imminent development of a MEGA payment facility, users will be able to sell their content (with a preview) directly to other end users. The content provider can choose to sell or share their content, and they can choose to supply it with or without advertising attached. This allows them to have a range of earning possibilities from their sub-domain.

The website includes video, pictures and mobile game sharing. Users can download video and pictures to their computer or smart phone. Users can also create an e-card from wallpaper on the site and send it to a friend's phone or as an email. E-cards sent in this way are charged at the Vodafone-to-Vodafone price which is cheaper than sending content across the network (e.g. Vodafone customer to Telecom customer). Users can also download games to their PCs or directly to their mobile phone. Because users need to register their mobile number to be able to upload content or carry out other functions, a database of active customers is automatically created in the MEGA system.

The MEGA process also provides a bundle of unique benefit to advertisers:

*   It enables advertisers to place their advertisements directly into the daily prime times of a target segment (for example, the young, mobile and connected segment).
*   Once downloaded, the advertisement stays with the viewer and will be seen every time that video or game is viewed by them or anyone else they share it with.
*   The advertisement system is linked to a proprietary automated response management system that links the viewer into a managed sales and promotion process. This RMS expands the offer into many other associated products and services. The advertiser gets two services for the price of one. The MEGA service allows advertisers to connect with prospective buyers by way of a mobile message, PXT and SMS, plus emails and a web link.
*   The advertiser manages their own budget and unit price by bidding into a pricing

mechanism based on cost per mille (1000) views. The advertiser can choose to advertise just on a particular category of content, or all of them. The payment method can be either pre- or post-paid.

- The advertiser pays:
  - \$2.50 per download of mobile games.
  - Videos are priced by auction price based on cost per mille views of videos. This system works in a similar way to the system used by Google (Adsense).
  - Cost per video download is 10 x auction price.

Marketing Plan

Market Research

A web search on social media and mobile integration provided data on the size of the mobile market and the trends in internet advertising revenues (See Appendices I and II).

Economics of the Mobile Integration Platform Market

The community/social media market works on a web and mobile phone platform that provides for sharing of user-generated content. The main global players at present are Wikipedia, Myspace, YouTube, Yahoo!, Flickr, CyWorld (South Korea), and Tencent (China).

From the data supplied by Universal McCann and Morgan Stanley, the key points are that global usage is doubling every seven months, and that the major percentage of global growth is in the Asia–Pacific region.

In the mobile phone markets there are over five billion camera-enabled mobiles globally. This has created a \$50 billion mobile data-services market that is based on a \$10 annual revenue-per-user factor. This factor is rising.

In the video market 60 per cent of internet usage is person-to-person file sharing of non-monetised video. This is the fastest-growing sector of video sharing. In the monetised sector growth is also extreme. Some indication of the size of this market is that PayPal has 123 million accounts with 41 per cent Y/Y growth. In regard to online advertising, internet advertising is rapidly growing. According to the latest report from eMarketer and Starcom MediaVest, global ad spend online is forecast to hit US\$96.8 billion by 2014, up from \$55.2 billion in 2009. At this point in time only 12 per cent of New Zealand's advertising is online (Interactive Advertising Bureau New Zealand) and this is thought to indicate an opportunity for MEGA to introduce existing New Zealand advertisers to this new wave of advertising media.

Customers

The target market for MEGA services is the 'Pod' generation. These are early adopters of social network services—sharing pictures and videos, and using multiplayer gaming products on mobile phones.

Demographically they can be identified as non-gender-specific 10–30 year olds who are high users of personal web/mobile technology and entertainment products (games and video/image sharing). Geographically they are located in New Zealand, Australia and Asian locations such as Singapore, Hong Kong and Taiwan where the fastest growth in mobile use is occurring.

The market's 'need and want' is to have the full functionality of the internet available on mobile phones. For advertisers they represent an attractive high dollar-volume market and advertising via mobile phones is an effective way of reaching them. This is because they self-identify by their usage of mobile products and services and they also self-select the prime time for the advertiser to reach them—every time they use the mobile service the advertiser is with them.

Competition

The competition can be classified in three types—mobile gaming; video sharing; and photo sharing. In each of these areas there are competitors who dominate the market with current products and services. MEGA's intention is to offer features to their customers and advertisers that the major operators don't have. The characteristics of each of the major competitors in each classification are outlined below.

Mobile Gaming

Vodafone is the main competitor in this field. Mobile games are available from Vodafone at a cost that ranges from $7–12 for each game depending on its complexity and quality. Although Vodafone represents a serious competitor, competitive advantage lies with MEGA's business model, which enables games to be available at no cost to the user other than the normal mobile phone charges.

The games are developed and provided to MEGA by gamers themselves. MEGA game developers receive 50 per cent of the advertising revenue arising from their game. Under this revenue-sharing model MEGA currently has the rights to seven games and is negotiating for rights to a further group.

Video Sharing

The main competitor in the field of video sharing is YouTube which, like Vodafone, is a powerful competitor.

A point of advantage for the MEGA business model is that YouTube has no payment to suppliers of content. The 50 per cent advertising revenue share by MEGA means that suppliers of content are motivated firstly to provide content and secondly to produce content of quality that attracts advertising revenues.

Finally, YouTube has limited support for personal blogs. In contrast MEGA provides users with their own MEGA website, with their own domain name, content and unlimited space.

Photo Sharing

Flickr is considered the best online photo management and photo sharing application in the photo sharing market

MEGA has the advantage of not only enabling the uploading of pictures to a PC but also the ability to download them to mobile phones. The same benefit applies to e-cards. On the MEGA system the card can be sent to a mobile phone so that the receiver gets the card immediately and not just when they are viewing email on a PC.

Sales Plan

Geographic Target Markets

MEGA sees its market development starting in New Zealand and then progressing quickly into the Australian market. The second target area will be Singapore and Hong Kong before finally moving to Taiwan. In each case the marketing strategy will be to develop groups of content suppliers and advertisers in parallel so that advertisers have content to attach their advertisements to, and content suppliers can quickly gain a share of the advertising revenue.

An Awareness Campaign

MEGA sees itself more of a technology and content provider. Therefore the lowest cost and most effective initial marketing and branding plan is to run some PXT campaigns in collaboration with selected advertisers. In this case MEGA will provide the technology (a central place where users can upload PXT video and picture content) to host user-provided content. The advertiser will promote themselves in the normal media with a PXT number and the MEGA web address included in their advertisements. People can then enter the MEGA site to view and rate the content which has been uploaded.

Content Development

To develop content contributions two or three full-time salespeople will be employed to find and encourage suppliers of content. These salespeople will have a high level of product and system knowledge, and a strong empathy with the target market of 10–30 year old social media users.

Initial content users and suppliers are likely to come from industry and educational groups who could get immediate benefit from using the facility of shared files and the convenience of connection to mobile phones. Examples of the sectors that would be targeted by the sales teams are school groups, real-estate companies, TV stations, the music industry, film companies, and the tourism industry.

Other non-specific content providers from the general public would come from personal contacts, networking and word-of-mouth promotion. Because the market in shared content is already well established, it is considered that once the advertising payment-share system is made known general public providers will be willing to participate.

Selling Advertising Space

Selling the concept to advertisers will also require salespeople with a high level of product and system knowledge. These salespeople will target advertisers who would normally promote and sell their products or services to the market of 10–30 year olds and they will be familiar with the marketing issues relevant to that market segment.

The strategy for building advertiser participation will be to start with those advertisers who already have strong product/service connections to the market of 10–30 year olds. The aim will be to get one or two strong brands to participate first and then move on to other, smaller, but still significant, advertisers. Prime targets in this strategy would be brands such as Coca-Cola, Vodafone and McDonald's.

Sales Forecast

Estimates of demand are based on the research studies done by Morgan Stanley Research, PWC (see Appendix I) and Universal McCann. These studies show that in New Zealand and Australia there are currently two million users of social media file sharing and that the average advertising spend is $10 per user. This suggests an advertising market size of $20 million. MEGA plan to reach a market share of 10 per cent after five years. The result of the research data on demand and the 10% market-share target leads to a fifth-year sales revenue forecast of $2–2.5 million, with an expected profit before tax of approximately $1.8 million.

Operational Plan

The MEGA system is a fully digital hosted e-commerce system of transactions for both content and revenue flows. In Figure 1.1 (see page 107) the system is hosted on the Amazon EC2 server. Games, video and other content are supplied to MEGA through the Amazon server. Advertisers bid for the right to add their advertisements to the content. Winning bidders then attach their advertising to the content and pay their fees into the MEGA bank account and 50 per cent of that fee is then transferred back to the content provider. Content can be downloaded by content users to a PC or to a mobile phone using an image enhancement process provided in the MEGA software. Advertisers have the ability to use the automated response management system offered by a third party to add functionality to their advertising campaigns.

The operational system requires few assets and minimal staffing or other overhead costs. The activities and costs of running the business are located in the software development activities and in the sales effort to recruit content suppliers and advertisers.

Figure 1.1: MEGA content and revenue flows

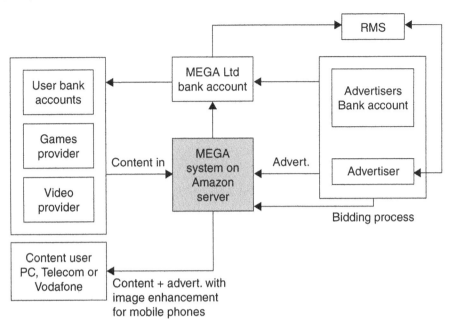

Management and organisation

The two activity streams dictate the organisational structure of the company (Figure 1.2). The two shareholders will run the company from their respective home offices in Auckland. Chae Wuwei is responsible for the sales and administration activities. A three-person sales team for each country will be developed starting with New Zealand before building the Australian team, and then expanding to deal with Asia. Chae Wuwei will also be responsible for building and maintaining a comprehensive customer-relationship-management system as outlined in Figure 1.2 (see page 108).

Lu Shiwei will manage the development of the software product and manage a software development team of two or three developers based in an R&D centre in China.

Professional and Advisory Support

The business will set up an informal board of advisors when size and growth require it. Until that point the two directors will manage the initial development of the MEGA initiative. The directors will appoint a lawyer and accountant to provide legal and accounting services and advice. The company banks with the Bank of New Zealand. For advisory services to date, the company has used help from the University of Auckland's business incubator—the ICEHOUSE.

Figure 1.2: MEGA organisational chart

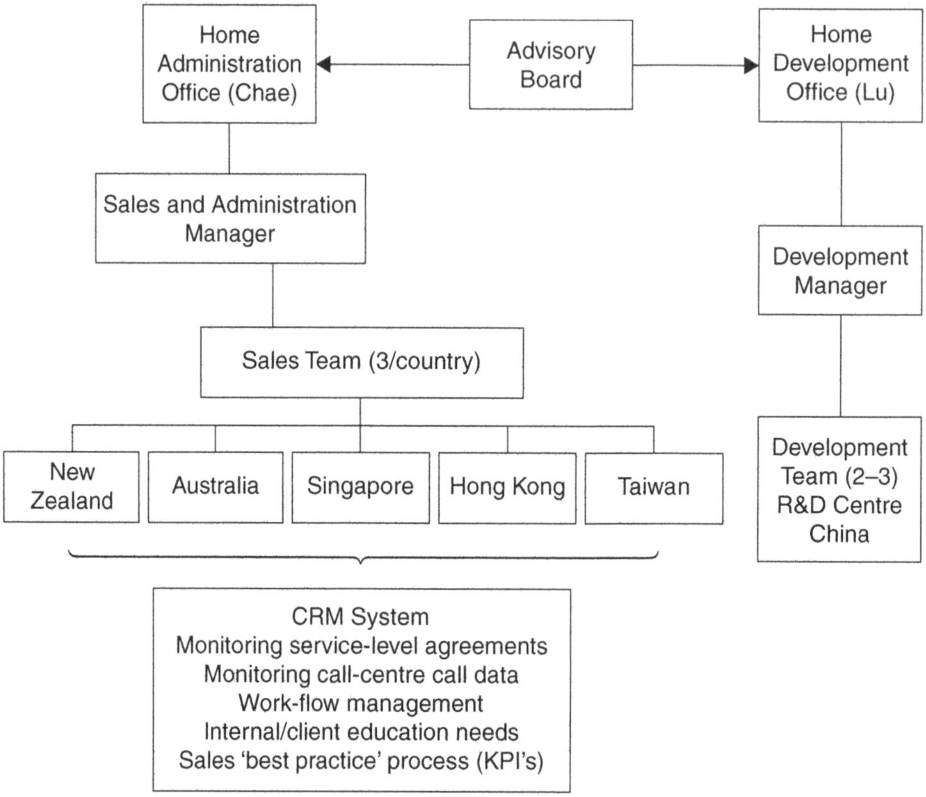

Financial Plan

Five-year Profit Projection

Revenue projections based on the research data on the size of the demand in New Zealand and Australia and market-share estimates are outlined in the five-year financial forecast in Table 1.1 (see page 109). Estimates of cost of sales (COS), research and development (R&D), marketing and sales (M&S), and general and administration (G&A) costs have been made for each of the first five years. The business will not carry any tangible assets, stock or debtors on its balance sheet, and for the first three years the salary of the two initial directors are included in the software development, sales and marketing, and administration budgets.

Table 1.1: Financial forecasts

Years	1	2	3	4	5
Revenue	14 000	300 000	600 000	800 000	2 400 000
COS	2700	4080	4080	4080	4080
R&D	77 000	120 000	120 000	120 000	120 000
M&S	360 000	200 000	200 000	200 000	200 000
G&A	4700	200 000	200 000	200 000	200 000
NPBT	(430 400)	(224 080)	75 920	275 920	1 875 920
Capital 650 000					
Dividends	0	0	0	200 000	500 000
Cash	219 600	(4480)	71 440	147 360	1 523 280

	5th-year Demand	Rev/Person	Tot Rev		Market Share
NZ	1 000 000	$10	$10 000 000	0.1	$1 000 000
Aust	1 000 000	$10	$10 000 000	0.1	$1 000 000
				Total	$2 000 000

Revenue/Profit Split

Years	1	2	3	4	5
Games	5600	120 000	240 000	480 000	960 000
Costs	177 760	209 632	209 632	209 632	209 632
NPBT	(172 160)	(89 632)	30 368	270 368	750 368
Video	8400	180 000	360 000	720 000	1 440 000
Costs	266 640	314 448	314 448	314 448	314 448
NPBT	(258 240)	(134 448)	45 552	405 552	1 125 552

Table 1.1 also shows the breakdown of revenues between New Zealand and Australia, and the annual split between the projected games revenue and video revenue.

Direct expenses include software development costs and the hosting service. The advertising spend increases rapidly as the sales and marketing effort builds into national and international campaigns. The cash flow forecast shows a need for seed funding in the order of approximately $500 000 in the first year which will be applied to the main costs of software development and the salaries and commissions paid to salespeople. To cover this seed funding the shareholders will seek an equity partner(s) who will invest in the company in return for a 40 per cent shareholding in MEGA Ltd.

The post-funding and 12-month balance sheets would then appear as follows in Tables 1.2 and 1.3.

Table 1.2: Post-funding balance sheet

Assets		Funding	
Current			
Cash	650 000	Current Liabilities	0
Intangible			
Intellectual Property	0	Shareholder Equity	650 000
Non-Current			
Fixed	0	Term Liabilities	0
Total	**650 000**	**Total**	**650 000**

Table 1.3: 5th year balance sheet

(IP is estimated at 3x development labour cost)

Assets		Funding	
Current			
Cash	1 523 280	Current Liabilities	0
Intangible			
Intellectual Property	500 000	Shareholder Equity	2 023 280
Non-Current			
Fixed	0	Term Liabilities	0
Total	**2 023 280**	**Total**	**2 023 280**

Appendix I: Mobile video and gaming

Research by the directors of MEGA has revealed the following profile and characteristics of the developments in mobile gaming. A PricewaterhouseCoopers survey of the industry shows that entertainment software remains one of the fastest-growing industries in the US economy. The sector is expected to remain one of the above-average growth segments of the global entertainment industries through 2011 and beyond.

The Entertainment Software Association (ESA) is the trade association that represents US computer and video game publishers. Their website contains data about the American gaming market. Their research shows that nearly three-quarters of all American households play games. This vast audience fuels the growth of this multibillion dollar industry and helps bring jobs to communities across the nation. Below is a list of the top eight entertainment software industry facts supplied by the ESA:

- Consumers spent $25.1 billion on video games, hardware and accessories in 2010.
- Purchases of digital content accounted for 24 per cent of game sales in 2010, generating $5.9 billion in revenue.
- Seventy-two per cent of American households play computer or video games.
- The average game player is 37 years old and has been playing games for twelve years.
- The average age of the most frequent game purchaser is 41 years old.
- Forty-two per cent of all game players are women. In fact, women over the age of eighteen represent a significantly greater portion of the game-playing population (37 per cent) than boys aged seventeen or younger (13 per cent).
- In 2011, 29 per cent of Americans over the age of 50 play video games, an increase from 9 per cent in 1999.
- Fifty-five per cent of gamers play games on their phones or handheld device.

The development of internet gaming has some identifiable trends that are important for businesses evaluating new marketing opportunities in social gaming and smartphone apps.

- Social Games. Social games are games with simple rules that require minimal time commitment and no special skills, making them popular with casual players. Parks Associates, a market intelligence company in America, predicts that social gaming is on track to become a $5 billion industry by 2015, primarily through the sale of virtual goods and new advertising revenues that will drive market growth.
- Smartphone Apps. The user base of smartphone gamers has expanded rapidly due to the popularity of mobile apps and the gaming products that have been developed for mobile technologies. According to Microsoft Research, games are among the most popular applications and constitute the vast majority of downloads to common smartphone software platforms. Although most smartphone-based games are single-player games, Microsoft have created Switchboard, a cloud service that enables smartphones to link to each other for multiplayer gaming.
- Digital Distribution. Digital (online) game distribution is growing in popularity with the practice of delivering content by streaming games or downloading everything from the Web directly to the consumer's hard drive or gaming device.
- Cloud Gaming. Cloud gaming involves making games available over the internet in a 'rentable' form as opposed to buying and owning the game. Game time is sold typically by the minute or the hour. The advantage to a game developer of using the

cloud to distribute their product is protection from pirate copying and replication. For users the user-pays element allows access to a wide variety of games without the up-front costs of purchasing them.

- Advergaming. Wikipedia describes advergaming as the practice of using video games to advertise products, organisations and even viewpoints. With the growth of the internet, advergames have proliferated, often becoming the most visited aspect of brand websites and turning into an integrated part of brand media planning in an increasingly fractured media environment. Advergames theoretically promote repeated traffic to websites and reinforce brands. Users choosing to register to be eligible for prizes can help marketers collect customer data. Gamers may also invite their friends to participate, which could assist promotion by word-of-mouth viral marketing.

Going with the trends

Mobile video gaming is enjoying significant growth along with the accelerated development of mobile smartphones and the proliferation of apps designed for mobile phones. Opportunities exist for developers in not only the sale or renting of games, but also in using games as a vehicle to carry advertising messages directly to those segments of the market where there is alignment of the gamer profile with target market characteristics.

Appendix II: Online advertising

Report: Global online ad spend to reach $96.8 billion in 2014
Posted by Leah McBride-Mensching on September 13, 2010

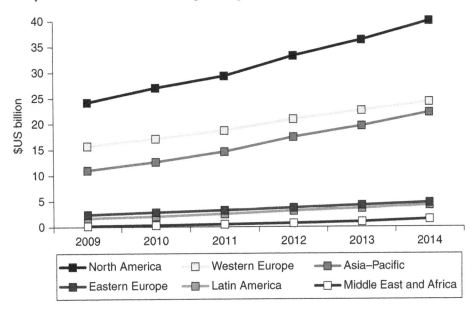

Spending on internet advertising is rapidly growing, according to the latest report from eMarketer and Starcom MediaVest, out today. Global ad spend online is forecast to hit US$96.8 billion by 2014, up from $55.2 billion in 2009, the Global Media Intelligence Report states.

'Companies worldwide will spend nearly half a trillion dollars on advertising this year. But spending that money wisely is more of a challenge now than ever before because of the changes brought about by the growing importance of digital media,' the report's summary states. 'To meet that challenge, marketers need dependable data about evolving economic conditions, consumer spending patterns, media consumption habits and competitor spending levels. And multinational corporations and their agencies need to compare and contrast these trends across regions and countries.

In 2014, total ad spending in the Asia–Pacific region will reach $173.2 billion, according to the report, Bloomberg noted. Meanwhile, North America will still have a larger overall share, at 33.8 percent, or $190.6 billion.

Thanks to a growth in consumer spending in China and India, Asia is stronger amidst the global economic downturn than the rest of the world, Bloomberg explained. Online spending in the region is expected to reach $22.2 billion, or 22.9 percent of the global total.

According to the press release, other key findings of the report include:

- The global recession sped up the shift of marketing dollars to digital in large developing markets such as China, India and Brazil.
- Asia–Pacific will eventually surpass North America as the world's biggest advertising market soon after 2014.
- While the Middle-East and Africa only receive 2.9% of total media spending worldwide, the $14 billion in spending estimated this year represents growth of 11.4%, the fastest of any major region in the world.
- Online ad spending in Latin America—though small compared to more mature regions—will more than double over the next four years, growing from $2 billion in 2010 to $4.2 billion in 2014.
- The aging of the large UK internet audience could be an early indicator of a trend that could lead to greater internet penetration throughout Western Europe.
- The disparate internet adoption rates throughout emerging regions like Central and Eastern Europe will make mobile an attractive option to marketers.

Self-development exercise A

The objective of these questions is to enable you to gain some insight into self-employment as a possible career choice. No questionnaire can claim to produce results that are absolutely accurate. What these questions can do is to help you make your own appraisal about your capacity for self-employment. Take as much time as you need to answer each question honestly. Use the answer sheet on page 124 to record your answers. Each question has two responses. Tick the box for the response that best reflects your feelings. When you are finished, turn to page 328 for feedback on the results.

1. Do you:
   a) usually offer your unsolicited opinions?
   b) offer your opinion only if asked?
2. Would you prefer the atmosphere in your business to be:
   a) one big happy family?
   b) strictly business?
3. Are you inclined to:
   a) get involved in too many projects at once?
   b) make sure that you do not get over-extended?
4. Do you find yourself using your imagination:
   a) occasionally?
   b) often?
5. Are you usually:
   a) comfortable with making plans?
   b) impatient with making plans?
6. Are you more likely to:
   a) keep the promises you make to yourself?
   b) break the promises you make to yourself?
7. Being able to live in a particular community is:
   a) very important to you?
   b) not important to you?

8. Competing and winning is:
   a) not very important to you?
   b) an important element in your life?
9. Building your business around a specific skill or technical area is:
   a) not important to you?
   b) very important to you?
10. Would you be more likely to:
    a) risk your lifestyle to start a promising venture?
    b) pass up a promising venture to protect your lifestyle?
11. Do you tend to find yourself doing most of the:
    a) talking?
    b) listening?
12. Would you be best described as a:
    a) sentimental person?
    b) calculating person?
13. Do you tend to:
    a) leave things unresolved for a while?
    b) look for quick resolution of issues?
14. Do you think you would run your business in a more:
    a) conventional manner?
    b) unconventional manner?
15. When you go into business, will you have a:
    a) detailed plan for getting started?
    b) rough plan for getting started?
16. Do you tend to:
    a) find it easy to finish the things that you begin?
    b) have some difficulty in finishing some things?
17. Work that is free from organisational restrictions is:
    a) moderately important to you?
    b) very important to you?
18. The real challenge in your life has been to:
    a) develop an overall lifestyle?
    b) confront and solve problems?
19. Becoming a business manager is:
    a) your main career goal?
    b) only a means to becoming self-employed?
20. Events in your life have been mostly determined by:
    a) yourself?
    b) forces outside your control?

21. Do you tend:
    a) to mix easily in a group?
    b) not to mix easily in a group?
22. In making business decisions, would you take:
    a) people into account most?
    b) facts into account most?
23. Would you tend to run your business with a:
    a) flexible approach?
    b) decisive approach?
24. Would you be more likely to run your business:
    a) in a tried or proven manner?
    b) in an untried or experimental manner?
25. Are you a person who:
    a) plans in advance?
    b) waits until the last minute?
26. Do you think you are:
    a) very motivated?
    b) moderately motivated?
27. A business that provides you with complete financial security is:
    a) extremely important to you?
    b) moderately important to you?
28. A successful business is worthwhile:
    a) only if it enables you to lead your life in your own way?
    b) even if you have to make some unpleasant changes to your lifestyle?
29. Pursuing your particular trade or specialty is:
    a) not as important to you as general management?
    b) more important to you than general management?
30. Are you more likely to:
    a) do whatever it may take to finish a job?
    b) apply only a reasonable amount of effort to finish a job?
31. In a group, do you tend to be more of:
    a) an organiser?
    b) a participator?
32. Would you prefer your staff to have personalities that are:
    a) warm and gentle?
    b) formal and business-like?
33. Would you prefer to run your business in a:
    a) flexible and spontaneous manner?
    b) planned and controlled manner?

34. Would you consider yourself to be more:
    a) practical?
    b) creative?
35. If you wanted to buy a used car, would you tend to talk it over with a:
    a) motor mechanic?
    b) few of your friends?
36. Have you:
    a) made some progress toward achieving your goals?
    b) not yet made much progress toward achieving your goals?
37. A business that will give you long-term job stability is:
    a) very important to you?
    b) only moderately important to you?
38. Choosing and maintaining a certain lifestyle is:
    a) more important than success in business?
    b) less important than success in business?
39. A management role in which you can supervise other people is:
    a) very important to you?
    b) not important to you?
40. In running your business, would you place more emphasis on:
    a) looking for new business opportunities?
    b) developing existing business opportunities?
41. Are you a person with a:
    a) considerable amount of social charm?
    b) modest amount of social charm?
42. Would you be best described as:
    a) emotional?
    b) logical?
43. Would you prefer to run your business with a:
    a) spontaneous approach, keeping your options open?
    b) predictable and controlled approach?
44. When you perform a task, do you like to:
    a) do it in the usual way?
    b) try to find another way?
45. When you begin a project, do you:
    a) plan it out first?
    b) work it out as you go along?
46. Do you:
    a) usually complete things on time?
    b) often run out of time?

47. Work that permits you to have complete freedom is:
    a) moderately important to you?
    b) very important to you?
48. Working on tough problems is:
    a) not usually enjoyable for you?
    b) almost always enjoyable for you?
49. Working in your particular trade or specialty for your entire career is:
    a) not important to you?
    b) very important to you?
50. Do you have a:
    a) considerable amount of self-confidence?
    b) moderate amount of self-confidence?
51. Would you describe yourself as more:
    a) outgoing?
    b) reserved?
52. When you make decisions, do you tend to use mostly:
    a) your feelings?
    b) facts and logic?
53. Does your thinking tend to be more:
    a) unstructured and free?
    b) structured and focused?
54. The most important quality you will bring to your business is:
    a) practical experience?
    b) a vision of the future?
55. If you had to plan an office party, would it be:
    a) enjoyable?
    b) a burden?
56. Do you consider yourself a:
    a) person who gets things done?
    b) bit of a procrastinator?
57. So far in your working life, have you been mostly concerned about:
    a) security and stability?
    b) your own sense of freedom?
58. Giving equal weight to your family life and your business life is:
    a) very important to you?
    b) moderately important to you?
59. Being a business manager is:
    a) more important than your trade or specialty?
    b) less important than your trade or specialty?

60. Having friends and business associates is:
    a) very important to you?
    b) only moderately important to you?
61. Are you:
    a) always willing to try something new?
    b) reluctant to try something new until you understand it first?
62. Are you more inclined to be a:
    a) warm and understanding person?
    b) firm but fair person?
63. Are you usually:
    a) open to the views of others?
    b) not easily influenced by others?
64. When you were in school, did you do better at:
    a) practical subjects?
    b) theoretical subjects?
65. Success in business depends mostly on:
    a) planning?
    b) a lucky break?
66. Are you a person with a bit:
    a) more than average initiative?
    b) less than average initiative?
67. A business that provides you with lifetime employment is:
    a) very important to you?
    b) not important to you?
68. Competing and winning is:
    a) not an important part of your life?
    b) the most exciting part of your life?
69. Do you want to be a manager:
    a) as soon as you possibly can?
    b) only if it is in your area of expertise?
70. Do you think that you would be best at:
    a) developing new products or services?
    b) refining existing products or services?
71. Are you more likely to:
    a) act spontaneously?
    b) think about something before acting?
72. As a boss, would you tend:
    a) to get upset by disagreements?
    b) not to get upset by disagreements?

73. Do you like to work in:
    a) an environment that is constantly changing?
    b) a more predictable environment?
74. When you think about the future, do you rely mostly on:
    a) known facts?
    b) your intuition?
75. Do you usually:
    a) plan your day in advance?
    b) wait to see what happens first?
76. If it was late at night and you were tired, would you be more likely to finish a job:
    a) that night?
    b) the next day?
77. Living in one particular place and not having to move is:
    a) very important to you?
    b) not important to you?
78. A business that permits you to pursue your own lifestyle is:
    a) very important to you?
    b) only moderately important to you?
79. To be in charge of a business organisation is:
    a) very important to you?
    b) not important to you?
80. Do you usually:
    a) feel comfortable taking moderate risks?
    b) avoid situations in which you have to take risks?
81. Do you have a tendency to react:
    a) quickly, according to your 'gut' reaction?
    b) only after you know all of the details?
82. In making business decisions, is it more important to:
    a) consider the feelings of everyone concerned?
    b) make logical and objective decisions that are not influenced by other people's feelings?
83. Do you:
    a) feel comfortable when you are involved in many projects at once?
    b) prefer to finish one project before starting another?
84. Would you describe yourself as more:
    a) practical?
    b) imaginative?

85. When you have to do several things, do you:
    a) make a list first, and then do them one at a time?
    b) attack them all simultaneously or in no particular order?
86. Do you:
    a) like to get things done ahead of time?
    b) usually put things off until they have to be done?
87. The thing you care about most in your working life is:
    a) security?
    b) freedom?
88. Being constantly confronted by problems or competitive situations:
    a) depresses you?
    b) excites you?
89. If you had less time for your specialty and you were forced to spend more time in general management, would you:
    a) be just as happy?
    b) possibly sell your business?
90. Would you prefer a business venture with:
    a) higher risk and greater possible rewards?
    b) lower risk and smaller guaranteed rewards?
91. Are you the sort of person who:
    a) is easy to get to know?
    b) reveals yourself slowly to others?
92. Do you think that you would be a:
    a) sympathetic boss who gets involved with your staff?
    b) firm boss who does not get involved with your staff?
93. Would you describe yourself as more:
    a) flexible?
    b) firm?
94. Do you like doing things in:
    a) tried and proven ways?
    b) new and different ways?
95. Have you:
    a) established your goals for the next five years?
    b) focused mainly on the initial steps toward establishing your goals?
96. Do you:
    a) like to set your own deadlines?
    b) dislike deadlines, even if you set them yourself?

97. The need to plan and organise your own work is:
    a) moderately important to you?
    b) very important to you?
98. In getting your business off the ground, would you:
    a) not be prepared to spend much time away from your family?
    b) be prepared to spend time away from your family?
99. The process of supervising and managing people is:
    a) very important to you?
    b) not important to you?
100. Would you prefer to:
    a) be your own boss with no guarantee of success?
    b) have a guaranteed career as a manager in a big company?

Answer sheet

	1	2	3	4	5	6	7	8	9	10
a	☐	☐	☐	☐	☐	☐	☐	☐	☐	☐
b	☐	☐	☐	☐	☐	☐	☐	☐	☐	☐

	11	12	13	14	15	16	17	18	19	20
a	☐	☐	☐	☐	☐	☐	☐	☐	☐	☐
b	☐	☐	☐	☐	☐	☐	☐	☐	☐	☐

	21	22	23	24	25	26	27	28	29	30
a	☐	☐	☐	☐	☐	☐	☐	☐	☐	☐
b	☐	☐	☐	☐	☐	☐	☐	☐	☐	☐

	31	32	33	34	35	36	37	38	39	40
a	☐	☐	☐	☐	☐	☐	☐	☐	☐	☐
b	☐	☐	☐	☐	☐	☐	☐	☐	☐	☐

	41	42	43	44	45	46	47	48	49	50
a	☐	☐	☐	☐	☐	☐	☐	☐	☐	☐
b	☐	☐	☐	☐	☐	☐	☐	☐	☐	☐

	51	52	53	54	55	56	57	58	59	60
a	☐	☐	☐	☐	☐	☐	☐	☐	☐	☐
b	☐	☐	☐	☐	☐	☐	☐	☐	☐	☐

	61	62	63	64	65	66	67	68	69	70
a	☐	☐	☐	☐	☐	☐	☐	☐	☐	☐
b	☐	☐	☐	☐	☐	☐	☐	☐	☐	☐

	71	72	73	74	75	76	77	78	79	80
a	☐	☐	☐	☐	☐	☐	☐	☐	☐	☐
b	☐	☐	☐	☐	☐	☐	☐	☐	☐	☐

	81	82	83	84	85	86	87	88	89	90
a	☐	☐	☐	☐	☐	☐	☐	☐	☐	☐
b	☐	☐	☐	☐	☐	☐	☐	☐	☐	☐

	91	92	93	94	95	96	97	98	99	100
a	☐	☐	☐	☐	☐	☐	☐	☐	☐	☐
b	☐	☐	☐	☐	☐	☐	☐	☐	☐	☐

Turn to page 328 to interpret your results.

Part B
Financial management

The purpose of Part B is to understand how a business is funded, how it creates a profit and how it depends on cash flow for survival. Chapter 7 examines the balance sheet and profit and loss statement together with methods for carrying out *financial analysis*. Chapter 8 explains the importance of forecasting and managing cash flow. Chapter 9 deals with sources of funding and the *financial structure* of a business. Chapter 10 is concerned with profit planning and describes the nature of fixed and variable costs, contribution margins, break-even points and how to establish and evaluate a profit plan.

7 Financial analysis

Success in a small business is significantly affected by the type of financial-information system you have and the use you make of it. Common sense will tell you that without current reliable financial information at your fingertips it is going to be difficult to make effective decisions. The purpose of this chapter is to describe the components of an accounting system, explain the nature of financial statements and demonstrate how to analyse financial information in order to plan and control your business.

Accounting systems

Your accounting system should be designed to reflect the type of business you operate. It is important to seek the advice of an accountant when you set up your accounting system. They can advise you about which accounting methods will suit your operation and what records you will need to keep for tax and statutory reporting purposes. Your accountant may design an accounting system especially for you or suggest that you use a prepackaged one. Low-volume systems can be run manually. If you have high volume you need to look at a computer-based accounting system. Even if your accountant is providing a full accounting service, it is important that you understand the basis of the system and the significance of the information it provides. Figure 7.1 illustrates how

Figure 7.1 Basic accounting system

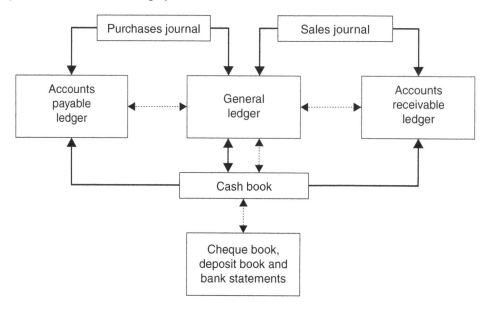

the components of a basic accounting system fit together. Following that, there is a description of the components and accounting principles.

Purchases journal

The purchases journal records the purchases you make in conducting your business. It includes the purchase of goods for resale, equipment, supplies and services. The summarised information from the purchases journal is transferred to the general ledger. Purchases you have made on credit are also transferred to the accounts payable ledger.

Sales journal

The sales journal records the sales you have made to your customers. It may contain an individual entry for each sale or a batch of daily sales. The summarised information from the sales journal is transferred to the general ledger. Sales you have made on credit are also transferred to the accounts receivable ledger.

Accounts payable ledger

The accounts payable ledger (sometimes called the creditors' ledger) records the goods and services you have purchased on credit from your suppliers and the amounts you owe them. From the cash book, the accounts payable ledger receives information on the amounts you have paid. The balance of the individual creditor accounts should equal the accounts payable total in the general ledger. This control feature helps you to detect mistakes. The accounts payable ledger provides you with the information you need to maintain a good relationship with your suppliers.

Accounts receivable ledger

The accounts receivable ledger (sometimes called the debtors' ledger) records the goods and services you have sold to your customers on credit and the amounts they owe you. From the cash book, the accounts receivable ledger receives information on the amounts that have been paid. The total of all the individual debtor accounts should equal the accounts receivable balance in the general ledger. This is another control feature to catch mistakes. The accounts receivable ledger provides you with the information you need to control credit and collections.

General ledger

The general ledger is the place where all transactions are ultimately recorded. Most transactions come from the journals and the cash book. At the end of each accounting period your accountant will make some further adjustments for non-cash items and accruals. The general ledger is where all of the information is gathered together to make up your financial reports.

Cash book

The cash book records cash receipts and payments—the transfer of cash into and out of the business. The cash received information is transferred to the general ledger and to the accounts receivable ledger. The cash paid information is also transferred to the general ledger and to the accounts payable ledger. The cash book is used to track the cash balance in the firm's bank account. It is regularly reconciled with the bank statement to ensure that they agree.

Accounting principles

Accounting systems are used to keep track of the property of the business (called assets). Accounting systems then distinguish between the property to which creditors have a claim (liabilities) and the property to which the owner has a claim (owner's equity). The basic accounting principle can be expressed as a simple equation.

What a business has	*equals*	that which creditors contribute	*plus*	that which the owner contributes
ASSETS	**=**	**LIABILITIES**	**+**	**OWNER'S EQUITY**

Each of the three categories in the accounting equation can consist of numerous subdivisions called accounts. Activities that affect the property of the firm change the accounting equation. They are called transactions and are recorded by noting what property is given up and what property is received. The simple mechanical procedure used to record transactions is called double-entry book-keeping.

The accounting system produces two principal financial reports called the balance sheet (a statement of financial position) and the profit and loss statement (a statement of financial performance). Essentially, the balance sheet shows what a business has, what it owes, and the investment of the owners in the business. It can be likened to a photograph, showing the financial position of the business at a point in time. The profit and loss statement is a summary of business operations. It is more like a moving picture. It reports the financial activity of a business over a certain period of time. In very general terms the balance sheet tells you where you are, and the profit and loss statement tells you how you got there since the last balance sheet was prepared.

Balance sheet

The balance sheet is an itemised listing of the basic accounting equation (Assets = Liabilities + Owner's equity). Figure 7.2 is an example of a balance sheet for 'Our Small Business' (OSB). Modern accounting practice is to present the balance sheet in a tabular form but for ease of understanding we will use a two-column layout.

Figure 7.2: Balance sheet

OUR SMALL BUSINESS
Balance sheet
31 March 20X1

	$	$		$	$
Current assets			Current liabilities		
Cash	1250		Overdraft	nil	
Trade debtors	93 750		Trade creditors	61 000	
Trading stock	100 000		Provision for taxes	30 000	
Prepaid expenses	5000	200 000	Accrued expenses	9000	100 000
Fixed assets			Term liabilities		
Plant and equipment	100 000		Term loan	100 000	
Accumulated			Mortgage	100 000	200 000
depreciation	(20 000)		Owner's equity		
Buildings	150 000		Contributed capital	175 000	
Land	70 000	300 000	Retained earnings	125 000	300 000
Intangible assets					
Business systems	100 000	100 000	TOTAL LIABILITIES &		
TOTAL ASSETS		600 000	OWNER'S EQUITY		600 000

Assets

Assets are what the business owns. They are recorded in descending order of their convertibility into cash. Those that can be converted into cash reasonably quickly are called current assets. Those that stay in the business over a longer period of time are called fixed assets.

Current assets

These are cash and other assets that can be converted into cash within one year from the balance sheet date. Lenders and others pay particular attention to current assets because they represent, to some extent, the amount of cash that might be raised quickly to meet current obligations. OSB's balance sheet contains the following current asset accounts:

- Cash consists of funds immediately available to use without restrictions. These are usually your cheque account balance at the bank, cash register money and petty cash.
- Trade debtors are amounts owed to the business by its customers as a result of credit sales. They are one step removed from cash. The time it takes for trade debtors to be converted to cash depends upon your credit policy and your customers' payment habits.
- Stock consists of raw materials, goods in the process of manufacture and finished trading stock that is held for resale. Trading stock is two steps removed from cash. First, a sale must take place to shift the current asset from trading stock to a trade debtor. Second, the trade debtor must be collected to turn it into cash.
- Prepaid expenses represent expenses that have been paid for in advance and whose usefulness will expire in a short time. A good example is prepaid insurance. You pay for insurance cover in advance and the right to this protection is an asset.

Fixed assets

Fixed assets are items owned by the business that have a relatively long life. In our example they consist of plant and equipment, buildings and land. With the exception of real estate, fixed assets are subject to depreciation. This is the process whereby the cost of a fixed asset is apportioned over its useful life. For example, in Figure 7.2 plant and equipment was acquired one year ago for $100 000. When it was purchased it was recorded on the balance sheet at its original cost. It has a useful life of five years, so each year one-fifth of its original cost goes into another account called accumulated depreciation. After one year there is $20 000 in accumulated depreciation. The difference between the original cost and the accumulated depreciation is the remaining book value for plant and equipment. There are several accepted ways to calculate how much of an asset's cost can be deducted for depreciation in a given year.

Other assets

This is a miscellaneous third category used only for assets that do not fit neatly into either current assets or fixed assets. These include intangible assets such as patents, intellectual property in business systems, trade names or goodwill.

Liabilities

Liabilities are debts owed by the business. They are recorded in order of increasing time to maturity. They are claims against the total assets although they are not usually claims against any specific assets except for mortgages. Liabilities are divided into current liabilities and long-term liabilities.

Current liabilities

Current liabilities consist of those debts that will fall due within one year from the balance sheet date. In Figure 7.2 OSB's balance sheet contains the following current liability accounts:

- An overdraft is a line of credit with your bank that allows you to write cheques for amounts in excess of your account balance. These are expected to be repaid in a short period of time.
- Trade creditors represent the amount you owe to vendors and suppliers from whom you have bought items on account and for which payment is expected in less than one year.
- Provision for taxes is the amount of income tax yet to be paid.
- Accrued expenses are obligations that the business has incurred but for which no formal account has been rendered. An example of this is accrued wages. Although wages may be paid fortnightly, they are being earned daily and constitute a valid claim against the business at any time between paydays. An accurate balance sheet will reflect these obligations.

Long-term liabilities

Claims of outsiders that do not come due within one year are called long-term liabilities. In Figure 7.2 long-term liabilities consist of a term loan and a mortgage. Any part of a long-term liability that falls due within one year from the balance sheet date would be listed as part of the current liabilities.

Owner's equity

Owner's equity consists of the capital contributed by the owners plus any earnings that have been retained in the business. Together, they represent the sum due to the owners if the assets were sold for the amounts appearing in the balance sheet, and the liabilities were paid off. Owner's equity is essentially a balancing figure in the sense that the owners get whatever is left over after the liability claims have been satisfied.

Profit and loss statement

The profit and loss statement summarises the activities of a business over a period of time. It reports sales revenue together with the expenses incurred in obtaining the revenue, and it shows the profit or loss resulting from these activities. The profit and loss statement can be tailored to fit the needs of a particular type of business. The amount of detail contained in the breakdown of revenue and expense depends on what you require to manage the firm effectively. Figure 7.3 is an example of a profit and loss statement for Our Small Business.

Sales revenue

The major activity of most businesses is the sale of products and/or services. The figure used is net sales after discounts, allowances and returned goods have been deducted.

Figure 7.3: Profit and loss statement

	$	$
OUR SMALL BUSINESS		
Profit and loss statement		
Year ending: 31 March 20X1		
SALES		1 000 000
Less cost of sales		
Opening stock	40 000	
Purchases	660 000	
Closing stock	(100 000)	600 000
GROSS PROFIT		400 000
Less operating expenses		
Salaries	35 000	
Wages	50 000	
Marketing	100 000	
Occupancy	45 000	
Administration	40 000	
Depreciation	20 000	
Interest	20 000	310 000
NET PROFIT BEFORE TAX		90 000
LESS PROVISION FOR INCOME TAX		27 000
NET PROFIT AFTER TAX		63 000

Cost of sales

An important item in calculating profit or loss is the cost of the goods or services that were sold. Large firms employing sophisticated cost accounting systems use some very complicated methods for calculating the cost of sales. There are much simpler, generally accepted ways of calculating average cost of sales for different types of small businesses.

In a retail firm the cost of sales can be found by adding the amount of stock purchases to the beginning stock and subtracting the ending stock. An example of calculating cost of sales in a retail firm can be found in Figure 7.3. Wholesale firms calculate cost of sales the same way except they include the cost of freight and cartage with their purchases. Service firms typically have a component of wages in addition to materials in their cost of sales. Only those wages and materials directly involved in providing the service are counted. Because manufacturing firms convert raw materials into finished goods, their method of accounting for cost of sales differs significantly from the others. In manufacturing, cost of sales involves not only raw materials, goods in the process of being manufactured and finished goods, but also direct wages and factory overhead costs.

Gross profit

The difference between sales and the cost of sales is the gross profit. It is also expressed as a percentage of sales. The gross profit percentage is significant because it represents the average profit margin on each dollar of sales before operating expenses.

Operating expenses

The other costs of running a business, besides the cost of sales, are operating expenses. The amount of detail that you include in your operating expenses is dictated by the requirements of your business. The profit and loss statement in Figure 7.3 contains the following operating expense accounts:

- *Salaries* include not only compensation for permanent staff, but also the associated forward costs such as leave loadings, long service leave accruals, superannuation contributions and payroll tax. Do not forget to include your own salary. To exclude the owner's compensation from operating expenses distorts the profitability of the business.
- *Wages* represent compensation for casual and hourly staff, including the associated forward costs.
- *Marketing* includes such things as advertising, promotion, commissions, travel and samples.
- *Occupancy* includes rent, insurance, heating/cooling, electricity, repairs and maintenance.
- *Administration* includes such things as telephone, stationery, postage, accounting and legal fees.

- *Depreciation* was first discussed when we described the balance sheet. Although no money changes hands, depreciation is a real expense because it represents an apportionment of the cost of fixed assets.
- *Interest* represents interest payments to lenders but not principal repayments.

Net profit before tax

When operating expenses have been subtracted from gross profit, the difference is net profit before tax. If the business receives revenue from non-operating sources such as rents, dividends on shares or interest on money loaned, it is added to net profit before tax at this point. This is the figure on which income tax is calculated.

Provision for income tax

This represents the amount of income tax payable on your net profit before tax. The amount of taxation, and how it is paid, will be affected by whether your business is organised as a proprietorship, a partnership or a company. In our example, the provision for income tax is also shown as a liability on the balance sheet until it is actually paid.

Net profit after tax

After the income tax liability has been provided for, the last entry is net profit after tax. It is from this amount that dividends or distributions of profits may be made to the owners. Any profits that are not paid out to the owners will be added to retained earnings in the balance sheet.

Financial ratios

The most widely practised method of analysing and interpreting financial reports is to use ratios. Financial ratios in isolation have little significance. What we need in order to evaluate financial ratios is something with which to compare them. There are three types of comparative ratio analysis:

- Comparisons with past financial ratios tells us whether the trends are getting better or worse.
- Comparisons with the financial ratios of similar firms or industry averages tell us how we stack up against the financial performance of others in the same line of business.
- Comparisons with 'rule of thumb' standards tell us how we compare with commonly accepted norms.

There are many ratios that can be derived from your financial statements. Eventually you will settle on the ones that help you the most in running your business. We shall look at eight ratios that have been shown to be useful for most small businesses.

Liquidity ratios

Liquidity ratios reflect the ability of the business to meet its current financial commitments. Inability to satisfy the legitimate demands of creditors is sufficient reason for a business to be wound up—irrespective of how profitable it may be! While these ratios help you and your creditors to monitor the liquidity of your business, they are not a substitute for cash flow budgeting.

Current ratio

The current ratio is a common test of liquidity. It looks at the level of current assets available to meet current liabilities. If you refer to the balance sheet in Figure 7.2 (see page 130) you will find the information necessary to calculate OSB's current ratio.

$$\text{Current ratio} = \frac{\text{Current assets}}{\text{Current liabilities}} = \frac{\$200\ 000}{\$100\ 000} = 2.0$$

OSB has a current ratio of 2.0. This means that the value of current assets equals twice the value of current liabilities, and the generally accepted rule of thumb is that the current ratio should be about 2.0 or better. If, however, the firm has growing sales and a short operating cycle, a lower current ratio can be quite satisfactory. Conversely, if the firm has a very long operating cycle, a current ratio of more than 2.0 may be considered prudent.

Liquid ratios

Creditors often question the liquidity of a firm's trading stock. They reason that since trading stock is two steps away from cash it should not be considered available to pay bills that are immediately due. On the other hand, because the bank overdraft does not usually have to be repaid in the immediate short term there is logic in leaving it out of the current liabilities for a test of liquidity. The liquid ratio relates current assets (less stock) to current liabilities (less the overdraft). If you refer to the balance sheet in Figure 7.2 (see page 130) you will find the information necessary to calculate OSB's liquid ratio.

$$\text{Liquid ratio} = \frac{\text{Current assets} - \text{Trading stock}}{\text{Current liabilities}}$$
$$= \frac{\$200\ 000 - \$100\ 000}{\$100\ 000} = 1.0$$

Because OSB has no overdraft the liquid ratio is 1.0. The rule of thumb for the liquid ratio is 1.0. While it needs to be interpreted with the same care as the current ratio, significant deviations below 1.0 are usually viewed with concern.

Profitability ratios

Profitability ratios consist of two types. First, there are profitability ratios that relate profit to sales. They are used to assess how each dollar of sales generates a profit. Second, there are profitability ratios that relate profit to assets. They are used to evaluate how each dollar of assets is working to generate a profit.

Gross profit margin

Gross profit margin represents the average profit on every dollar of sales before operating expenses expressed as a percentage. If you refer to the profit and loss statement in Figure 7.3 (see page 133) you will find the information necessary to calculate OSB's gross profit margin ratio.

$$\text{Gross profit margin} = \frac{\text{Gross profit}}{\text{Sales}} = \frac{\$400\ 000}{\$1\ 000\ 000} = 40\%$$

The gross profit margin can vary tremendously from one type of business to another so there is no rule of thumb. However, it is the only point at which the business generates profit and so it is a critically important figure. It is compared from one point in time to another to detect trends, and it is compared to industry averages to assess performance relative to similar firms. A lower-than-expected margin needs to be investigated to identify and remedy the causes.

You need to maximise the gross profit margin and protect it carefully because many factors can erode gross margin. Adding product lines of lower margins will drop the overall margin, while adding product lines with higher margins will increase the overall margin. If you can charge for a service that costs very little in extra labour costs, this will add significantly to the gross profit margin.

Common causes of gross margin erosion are waste and rework, damage to goods, quality claims and replacements, short delivery from suppliers, ad hoc discounting or undercharging, and theft of stock or cash. These costs directly affect the owner's returns. Particular attention should be focused on achieving the best possible margin and eliminating causes of erosion.

Net profit margin

Net profit margin represents the profitability of sales after the operating expenses have been subtracted from the gross profit. The net profit margin is expressed as a percentage and can also vary significantly from one type of business to another. If you refer to Figure 7.3 (see page 133) you will find the information necessary to calculate OSB's net profit margin.

$$\text{Net profit margin} = \frac{\text{Net profit before tax}}{\text{Sales}} = \frac{\$90\ 000}{\$1\ 000\ 000} = 9\%$$

Return on assets

Return on assets is used to assess the profit-earning performance of the firm's assets. It relates the net profit before tax in the profit and loss statement to the assets in the balance sheet and is expressed as a percentage. If you refer to Figure 7.3 (see page 133) you will find the information necessary to calculate OSB's return on assets.

$$\text{Return on assets} = \frac{\text{Net profit before tax}}{\text{Total assets}} = \frac{\$90\ 000}{\$600\ 000} = 15\%$$

A decline in the return on assets will occur if expenses rise faster than sales. Therefore, this ratio should always be examined in conjunction with the gross and net profit margins. A decline may also occur if the asset base increases at a faster rate than net profit or if the assets are not used productively.

Return on owner's equity

Return on owner's equity is considered one of the best indicators of profitability. It reflects the earning power of the owner's investment in the business. If there were no liabilities, the return on owner's equity would be the same as the return on assets. Return on owner's equity is influenced by the extent to which the firm borrows, or leverages the owner's equity. Leveraged firms are more profitable when earnings are positive, but they are also exposed to greater losses when earnings are negative. OSB's return on owner's equity is 30 per cent.

$$\text{Return on owner's equity} = \frac{\text{Net profit before tax}}{\text{Owner's equity}} = \frac{\$90\ 000}{\$300\ 000} = 30\%$$

If we are interested solely in comparing the earning capacity of different firms, the return on assets is a more appropriate ratio. The return on owner's equity is used to compare the earning capacity of the owner's investment in the business with the returns that could be earned from alternative investments. Risk and return are directly related, and small business is considered by financial analysts to have a high-risk profile requiring returns of 30 per cent or more to justify the investment.

Efficiency ratios

If all of your assets were used efficiently, then you would expect the return on assets to be maximised. One way of assessing how efficiently assets are being used is to measure their frequency of turnover. This measure relates the investment in assets to the level of activity that they support.

Asset turnover

Asset turnover measures how hard the firm's total asset base is working to generate sales. One of the key management tasks is to maximise the asset turns. Greater asset turnover indicates a more efficient use of assets to generate sales, and lower asset turnover indicates a less efficient use of assets to generate sales. Low asset turns means unnecessary funding burdens and pressure on the cash flow. Asset turnover varies significantly from one type of business to another but businesses that can generate high sales from a low asset base have an advantage. If you refer to Figures 7.2 and 7.3 (see pages 130 and 133) you will find the information necessary to calculate OSB's asset turnover ratio.

$$\text{Asset turnover} = \frac{\text{Sales}}{\text{Total assets}} = \frac{\$1\ 000\ 000}{\$600\ 000} = 1.66 \text{ times}$$

At OSB, asset turnover is 1.66 times per year. For every $1 of assets, $1.66 of sales are generated annually. Many small business operators are interested in a more detailed analysis of debtors and trading stock. These two current assets are key variables in overall asset turnover and cash flow budgeting.

Financial structure ratios

Most small businesses borrow money. Borrowing not only makes it possible to leverage the owner's equity, but it also enables the business to take advantage of opportunities that would otherwise have to be forgone. The relationship between the proportion of borrowed money and equity capital is referred to as financial structure.

Ownership ratio

One way of looking at financial structure is to focus on the proportion of total assets represented by the owner's equity. We call this the ownership ratio. If you refer to Figure 7.2 (see page 130) you will find the information necessary to calculate OSB's ownership ratio.

$$\text{Ownership ratio} = \frac{\text{Owner's equity}}{\text{Total assets}} = \frac{\$300\ 000}{\$600\ 000} = 50\%$$

OSB's ownership ratio is 50 per cent. An important and difficult question in financial management is how much debt a firm can afford to take on. The acceptable proportion of debt varies between different types of businesses. Debt finance will enable a firm to grow and to improve its profitability, but too much debt exposes the firm to the risk of financial loss and bankruptcy. When the ownership ratio is below 50 per cent, the creditors have a greater financial stake in the business than the owners.

Business performance analysis

The business performance model analyses the return on owner's equity. It is like the interest rate on a bank savings account. In other words, return on owner's equity represents the interest rate earned by your investment in the business. Knowing the return on owner's equity is valuable, because it allows you to compare the rate of return from your investment in the business with the returns you could earn from other investment opportunities.

The real value of the business performance model, however, is that it represents a framework for organising the analysis of your financial information. It is a powerful tool that can be used to identify the important variables in your business, determine the cause and effect between them, and direct your attention toward the best areas for improvement. Figure 7.4 (see below) is an overview of the business performance model.

Return on owner's equity is divided into its two constituents—return on assets and the ownership ratio:

* Return on assets is an overall measure of how well the asset base produces a profit. It reflects *operating decisions* over buying, selling, expense control and asset management.
* The ownership ratio is a measure of the owner's investment in the business. It reflects *financing decisions* over how much capital has been borrowed and how highly the firm is leveraged.

Return on owner's equity, therefore, is affected by two types of decision-making. Operating decisions affect the income-producing capacity of the business and are reflected in the firm's return on assets. Financing decisions affect the ownership ratio, which amplifies the return on assets to arrive at the rate of return on the funds the owners have invested in the business.

When read from left to right, the business performance model is a framework for analysing return on owner's equity. When read from right to left, it enables you to determine the effects of various operating and financing decisions. It is a systematic method

Figure 7.4: Business performance model overview

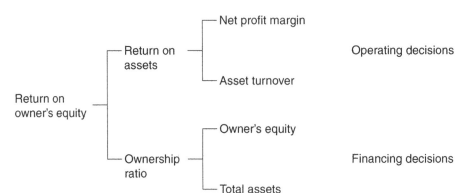

for keeping all of the variables in focus in order to find the best way to maximise the return on your equity. Figure 7.5 (see below) represents the application of the business performance model to OSB's financial statements. It demonstrates how each item in the balance sheet and the profit and loss statement is related to return on owner's equity and applies the ratios calculated in the previous section. The return on owner's equity at OSB is 30 per cent. To understand why, and how it can be improved, we shall examine the return on assets and the ownership ratio for the factors that influence them.

Analysing the return on assets

Return on assets reflects the effects of operating decisions. (OSB's return on assets is 15 per cent.) It is influenced by two interdependent factors: net profit margin and asset turnover. OSB's net profit margin, the proportion of net profit to sales, is 9 per cent. It represents the combined effects of pricing, the effectiveness of the marketing mix in creating sales, and control of the costs incurred in the process of doing business. Since it is the percentage of each dollar of sales going to the owner, we would like to see it as high as possible. OSB's asset turnover is 1.66 times. It measures the efficiency of the assets in generating sales. If the asset turnover were higher, then the same asset base

Figure 7.5 OSB's business performance analysis

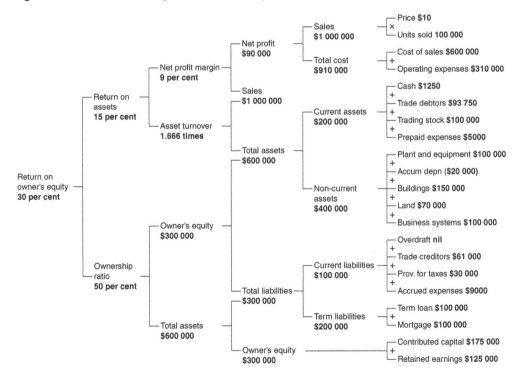

would be generating greater sales. Therefore, we would also like to see asset turnover as high as possible.

Both the net profit margin and the asset turnover are important, but it is their combined effect on the return on assets that matters most. When net profit margin is low, asset turnover must be high in order to achieve an acceptable return on assets. If a firm is operating on a low net profit margin and allows total assets to increase significantly, there will be a consequent drop in the return on assets. A fall in sales will have the same effect. Therefore, it is critical for a firm operating on a low net profit margin to carefully monitor the rate of asset turnover. A firm that is operating on a high net profit margin can afford to have a lower rate of asset turnover and still achieve a good return on assets. This firm is also less sensitive to variations in the net profit margin because it is turning its assets over less frequently.

A firm with a high proportion of fixed assets to total assets usually finds it difficult to maintain a stable rate of asset turnover in the face of fluctuating sales. This firm has to pay special attention to its net profit margin. Conversely, a firm with a low proportion of fixed assets to total assets can easily adapt to changes in sales. If sales fall, they can take steps to reduce stock and debtors. This enables them to reduce total assets, maintain asset turnover, and preserve their return on assets.

Business performance analysis gives us the means to look at every possible strategy for improving the return on assets. First, we can increase the net profit margin in one or more of the following ways:

- Increase the selling price on the same unit sales volume.
- Decrease cost of sales:
  - by more efficient purchasing
  - by more efficient management of quality
  - by eliminating waste and rework
  - by identifying short delivery by suppliers
  - by maximising security of stock and cash
  - by eliminating undercharging errors and omissions.
- Decrease operating expenses through more productive operations.

Alternatively, we can improve return on assets by increasing the asset turnover in one or more of the following ways:

- Increase the selling price on the same unit sales volume.
- Increase unit sales volume at the same selling price and with the same operating expenses.
- Reducing the assets.

If the assets are reduced we have the added options of:

- Reducing liabilities by the same extent.
- Reducing the equity by the same extent.
- Reducing a balance of liabilities and equity.

Reducing the assets while maintaining the net profit will automatically produce a higher return on assets (ROA). This higher ROA gives us a higher threshold of acceptable debt financing and makes the option of reducing equity more attractive. However, as we will see, reduced equity means higher risk of failure should the net profit suffer a drop for any reason.

Depending on the circumstances, some strategies will produce more effective results than others. For example, the first strategy in each category benefits both net profit margin and asset turnover, while some of the other strategies benefit only one.

Analysing the ownership ratio

OSB's ownership ratio is 50 per cent. If the owner had funded the entire asset base him or herself the ownership ratio would have been 100 per cent, and the return on owner's equity would have been the same as the return on assets—only 15 per cent. The fact that the owners have elected to finance part of the asset base with borrowed funds has effectively increased the return on their equity.

The ownership ratio also tells us who has the greatest financial stake in the business and in what proportion. At OSB, for every dollar of assets, the owner has contributed 50 cents and the remaining 50 cents has been borrowed. If the ownership ratio goes below 50 per cent, then the creditors will have a greater financial stake in the business than the owners. It is easy to see why this area tends to be of great importance to lenders and financial advisers.

An optimal ownership ratio is a compromise between the costs and benefits of borrowing. If the interest cost of borrowing is less than the return on assets, then borrowing is usually a good financing option. OSB's return on assets is 15 per cent, so this is the maximum interest rate it can pay for borrowed funds. Debt financing will decrease the ownership ratio, increase financial leverage, and improve the return on owner's equity. Too much debt, however, will also increase the risk of failure if sales fall unexpectedly.

If the interest cost of borrowing is greater than the return on assets, then borrowing will actually decrease the return on owner's equity. In this situation the only other source of finance is owner's equity. This consists of the owner contributing more capital or retaining some of the profits in the business.

Using the analysis to improve returns

We have established that return on owner's equity (ROE) is the prime financial result for small business owners and we now have an understanding of the key drivers that influence ROE. OSB is producing a reasonable ROE and it appears that it is well managed. However, we can make some further improvements that will result in a higher net profit, including:

- Raising prices by 2 per cent per unit
- Raising unit volume by 2 per cent with a 5 per cent increase in advertising spending
- Decreasing the cost of sales by improving procedures—target gain in gross margin 2 per cent
- Find a 5 per cent saving in administration expenses.

These relatively minor changes will produce the forecast profit and loss statement in Figure 7.6 resulting in a rise in net profit margin from 9 per cent to 11.9 per cent and an improvement in ROE from 30 per cent to 41.3 per cent.

Figure 7.6: Changed profit and loss statement for OSB

	CURRENT		CHANGED	
	$	$	$	$
SALES		1 000 000		1 040 400
Less cost of sales				
Opening stock	40 000		40 000	
Purchases	660 000		663 432	
Closing stock	(100 000)	600 000	(100 000)	603 432
GROSS PROFIT		400 000		436 968
Less operating expenses				
Salaries	35 000		35 000	
Wages	50 000		50 000	
Marketing	100 000		105 000	
Occupancy	45 000		45 000	
Administration	40 000		38 000	
Depreciation	20 000		20 000	
Interest	20 000	310 000	20 000	313 000
NET PROFIT BEFORE TAX		90 000		123 968
PROVISION FOR INCOME TAX		27 000		37 190
NET PROFIT AFTER TAX		63 000		86 778

If we look at the balance sheet for opportunities to reduce assets we find some more interesting possibilities. The current assets are well managed and there is little room for reduction. This is not common in small businesses and often large reductions in current assets can be achieved by improved stock and debtor control. We will accept that the plant and equipment is necessary for normal operations and so it cannot be reduced. However, there is $220 000 of land and buildings on this balance sheet, causing a major distortion to the analysis of performance. Real-estate investment is not the activity of this business and ownership of the land and buildings could be transferred to a separate legal entity such as a company or family trust and leased back to the business. So the aim here is to reduce fixed assets by, say, $200 000 so that total assets would drop to $400 000. Now we see that the return on assets has jumped to 31 per cent, meaning that high debt funding is more acceptable. The logical consequence is that the reduction in assets can allow a significant reduction in equity. Figure 7.7 represents the resulting forecast balance sheet.

Figure 7.8 (see page 146) lists the changes and shows the combined effect on the key ratios. The overall result is an improvement of ROE to a new level of 77.5 per cent. Results like this can happen in many businesses and the procedure is one of changing each key input variables by an achievable amount. Always take care to consider the impact of secondary effects that may counterbalance your attempts to create improvements.

To be of any practical use, the information you are working with must be current. Analysing annual accounts that are up to 18 months old has very limited use. As with any journey, you need to check your position frequently and 'steer the ship' as you go. We recommend that you use small business accounting software to produce regular financial reports.

Figure 7.7: Balance sheet for OSB with reduced assets

	$	$		$	$
Current assets			*Current liabilities*		
Cash	1250		Overdraft	20 000	
Trade debtors	93 750		Trade creditors	61 000	
Trading stock	100 000		Provision for taxes	30 000	
Prepaid expenses	5000	200 000	Accrued expenses	9000	120 000
Fixed assets			*Long-term liabilities*		
Plant and equipment	120 000		Term loan	120 000	120 000
Accumulated			*Owner's equity*		
depreciation	(20 000)	100 000	Contributed capital	35 000	
Intangible assets			Retained earnings	125 000	160 000
Business systems	100 000	100 000	TOTAL LIABILITIES &		
TOTAL ASSETS		400 000	OWNER'S EQUITY		400 000

Figure 7.8: Financial improvement plan

Key input variable	Change	Net profit before tax	N/profit margin	Asset turn	ROA per cent	ROE per cent	Change in ROE
Raise unit price	+2%						
Increase unit sales	+2%						
Gross margin	+2%						
Marketing expenses	+5%	123 968	11.9%	2.6	31%	77.5%	47.5%
Admin. expenses	–5%						
Assets	–33%						
Equity	–46.6%						

8 Cash flow

If the cash flowing into your business exceeds the cash flowing out, then you can continue to operate. But if the cash flowing out of your business exceeds the cash flowing in, your business will eventually run out of cash and grind to a halt. Even if a cash deficit is only for a short time, it can put you out of business. Small businesses are especially vulnerable to cash flow problems because they not only tend to operate with inadequate cash reserves, but they also tend to miss the implications of a cash flow deficit until it is too late. The purpose of this chapter is to explain how to plan your cash flow. It illustrates why profits are not cash, describes the operating cycle and cash flow budgeting, demonstrates how to control trade debtors and trading stock, and considers ways to overcome cash flow problems.

Profits are not cash

Financial accounting systems measure profit by matching *revenues* and *expenses*. Unfortunately, the financial accounting process does not distinguish between financial transactions and cash transactions. To understand how cash flows into and out of your business, you need to be able to match the cash *receipts* and *disbursements*. The following example clearly illustrates why profits are not cash.

You have discovered a fantastic new business opportunity. If you give your customers 30 days' credit on their purchases, sales will be $10 000 in the first month of trading and will double every month thereafter! Your stock is to be paid for in cash and it will cost you 50 per cent of the retail price. Your operating expenses will be 10 per cent of sales revenue and must also be paid in cash. The result is that you will have a net profit margin of 40 per cent and after four months of trading your profit will be $60 000. (See Figure 8.1.)

Your accountant will be so impressed by your trading results that she will probably double her fees. Your bank manager, however, will not be so impressed. In fact, he will be downright disturbed by what has happened to the balance in your bank account. Remember, your customers do not have to pay for their purchases for 30 days, but you have to pay your expenses immediately. After the same four months of trading you will have a $20 000 overdraft! (See Figure 8.2.)

How can a business with a $60 000 profit end up with a $20 000 overdraft? The answer is because $80 000 of cash flow is tied up in trade debtors. Profits are not cash. Without cash flow planning, this profitable operation could run out of cash and go out of business.

Operating cycle

The operating cycle is a series of activities that continuously transforms the components of working capital. Figure 8.3 (see page 149) is a diagram of the cash cycle.

Figure 8.1: Four-month start-up profits

	Month 1	Month 2	Month 3	Month 4	Total
Sales revenue	10 000	20 000	40 000	80 000	150 000
Expenses					
Stock	5000	10 000	20 000	40 000	75 000
Operating	1000	2000	4000	8000	15 000
Profit	4000	8000	16 000	32 000	60 000

Figure 8.2: Four-month start-up cash flow

	Month 1	Month 2	Month 3	Month 4	Total
Receipts	0	10 000	20 000	40 000	70 000
Payments	6000	12 000	24 000	48 000	90 000
Cash flow	(6000)	(2000)	(4000)	(8000)	(20 000)

Figure 8.3: Cash cycle

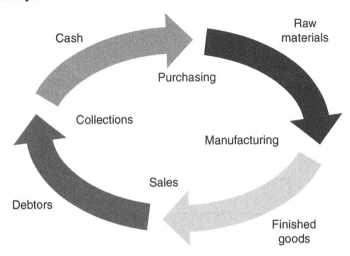

Cash is transformed into stock and services by purchasing but the impact is delayed by supplier credit. Stock is transformed into debtors by selling on credit. And debtors are transformed back into cash when payment is collected. The cycle repeats itself continuously so long as there are no bottlenecks to restrict its flow.

When bottlenecks do occur, they cause a stop–start reaction that disrupts the smooth flow of the operating cycle. For example, if collections slow down debtors will increase and cash will dry up. Without cash, purchases will have to be curtailed. Once purchases have been curtailed, sales will fall off when stock runs out. One of the important objectives of cash flow budgeting is to keep the operating cycle running smoothly.

The length of the operating cycle is the average amount of time it takes for one revolution of the cycle (days in stock, minus days in creditors, plus days in debtors). The shorter the operating cycle, the less cash is required to invest in stock and debtors, and the easier it is to maintain cash flow. *Your ability to control the length of the operating cycle plays an important part in cash flow management.*

There are also non-operating cash flows that should not be overlooked. They consist of one-off transactions such as an injection of equity capital, borrowings, the acquisition or disposal of fixed assets, debt repayments, and the distribution of profits.

Cash flow budgeting

The following five steps are simple in theory, but it takes a little time and effort to make them work. A controlled cash flow, the end result of this process, will more than repay the time and effort you give to it. We shall refer to Figure 8.4 (see page 153) to demonstrate cash flow budgeting. It represents the cash flows for Our Small Business (OSB) during its first year of operation.

Step 1: Forecasting sales

Forecasting sales is the first and most important step in cash flow budgeting. Begin by making a physical forecast of sales in terms of the number of units sold, the number of transactions completed or the number of customers served. Then translate the physical figures into dollar figures according to your pricing schedule.

Actual sales will inevitably be different from the forecast. Nevertheless, an imprecise sales forecast does not make the cash flow budget useless. What we are looking for is a forecast that is within the relevant range of possible outcomes. Using last year's sales adjusted for anticipated changes will usually enable you to forecast the major cash flow implications. Of course, the more accurate you can make the sales forecast, the more accurate will be your cash flow budget.

In Figure 8.4, OSB's sales forecast is based on estimates of unit sales at an average price of $10 each (including 15% GST). A forecast has been made for each month and it has been divided into cash sales and credit sales.

Step 2: Identifying cash receipts

Cash receipts can be divided into two categories: operating cash receipts and non-operating cash receipts. The non-operating cash receipts are associated with one-off transactions such as obtaining new equity capital, borrowing money or selling an asset. Figure 8.4 (see page 153) shows three non-operating cash receipts in the month before start-up. They are $175 000 in owner's equity, a $100 000 mortgage and a term loan of $100 000.

The operating cash receipts are directly related to the operating cycle. If you sell on a cash basis only, then your operating cash receipts will be the same as your sales forecast. If you sell on credit, however, your operating cash receipts will depend not only on the proportion of credit sales, but also on when you collect from your debtors.

In cash flow forecasting it is the timing of the flow that is important. You are trying to predict when you will actually bank the money from making a sale. Cash sales are immediately bankable but credit sales are not. To estimate when you will receive the money from credit sales you need to make some realistic assumptions about the promptness of your debtors in paying their accounts. If, for example, your invoices are due for payment in the month following the invoice date, you might find that you collect payment on only 50 per cent of the outstanding balance one month after the sales were made. A further 30 per cent arrives in the second month and the remaining 20 per cent in month three. In some industries, especially those associated with agriculture, the seasons may affect the pattern of payments. You may find your customers are slow to pay their accounts in winter but then get up to date in summer or it may be the other way around. In any case your cash flow forecast will only be as good as your ability to judge the payment performance of your debtors.

The example in Figure 8.4 shows forecasted cash receipts based on the sales forecast including GST. Cash sales are estimated to be 25 per cent of total sales. Credit sales are estimated to be 75 per cent of total sales and they are expected to be collected on an average of 45 days. For example, September cash receipts are estimated at $67 875, consisting of September cash sales of $19 688 and debtors' collections of $42 188. The debtors' collections are based on half of July credit sales ($16 875) plus half of August credit sales ($25 312).

Step 3: Identifying cash disbursements

Cash disbursements can also be categorised as operating and non-operating disbursements. Operating disbursements consist of two groups: *variable* operating disbursements and *fixed* operating disbursements. Variable operating disbursements are directly related to the operating cycle and depend upon forecasted sales. An example is stock purchases. At OSB the cost of sales is 60 per cent, and the average elapsed time from delivery of stock to paying the supplier is one month. For September sales, OSB will order stock in August, and make payment for that stock in September. OSB currently has a policy of ordering 10 per cent more stock than the sales forecast indicates in order to build up a cushion for unexpected increases in sales. Therefore the purchases disbursement for September is 0.60 ($70 000 + $7000) = $46 200.

Wages and marketing are also variable operating disbursements that depend on the sales forecast. Wages are forecast to be 5 per cent of sales and marketing is forecast to be 10 per cent of sales.

Fixed operating disbursements are not directly related to the operating cycle and take place regardless of the level of sales. For example, quarterly interest payments of $5000 are due regardless of the level of sales. OSB's remaining fixed operating disbursements are lumped together for each month. Depreciation is not included in the cash flow budget because it is not a cash disbursement.

OSB also has five non-operating disbursements. These are usually one-off transactions. In Figure 8.4 they consist of the initial purchases of stock, plant and equipment, buildings and land in the month before start-up, and a dividend payment at the end of the year. GST has a cash flow impact and must be accounted for in the forecast. OSB has elected to pay on a cash basis and on a monthly schedule. This means that the net effects of GST in each month will be paid in the following month, as shown at the bottom of Figure 8.4. Negative figures indicate a GST refund.

Step 4: Determining net cash flow

This step consists of summarising the cash receipts and the cash disbursements to determine their net effect. In Figure 8.4 you can see that OSB has negative net cash flows in the first half of the financial year (except for November) that becomes positive in the second half of the financial year (except for June). This tells us OSB needs to make provision for a cash drain during the first six months of operations, and will have a positive cash flow to repay loans or expand operations thereafter.

At this point OSB can identify the major consequences of its expected cash flow. If the net cash outflows appear to be excessively heavy, then OSB can examine ways to reschedule or eliminate some disbursements. On the other hand, if OSB foresees large net cash inflows, then it can start to think about building some cash reserves or perhaps looking for new investment opportunities.

Step 5: Determining the future cash position

In this last step we simply relate the monthly net cash flow to the bank balance. In Figure 8.4 OSB has $375 000 with which to finance the business in the month before start-up. By adjusting the bank balance by the net cash flow in each month, we can forecast how it will look at the end of each month during the first year.

OSB does not have enough cash to sustain operations. The cash flow budget reveals that OSB will reach a maximum cash deficit of $52 941 in December, but it will also generate enough positive cash flow to repay an overdraft by March. This is exactly the information that OSB's bank would like to see when it gets an application for an over-draft. It tells the bank how much money OSB requires, when it will be needed, and when it will be repaid.

Without a cash flow budget OSB may not foresee the cash deficit. The cash drain projected by the cash flow budget emphasises the critical need for cash flow budgeting. Failure to anticipate the cash deficit could put OSB out of business. Profits are simply not the same thing as cash in the bank. Using the data from Figure 8.4 a graph of the relationship between sales, net profit and cash flow for OSB's first year is shown in Figure 8.5 (see page 154).

In Figure 8.5, the healthy opening cash flow position evaporates immediately after the business starts trading. The GST paid on the fixed asset purchases prior to start-up is claimed back in one month, causing a $53 000 'wobble' in the cash flow at the start. Note that although sales climb rapidly and net profit is positive, cash flow continues to fall through December. This illustrates the typical relationship between growth and cash flow. If it is not managed, it will result in a cash flow crisis. This is known as 'overtrading'. Many business operators who have suffered a severe and unexpected cash-flow crisis are puzzled by the mysterious and sudden arrival of financial trouble. The three most common causes of a cash flow crisis are excessive owner's drawings, poor control over debtors and over-investment in trading stock.

Trade debtors

If you sell for cash only, then you will not have any trade debtors. When you sell on credit, your selling terms define the period of time for which you agree to defer payment

Figure 8.4: OSB's cash flow budget

	Month before start-up	July	Aug	Sept	Oct	Nov	Dec	Jan	Feb	Mar	Apr	May	June	Total
Sales forecast														
Unit sales		4000	6000	7000	8000	9000	12 000	10 000	9000	9000	9000	9000	8000	100 000
Dollar sales		45 000	67 500	78 750	90 000	101 250	135 000	112 500	101 250	101 250	101 250	101 250	90 000	1 125 000
Cash sales		11 250	16 875	19 688	22 500	25 313	33 750	28 125	25 313	25 313	25 313	25 313	22 500	281 250
Credit sales		33 750	50 625	59 063	67 500	75 938	101 250	84 375	75 938	75 938	75 938	75 938	67 500	843 750
Receipts														
Cash sales		11 250	16 875	19 688	22 500	25 313	33 750	28 125	25 313	25 313	25 313	25 313	22 500	281 250
Collections			16 875	42 188	54 844	63 281	71 719	88 594	92 813	80 156	75 938	75 938	75 938	738 281
Term loan	100 000													100 000
Mortgage	100 000													100 000
Owner's equity	175 000													175 000
TOTAL	375 000	11 250	33 750	61 875	77 344	88 594	105 469	116 719	118 125	105 469	101 250	101 250	98 438	1 394 531
Disbursements														
Purchases	45 000	29 700	44 550	51 975	59 400	66 825	89 100	74 250	66 825	66 825	66 825	66 825	59 400	787 500
Wages		2000	3000	3500	4000	4500	6000	5000	4500	4500	4500	4500	4000	50 000
Marketing		4500	6750	7875	9000	10 125	13 500	11 250	10 125	10 125	10 125	10 125	9000	112 500
Interest				5000			5000			5000			5000	20 000
Fixed costs		5625	5625	5625	5625	5625	5625	5625	5625	5625	5625	5625	6750	68 625
Equipment	112 500													112 500
Buildings	168 750													168 750
Land	78 750													78 750
Dividend													29 000	29 000
GST payments		(52 826)	(3727)	(3023)	(470)	433	785	(360)	3338	4637	2986	2436	2436	(43 354)
TOTAL	405 000	(11 001)	56 198	70 952	77 555	87 508	120 010	95 765	90 413	96 712	90 061	89 511	115 586	1 384 271
Net cash flow	(30 000)	22 251	(22 448)	(9077)	(212)	1086	(14 541)	20 953	27 712	8757	11 189	11 739	(17 148)	10 260
Cash position	(30 000)	(7749)	(30 197)	(39 274)	(39 486)	(38 400)	(52 941)	(31 988)	(4276)	4481	15 670	27 409	10 260	10 260
GST calculator														
GST IN	0	1467	4402	8071	10 088	11 556	13 757	15 224	15 408	13 757	13 207	13 207	12 840	132 982
GST OUT	52 826	5195	7425	8540	9655	10 771	14 116	11 886	10 771	10 771	10 771	10 771	9802	173 299
Net GST	(52 826)	(3727)	(3023)	(470)	433	785	(360)	3338	4637	2986	2436	2436	3038	(40 317)
GST Payment		(52 826)	(3727)	(3023)	(470)	433	785	(360)	3338	4637	2986	2436	2436	(43 354)

Figure 8.5: Sales, profits and cash flow

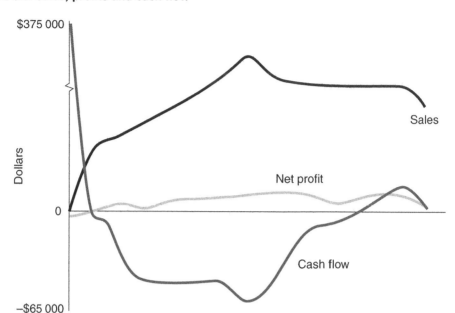

for a customer's purchases. If some customers take longer to pay than expected, then the actual collection period may be longer than your selling terms. Your selling terms and your collection policy are key components of the operating cycle and directly affect your cash flow.

Average collection period

The average collection period is the average length of time that sales dollars remain in the form of trade debtors. The longer the average collection period, the longer the operating cycle, and the greater the investment in trade debtors. The average collection period is calculated by dividing total trade debtors by average daily credit sales. If credit sales for the year were $730 000, then the average daily credit sales would be $2000.

$$\text{Average daily credit sales} = \frac{\text{Annual credit sales}}{365 \text{ days}} = \frac{\$730\ 000}{365 \text{ days}} = \$2000$$

If we have $120 000 in trade debtors, then the average collection period indicates that, on average, customers are taking 60 days to pay their bills.

$$\text{Average collection period} = \frac{\text{Trade debtors}}{\text{Average daily credit sales}} = \frac{\$120\ 000}{\$2000} = 60 \text{ days}$$

Offering customers better credit terms usually leads to greater sales, but better credit terms also lengthen the average collection period. The longer the average collection period, the greater the required investment in trade debtors. Similarly, the greater average daily credit sales, the greater the required investment in trade debtors. Concurrent changes in both have a compound effect on the required investment in trade debtors. In our example, if customers are allowed extended payment terms of 90 days and credit sales increase to $3000 per day, then we will need to increase the amount of cash invested in trade debtors from $120 000 to $270 000.

Trade debtors = Average daily credit sales × Average collection period
= $3000 × 90 days = $270 000

Comparing your average collection period with the following benchmarks will help to determine if you are over-invested or under-invested in trade debtors.

Payment experience vs selling terms
If your selling terms specify payment within 30 days and your average collection period is 45 days, it indicates some customers are not complying with your selling terms and a problem exists.

Past history
Comparing your present average collection period with previous experience will tell you if it is getting longer or shorter. A longer average collection period indicates a lengthening operating cycle and increased investment in trade debtors, while a shorter average collection period indicates a shorter operating cycle and reduced investment in trade debtors.

Industry averages
Comparison with industry averages will show you the extent to which your average collection period differs from other businesses like yours. Keep in mind that industry averages may not account for unique circumstances in your business. For example, if you are boosting sales by extending selling terms, then your average collection period will naturally be longer than the industry average.

Controlling trade debtors
Analysis of the average collection period will help to identify overall trade debtors' problems. In order to control your trade debtors effectively, you need to identify individual customers. Problems in individual accounts are detected through ageing analysis. Ageing analysis divides each customer's account into the amounts that fall into each ageing category. In Figure 8.6 (see page 156) an aged analysis of trade debtors divides customers' account balances into 0–30 days, 31–60 days, 61–90 days, and over 90 days.

Figure 8.6: Aged analysis of trade debtors

Customer	Balance	0–30 days	31–60 days	61–90 days	Over 90 days
A	5000	5000			
B	13 000	6000	7000		
C	4000	4000			
D	7000	7000			
E	3250	3250			
F	21 000	5000	6250	4500	5250
G	12 000	12 000			
H	9000	9000			
I	17 250	5000	5500	6750	2250
J	2250				
TOTAL	93 750	56 250	18 750	11 250	7500
Per cent	100	60	20	12	8

In this example it is clear that Customer F and Customer I are serious collection problems, and Customer B should be prevented from becoming one as well. Customer J is no longer an active account and the over 90 days balance could be an unresolved dispute or a bad debt. The longer an account is past due, the more serious the problem is likely to be. Ageing analysis pinpoints accounts that are tying up your cash flow so that corrective action can be taken.

The best time to pursue an overdue account is as soon as the customer exceeds your selling terms. As an account gets further behind, the balance may continue to increase while the chances of collection decrease. Many small business operators are reluctant to enforce strict collection procedures. Some are simply embarrassed to ask for money even though it is a legitimate debt. Others are afraid they will alienate a 'good' customer and lose the account. And still others feel that a rigid collections policy will damage their reputation. These reasons are not valid. What good is a customer if you are not paid? Wouldn't you be reluctant to accept further orders from a customer with an overdue account anyway? And would you really expect a customer who owes you money to spread this news around? It is your cash flow that is at stake, and you need to protect it.

Credit cards

Credit cards are an established way of doing business. When you offer to accept credit card purchases you do not need to invest cash in trade debtors and the costs and risks of credit and collection are practically eliminated. Credit card services are available from the trading banks and specialist credit card companies. Trading-bank credit cards include Bankcard, MasterCard and Visa. Examples of specialist credit card companies are American Express and Diners Club.

Receipts from bank credit card sales can be deposited daily and are immediately credited to your cheque account. The bank assumes all of the credit risks provided that you follow their instructions. These instructions usually require you to check the validity of the card against a list of cancelled cards, and to get approval before accepting the card for purchases above a certain limit. In return for this service the bank charges a fee called a *discount*. The amount of the discount is negotiable and you should shop around for the best deal.

The specialist credit card companies operate on a similar basis. They do not, however, offer the advantage of daily credits to your cheque account. Instead, you get paid some time after you have submitted the credit card vouchers to them. Some small-business operators do not like to use non-bank credit cards because of the length of time it sometimes takes to get paid.

Credit card services are particularly important for businesses with a large number of relatively small accounts. They eliminate the paperwork involved in credit approval, invoice preparation, debtors' records and collections. They avoid the need to commit cash to debtors and the risk of uncollectable accounts. And don't forget that the availability of instant credit is an indispensable marketing tool. Although credit cards are most often used for retail accounts, they can also be used successfully in selling to small commercial accounts.

Trading stock

For most retail and wholesale businesses the single largest asset is trading stock. Like trade debtors, trading stock is a key element in the operating cycle and a major influence on cash flow.

Stockturn

One way to evaluate your trading stock position is to calculate the stockturn. It measures the number of times your business sells, or turns, its investment in stock in one year. Stockturn is calculated by dividing the annual cost of sales by the average amount of stock on hand. For example, if your annual cost for the goods you sell is $500 000 and the usual amount of stock you keep on hand is worth $100 000 at cost, then your stockturn is five times per year.

$$\text{Stockturn} = \frac{\text{Annual cost of sales}}{\text{Trading stock}} = \frac{\$500\,000}{\$100\,000} = 5 \text{ times per year}$$

The higher your stockturn, the more sales volume you are producing from a given investment in trading stock. When you increase your stockturn, you shorten the operating cycle and increase your cash flow. Conversely, when you decrease your stock-turn, you lengthen the operating cycle and decrease your cash flow.

How you manage your trading stock has a tremendous impact on your sales effort. Having the right assortments in the right quantities is one of the keys to maximising sales. The more trading stock you carry, however, the longer the operating cycle will become and the more cash you will need. The investment in trading stock is dependent not only on the stockturn but also on the level of sales. For example, if sales doubled (resulting in $1 000 000 cost of sales) and stockturn slowed to four times per year, then the investment in trading stock would need to increase from $100 000 to $250 000.

$$\text{Trading stock} = \frac{\text{Annual cost of sales}}{\text{Stockturn}} = \frac{\$1\,000\,000}{4} = \$250\,000$$

You can determine if you are over-invested or under-invested in trading stock. First, you can compare your stockturn with other firms and industry averages. Second, you can track your stockturn over time to determine whether your investment in trading stock is increasing or decreasing relative to your sales volume. Both of these comparisons will enable you to monitor your overall investment in trading stock. Keep in mind that unique circumstances, such as a special promotion or a seasonal increase in sales, may justify a temporary deviation from your normal stockturn.

Controlling trading stock

Analysis of your stockturn helps to identify and evaluate your overall trading-stock position. Most businesses, however, carry a variety of products, each of which turns over at a different rate. In order to control your trading stock you need to analyse each product individually. Item analysis compares the number of units of each item held in stock against the amount actually required based on the most recent sales experience. Figure 8.7 is an example of an item analysis based on a target of 60 days' supply for all products.

Figure 8.7: Item analysis of trading stock

Product	Quantity on hand	Sales during past 60 days	Days' supply on hand	Required action
A	500	150	200	Reduce by 350 units
B	200	300	40	Increase by 100 units
C	50	100	30	Increase by 50 units
D	165	165	60	None
E	600	150	240	Reduce by 450 units
F	125	100	75	Reduce by 25 units

Overcoming a cash flow crisis

If your cash flow remains positive there is no need for concern. However, nearly all businesses experience negative cash flow at one time or another. When negative cash flow drives your bank balance into the red, you have a number of options.

Shorten the operating cycle

Essentially this means increasing the efficiency of the components in the operating cycle and reducing the cash committed to them. Increasing the stockturn or reducing the average age of trade debtors, while maintaining the same level of sales, will release cash. This requires more aggressive collection of trade debts and tighter control of trading stock. Good stock control systems require analysis of your sales so that you can build sales on fast-moving lines and eliminate the non-performers.

Increase the net profit margin

Increasing the net profit margin provides a greater number of surplus dollars for the same level of sales. This can be done by increasing price, reducing cost of sales or reducing operating expenses. Increasing sales volume at the same net profit margin, however, will only make a cash flow problem worse.

Reduce the sales volume

Reducing the sales volume decreases the investment required in the components that make up the operating cycle. In the 'profits are not cash' example at the beginning of this chapter (see page 148), notice that the cash flow deficit would not increase if sales were held steady. Reducing sales is difficult for most small business operators to contemplate, but holding growth in check is a rational way to resolve a cash flow crisis. One way to slow down sales while increasing both net profit margin and cash flow is to selectively increase prices.

Increase trade payables

In order to slow down your cash disbursements, you can rely more heavily on the credit available from your suppliers. Ask them to consider extending their credit terms. Look into acquiring stock on consignment, which means you do not need to pay for it until it is sold. Stretching payments to your suppliers beyond their selling terms may temporarily solve today's cash flow problem, but it may also risk your credit reputation in the future.

Borrow money

Borrowing can be used to solve short-term and long-term cash flow problems. Short-term borrowing is used to finance temporary increases in working capital such as a seasonal build-up of stock financed by an overdraft. Short-term borrowing should be self-liquidating, so that when the operating cycle returns to normal it automatically produces the cash flow necessary to repay the loan. Long-term borrowing can be used for permanent increases in working capital or for the acquisition of fixed assets. These needs are usually the result of a permanent increase in sales volume. Long-term borrowing is repaid over a longer period to give the assets enough time to generate the cash flow necessary for repayment.

Look for equity capital

Equity capital consists of putting more of your own money into the business or taking in new owners in the form of partners or shareholders. Equity capital is long-term capital and should normally be used for long-term purposes.

Maintain a minimum cash reserve

Cash is an idle asset. It makes no direct contribution to profits. The best cash position is a zero cash balance. However, in order to ensure that enough cash is on hand to pay the bills as they come due, you should consider some minimum cash reserve. The size of the minimum cash reserve is influenced by the extent to which you can count on collections from your debtors, the flexibility of your disbursements and the availability of outside finance. The more certain you can be about your cash flow, the less cash reserves you need.

9 Financing the business

Finance is needed for many different purposes, and it will be needed at several key points in the life of your business. This chapter surveys the essential components of financing a business. We begin with a discussion about financing a start-up and how to establish why we need financing. Then we examine the effects of borrowing on financial structure and earnings performance. The remainder of the chapter investigates sources of borrowing, leasing and equity capital.

Financing at start-up

A common cause of financial difficulties in the first few years of a business start-up is a lack of adequate capital. It is easy to overlook or underestimate some of the initial expenses. If you miss some critical expenses, your business could be short of money right from the start and surviving the first few years will be more difficult. Some of the expenses that are commonly missed or underestimated are real-estate agents fees, legal fees, rent in advance, bonds for power supply, local body permit and licence fees, compliance with health regulations in food businesses, and compliance costs for Occupational Safety and Health (OSH) regulations.

The first step is to develop a list of all the asset purchases and initial expenses required for the start-up. The asset list will include plant and equipment, vehicles and machines, computer hardware and software, the initial stock holding, and furniture and fittings. Initial expenses will include legal fees, location selection and fit-out costs, signage, local authority bonds, licences and fees, service bonds and connection fees, staff recruitment and training, and initial promotion and advertising.

The second step is to assess the business's need for operating cash flow during the start-up period by doing a cash flow budget. It will forecast the need for finance to cover negative cash flow in the early stages. Banks look more favourably at a business that has done cash flow planning and knows that it will need extra funds to carry it through the start-up phase. Banks are not impressed by a firm that strikes an unexpected cash shortage and then expects the bank to cover the problem.

Once the start-up costs are identified, the third step is to determine where the necessary funds are going to come from. Figure 8.4, the cash flow budget in the last chapter (see page 153), tells us that OSB uses all of its initial funding, which consists of $175 000 in equity, a term loan of $100 000 and a mortgage for $100 000. OSB also requires a bank overdraft for $52 941 to cover the first year's operations. This is the result of a cash deficit of $30 000 at start-up, plus accumulating cash deficits from trading through the first six months.

Justifying new investment

Before we begin the process of financing new investment in a going concern, we need to be sure we really need the money. Does the level of activity in the profit plan indicate the need for new investment? For the majority of small businesses, the most likely new investments will be in trade debtors, trading stock and fixed assets.

Trade debtors

The level of investment in trade debtors depends on the volume of credit sales, selling terms, the payment practices of customers and how effectively overdue accounts are collected. It can be estimated by looking at the expected average daily credit sales and the expected average collection period.

Trading stock

The level of investment in trading stock depends upon changes in sales volume and how effectively inventory is managed. It can be estimated by looking at the expected cost of sales and the expected stockturn.

Fixed assets

The purchase of fixed assets is not as closely tied to the profit plan as trade debtors and trading stock. The need for investment in fixed assets occurs when plant and equipment wears out and needs replacement, or when there is a significant change in business activity that requires more capacity. An investment in fixed assets usually represents a large financial commitment over a number of years. For this reason, you need to carefully evaluate the costs and the benefits because you will be living with the results of your decision for some time.

In general, the primary focus of asset management should be to optimise asset levels relative to the sales level. Getting the existing assets to work harder will reduce the need for new assets and, in turn, reduce the need for extra funding and take pressure off the cash flow. Optimising asset levels involves high capacity utilisation of fixed assets and short cycle times in the life of current assets.

If a business experiences a sustained period of growth it may not be able to fund that growth out of trading profits. Rapid growth in sales may cause the stock levels and debtors' balances to 'blow-out', catching the business in an unexpected cash flow crisis. In some cases this is made worse by decisions to buy more fixed assets, such as vehicles and equipment, in response to the growth in sales. Increasing sales faster than your ability to fund the growth is known as 'overtrading'.

You can take a variety of actions to deal with this situation, but time is against you and your remedy must be swift. The recommended action is to raise prices. This immediately dampens demand and takes pressure off the need for more and more assets. At the same time it provides more profit to fund whatever growth is still occurring. You may also be able to inject more funds or take steps to control the assets more tightly. In any case the problem of overtrading adds strong support to the argument that you need to manage the growth in assets carefully and have finance arranged in time to cover the needs of growth.

Financial structure

Deciding on financial structure means deciding what proportion of your capital should be borrowed. The greater the borrowings, the greater the degree of financial leverage and the return on owner's equity. Greater borrowings, however, also mean greater fixed-interest expense. If sales decline sharply, a leveraged firm will drop below its break-even point before a firm that is not leveraged. Figure 9.1 (see page 164) illustrates the effects of borrowing. It represents five alternative financial structures that OSB could adopt for 20X2. As we move from financial structure A to financial structure E, total liabilities become a greater proportion of total capital.

Let's use 10 per cent as the average interest rate for borrowed money. The amount of interest expense increases as the proportion (and amount) of total liabilities increases. Therefore, net profit before tax is reduced when the proportion of liabilities in the financial structure increases.

The return on assets decreases as the proportion of liabilities increases because net profit is decreasing. Similarly, the ownership ratio decreases as the proportion of

Figure 9.1: Effects of borrowing

Financial structure	($000)				
	A	B	C	D	E
Total assets	1000	1000	1000	1000	1000
Total liabilities	0	200	400	600	800
Owner's equity	1000	800	600	400	200
Net profit before interest	270	270	270	270	270
Interest expense	0	20	40	60	80
Net profit before tax	270	250	230	210	190
Return on assets	27%	25%	23%	21%	19%
Ownership ratio	100%	80%	60%	40%	20%
Return on owner's equity	27%	31.25%	38.33%	52.5%	95%

liability increases. The return on owner's equity, however, *increases* as the proportion of liabilities increases because of the effects of financial leverage. If we use net profit as the criterion for the best financial structure, then we would conclude that a firm should never borrow. If we use return on owner's equity as the criterion for the best financial structure, then we would conclude that a firm should borrow virtually all of its capital. So what is the best financial structure?

The optimal financial structure is a compromise between the costs and the benefits of borrowing. In order to benefit from the effects of financial leverage, a firm's return on assets must exceed the overall interest rate on its borrowings. The optimal capital structure also depends on the stability of the return on assets. If return on assets is stable, the uncertainty about the negative effects of leverage is reduced. If the return on assets is unstable, then any unexpected dip in sales or profit margins may drive a profit into a loss.

Important sources of information about financial structure are inter-firm comparisons and industry profiles. They not only give you an idea about the ownership ratio for an average firm in your industry, but they also tell you something about the relative proportions of short-term versus long-term borrowing.

Debt finance

The ability to borrow money when you need it is important. For that reason you should always maintain a good relationship with your bank and other potential lenders. The better they know you, the more inclined they will be to lend you money when you need it. Potential lenders want to know the answers to a number of questions.

- What is your character? Are you a good business manager? Are you the sort of person in whom the lender can feel confident?
- What are you going to do with the money? Will you need the money for a short time or a long time?
- When do you plan to pay back the loan? How will you generate the money for the repayments?
- Do you have assets that you can offer as security? Are you willing to personally guarantee the loan?
- What is the outlook for your business? Are you likely to stay in business for the duration of the loan?

Lenders only want to lend to businesses that are solvent, profitable and liquid. The balance sheet, profit and loss statement and cash flow budget are the lender's tools for determining how you meet these criteria. The balance sheet is used to determine solvency, the profit and loss statement is used to determine profitability, and the cash flow budget is used to forecast liquidity. Regular financial reports over a period of time are the best way to convince a lender about your financial stability.

Sometimes your signature is all a lender will require to lend you money if they know you already and the loan is for a short period. However, most lenders require some form of security, particularly for longer-term loans. There are a number of ways in which you can offer security. These include a guarantor, assignment of lease, trading stock, trade debtors, chattel mortgages, real-estate mortgages, cash value of a life insurance policy, or marketable assets such as shares or other investments.

Whether or not security is required for a loan, lenders may want to impose conditions in order to protect themselves against poor management practices. Examples of loan conditions include no further borrowing without the lender's agreement, maintaining working capital, carrying adequate insurance and supplying the lender with regular financial reports.

Lenders want to match the term of a loan with the useful life of the asset that it is financing. If you borrow short-term funds to invest in fixed assets, you will be faced with the prospect of having to repay the loan before the assets can generate enough cash to do so. If you borrow long-term funds to invest in temporary current assets, you will be paying for the finance long after you need it. This distinction between short-term borrowing and long-term borrowing is an important factor in determining the most suitable type of finance for your circumstances.

Short-term borrowing

Short-term borrowing is used to finance assets that turn over quickly, such as trade debtors and trading stock. It is usually repaid within one year. Contractors with substantial work in progress sometimes need short-term finance until they receive their next progress payment. Wholesalers and manufacturers with seasonal sales need short-term finance to carry the increases in debtors and stock until the end of the selling season. Therefore, short-term borrowing is usually self-liquidating because it is used to finance temporary assets that will generate the cash flow to repay the loan. The main sources of short-term borrowing for small businesses are trade credit, overdrafts, accounts receivable financing, floor plans, bridging finance, commercial bills and import-export finance.

Trade credit

Trade credit occurs when your supplier gives you time to pay for goods after they have been delivered. Essentially, this is an interest-free, short-term loan. Trade credit is the most easily accessible external source of finance for a small business. Unlike other sources of finance, it seldom involves complex and time-consuming negotiations. A planned program of trade-credit extensions can help a business to secure finance without resorting to lenders or equity capital investors. Here are a few points to keep in mind:

- Take full advantage of available payment terms. If no cash discount is offered for early payment, and the payment is due 30 days after delivery, do not make your payment until the thirtieth day.
- Whenever possible, negotiate extended payment terms with your suppliers. For example, if a supplier's regular payment terms are 30 days from the receipt of goods, try to get them extended to 30 days from the end of the month. That amounts to an extra 15 days' credit on average.
- If you are looking for a significant increase in trade credit, you should talk to your suppliers about extending your terms another 30 or 60 days. Remember that your request will put pressure on their cash flow. If you are a good customer, they may agree to your request.

Overdraft

An overdraft is an arrangement with your bank in which you may borrow through your cheque account up to a certain limit. It may be secured or unsecured. Overdrafts are the most flexible form of short-term finance because you borrow only when the need arises and interest is charged only on the daily balance outstanding, not the total overdraft limit. An establishment fee is usually charged by the bank, plus a periodic administration charge. Together, these extra charges increase the effective cost of an overdraft. In theory, the bank can ask a customer to repay their overdraft on demand. In practice, the bank either asks the customer to refinance their overdraft with secured longer-term borrowings or they reduce the overdraft limit.

A less expensive alternative to an overdraft is the home equity loan. The bank establishes the equity that you have in your home by taking the difference between its market value and the amount outstanding on your mortgage. The bank offers you a revolving line of credit secured by your home equity. You can draw it down and repay it in the same way as an overdraft. The interest rate is significantly lower than overdraft rates and only slightly higher than mortgage rates.

Accounts receivable financing

Accounts receivable financing can occur in two ways. Accounts receivable lending consists of cash advances of up to a percentage of eligible invoices. The lender takes a registered security over your debtors and will insist upon proper debtor control procedures. Accounts receivable lending is offered by banks and finance companies. Factoring is the cash purchase of your sales invoices at a discount. The factor advances you a percentage of the value of your invoices and takes over the collection of accounts from your customers. The balance, less the factoring fee, is paid to you when the factor receives the customer's remittance. Generally, you are still responsible for bad debts. Factoring is one way that manufacturers and wholesalers can improve their cash flow and maximise the use of their working capital. Factoring is available from finance companies and factoring companies. Businesses that deal with the public, however, are more likely to use consumer-credit factoring services available through the banks, such as Bankcard, MasterCard and Visa.

Floor plan

The term floor plan is used to describe finance especially designed for wholesalers and retailers who carry expensive items in stock such as cars, trucks, boats and caravans. Funds are advanced so that the dealer can have a suitable range of stock on the showroom floor. The stock is security for the advance. When an item is sold, that part of the advance is repaid. There are a number of different floor-plan arrangements available so it is good practice to shop around before you make a deal. For example, many finance companies allow a rebate on floor-plan interest charges depending on the volume of consumer finance written by the dealer on behalf of the finance company.

Bridging finance

Bridging finance is money borrowed for a short time until the proceeds from another transaction become available or more permanent financing is arranged. Bridging finance is commonly used in land and property development and it can also be used to finance the purchase of a business pending the sale of another business or some other asset. Bridging finance is generally secured and the interest rate varies depending upon the lender. It is available from banks, finance companies and solicitors' trust funds.

Commercial bills

Commercial bills are generally associated with business lending or high-end investment lending. They provide an injection of cash for borrowers who need more than $100 000. These types of loans are generally rolled over until the borrower has the funds to repay the loan amount in full. The bills can be either variable rate or fixed rate, with periods varying between one and ten years. During the loan term there are 'rollover' periods, at which time the interest rate and the amount borrowed may be recalculated. The rollover period may be 30, 60, 90, 180 days, six-monthly or even annually. Interest is paid at each rollover and you may negotiate with your bank to find a structure of time and interest to suit your needs.

Import–export finance

Import finance consists of a lender making payment to your overseas supplier for goods when they are shipped. The repayment terms usually extend 60 to 120 days after the goods have landed in New Zealand. Export finance consists of extending credit terms to an overseas buyer evidenced by a commercial bill that is discounted in the short-term money market. Import–export finance is available through banks and finance companies.

Long-term borrowing

Long-term borrowing is used to finance fixed assets such as vehicles, equipment, plant, buildings and property. It can also be used to provide funds for the purchase of an existing business, to help establish a new one, or to finance permanent additions to working capital. These assets need to produce enough income to meet the interest and principal repayments in addition to earning a profit for the owner. Therefore, when it comes to long-term borrowing, the lender looks for assurances that the business will be able to repay the loan out of earnings over the period of the loan. The main types of long-term borrowing for small businesses are personal loans, hire purchase, term loans, mortgages and debentures.

Personal loans

Personal loans are normally used to finance the purchase of consumer goods. They can also be used to finance a business. A personal loan can be used to pay for a motor vehicle, shop fixtures or perhaps the initial stock. Personal loans are repaid in regular instalments including principal and interest, and they are often unsecured if your credit reputation is established. Personal loans are available from banks and finance companies. You can also borrow money against the cash value of your life insurance policy.

Hire purchase

Hire purchase is widely used to acquire fixed assets such as equipment, shop fittings or motor vehicles. A deposit is required and the balance is financed with a hire-purchase agreement that calls for regular instalments including principal and interest. The amount of the deposit and the term of the hire-purchase agreement vary with the type of goods. Legal ownership of the goods remains with the lender until the instalments have been paid. Some hire-purchase finance is available from banks, but most of it is provided by finance companies.

Term loans

Term loans are available for fixed periods of one to 10 years. The purposes for which term loans are made include purchases of a business, land, buildings and equipment. They are generally secured and repaid in regular instalments including principal and interest. Sometimes a term loan is interest only, requiring only regular interest payments, with the principal repaid in a lump sum at the end of the loan period. The interest rate may be fixed or variable. Term loans are available through banks, finance companies, solicitors' trust funds, insurance companies and some building societies.

Mortgages

Mortgages are used to finance the purchase of land and buildings. Mortgage finance is long-term finance and it is secured by the property it is financing. It is generally repaid by regular instalments including principal and interest. The interest rate may be fixed or variable. It is possible to have second and third mortgages on the same property. Mortgages are available through banks, finance companies, solicitors' trust funds, insurance companies and building societies.

Equity finance

Equity finance is money invested in the business by its owners. It is a permanent part of the capital structure. You obtain equity capital in the first instance by investing your own money in the business. You can increase the equity capital by investing more of your own money, reinvesting some of the profits, or taking other people into the business as partners or by selling part of it in the form of shares.

Internal equity capital

The principal source of internal equity capital for a small business is the owner's money. For some individuals, it will be their life's savings. For others, it will be money that has been borrowed on a personal basis in order to provide equity capital for the business.

Another source of internal equity capital that is overlooked by some small business operators is retained earnings. Many business owners have gone to their bank to borrow money only to be shown that they did not need a loan because they could finance their needs out of profits if they budgeted carefully.

External equity capital

If the need for equity capital exceeds the capacity of the owner and the retained earnings of the business, then external equity capital will need to be considered. If the business is unable to borrow money, then external equity capital may offer the only means by which the firm can expand its financial base.

Some individuals have relatives, friends or acquaintances who have some spare cash to invest in the business. This can have some fish-hooks: while these people may be a great source of financial and emotional support, they may also meddle in the business by annoying you with incessant questions or unwanted advice.

The main source of external equity capital for small businesses is private investors known as business angels. These are individuals who are prepared to provide equity capital in the form of share capital or partnership capital for a worthwhile venture. Business angels tend to seek investment opportunities through a network of personal contacts or associations such as the ICE Angels.

There are various kinds of shares to suit the needs of a situation. The common classes of shares are 'ordinary', 'non-voting', 'preference' and 'redeemable' shares. Outside investors usually favour redeemable preference shares because they can be redeemed for cash at a certain date and they hold preferred payout status ahead of ordinary shares.

Selling equity in your business generally triggers various legal, taxation and accounting consequences. Make sure you get professional advice before you accept any money from an investor. You may also want to ask your accountant, solicitor and other financial advisers or your local business incubator if they could help you locate a business angel.

Getting ready to seek equity finance

Your bargaining power may be limited but a well-organised approach can help. The following attributes are considered necessary for a company seeking equity finance to qualify as an 'investment ready' company:

- Good governance and advisers
- A clear separation of personal and business affairs
- A planned entry and exit strategy for both the investors and the founders
- A simple company structure and capital structure
- Timely and accurate management accounts
- Declaration of full accounting profits (supported by tax returns)
- Reinvestment of earlier profits back into the business
- A depth of management skills and good quality of key personnel.

If you make it through the investor's door the next challenge you will face is a request by the investor for a due-diligence report. This is a detailed disclosure of company and market information that is required for the investor to make a 'go/no-go' decision on proceeding with the investment.

Valuation

If the angel investor is interested in proceeding, the value of the company must be established. An example is given below of a method that includes future profit estimates, the time value of money, market P/E rates and the angel's required Rate of Return (ROR) percentage. The basic formula is the investment required by you divided by the valuation of future earnings.

$$\text{Current investment required} \left/ \frac{\text{NPAIT }(n) \times \text{Market P/E ratio}}{(1 + i)^n} \right.$$

Where:

NPAIT = Net profit after interest and tax

n = Future point in years

P/E rate is taken from common market P/E rates paid for comparable companies

i = Interest rate required (ROR)

So for an example where five-year profits are forecast as $1 000 000 and you want an investment of $800 000 for five years, in an industry where the comparable P/E ratio is 15 and the investor wants a compound return rate of 50 per cent, the calculation is as follows:

$$\$800\,000 \left/ \frac{\$1\,000\,000 \times 15}{(1 + 0.5)^5} \right.$$

$$= \frac{\$800\,000}{\$1\,975\,000} = 0.41\%$$

which means that 41 per cent of the company will have to be given up to get the $800 000.

However, if all you get is the money, it is not a good deal. Your angel should be an experienced business manager with significant experience and knowledge to add to the management capability of the company.

The ICE Angels

The ICE Angels (currently 75 members) working in partnership with the ICEHOUSE business incubator, provide development funding for entrepreneurial ventures. Typically the start-up company will be seeking $500–750k in return for 20–40 per cent of the business. Examples of appropriate use of the funds are:

*   Establishing 'proof-of-concept'
*   Filing patents

- Market research and validation
- Product development
- Prototyping and product launches.

The deal will typically involve a syndication of investors often including government funds. By 2010 the ICE Angels had invested a total of $29 million with 18 companies.

Angel investors form a very necessary part of the business financing environment. Their focus is to provide funding for entrepreneurial ventures in the early stage start-up phase of business growth. They cover the deals that are considered too risky for normal bank lending or too small for the larger venture-capital companies. In New Zealand the market now provides approximately $60 million of entrepreneurial finance annually. Although the terms can seem tough and the process protracted and taxing for the entrepreneur, well-presented cases do get investment that may not be available elsewhere.

Leasing

Leasing is another way to finance vehicles and equipment without having to make a down payment. The leasing organisation (lessor) buys the equipment and leases it to you (lessee) in return for regular lease payments. The lease payments are tax deductible when the equipment is used to produce income. Leasing can be a very flexible method of finance that enables a variety of cash flow and tax advantages to be achieved. Leasing is offered by some suppliers, third-party leasing companies, finance companies and (occasionally) banks.

Finance lease

A finance lease is an alternative to hire purchase. As with hire purchase, the ownership of the leased asset remains with the lessor. At the end of the lease period you may either return the leased asset to the lessor or offer to purchase it for a previously stipulated residual value. If you decide to return the leased asset, the lessor will sell it on the open market. If the sale price is less than the residual value, then you will have to pay the difference.

A finance lease is a long-term contract that covers most of the useful life of the leased asset. The lessee is generally responsible for maintaining the asset for the lease period. If a lessee wants to get out of a finance lease before it expires, they will incur a hefty penalty. Despite many claims about the advantages of finance leases, they are simply an alternative to borrowing. In order to determine whether leasing or borrowing is best for your circumstances, ask your accountant to analyse the after-tax cost of each option.

Operating lease

An operating lease is a short-term rental agreement on an asset such as a vehicle. The vehicle is registered, insured and maintained by the rental company and the customer is entitled to possession and use of it in return for the lease payment. An operating lease can be cancelled at short notice and you do not have to guarantee the residual value.

Fleet leasing

Fleet leasing applies if your business has five or more passenger and light-commercial vehicles. The services generally included with fleet leasing are vehicle sourcing, maintenance, management and disposal. One fixed monthly rental payment is made for the entire fleet.

Sale and leaseback

An alternative to mortgage finance is the sale and leaseback of existing properties. The procedure is to sell your freehold property to a financial institution, such as an insurance company or a pension fund, and then lease it back. You get the use of the property, you have the cash in hand, and the lease payments are tax deductible. Some agreements also provide for the repurchase of the property at the end of the lease period. Similar leasing arrangements are available for the construction of new properties.

10 Profit planning

Profit planning is a systematic method for developing an operating strategy for the future. It takes the form of a forecast profit and loss statement that incorporates your sales objectives, your budgeted costs and your expected profit.

The purpose of this chapter is twofold. First, we shall examine the relationship between a firm's cost structure, pricing policy and sales volume with a view to the effect each has on profitability. Second, we shall use this information to help us to develop and evaluate a profit plan.

Your profit plan

Your profit plan is one of the most important operating tools at your disposal because it can be used for a number of purposes.

Thinking about the future

It is easy to get lost when you think about the future. Profit planning prevents you from viewing the future in ways that the facts do not support. It helps you to recognise opportunities and avoid crises. With this information, alternative strategies can be more easily and accurately evaluated.

Identifying resource requirements

Knowing the expected volume and mix of sales will help you to ensure that the right stock is available when it is needed. You may also need other resources such as more staff, equipment or floor space. The profit plan will show you in advance what is needed and when.

Anticipating financing needs

Knowing what resources will be needed in the future enables you to begin the search for capital as soon as possible. A realistic profit plan will inspire the confidence of potential lenders or investors. Financial crises are more easily avoided and funds can be arranged on favourable terms.

Evaluating operations

Each time you prepare a profit and loss statement you can compare it with the projections in the profit plan. This provides you with a standard against which sales performance and cost control can be evaluated.

Fixed and variable costs

We can illustrate the concept of fixed and variable costs by examining the costs of operating a car that has been driven 20 000 kilometres over the past year.

	$	¢/km
Depreciation	5000	25.0
Interest on loan	1000	5.0
Insurance	1600	8.0
Maintenance	1000	5.0
Registration	200	1.0
Petrol	2500	12.5
Total	11 300	56.5

Based on this information you could say the total cost to operate the car for one year is $11 300, or you could say that the average cost is 56.5 cents per kilometre. Both answers are correct, but only if the car is driven exactly 20 000 kilometres for exactly one year. Neither answer provides enough information to understand what happens to our costs when the car is driven for more or less than 20 000 kilometres or for more or less than one year.

A more useful way of looking at the operating costs for the car is to separate them into two components. The first is a fixed component, which remains about the same regardless of how many kilometres the car is driven. The second is a variable component, which changes in direct proportion to the number of kilometres the car is driven. In our example, the following costs are fixed.

	$
Depreciation	5000
Interest	1000
Insurance	1600
Maintenance	1000
Registration	200
Total fixed cost	8800

The only remaining cost is petrol. This represents the variable component of 12.5 cents per kilometre. Every extra kilometre driven will require an added cost of 12.5 cents for petrol. Therefore, the total annual cost for petrol will vary in direct proportion to the number of kilometres driven. A more useful statement of the operating costs for the car would be to identify the fixed and variable components separately. It costs $8800 per year plus 12.5 cents per kilometre to operate the car.

In practice, some costs are neither totally fixed nor totally variable. For example, maintenance costs would probably stay the same if we drove the car an extra 5000 kilometres, but might go up if the number of kilometres driven is doubled. Moreover, fixed costs are really only fixed for a limited range. The more closely we can identify the fixed and variable cost components, the better we can understand our cost structure. Let's apply the concepts of fixed and variable costs to OSB.

Fixed costs tend to remain about the same. They include items such as rent, salaries, insurance, rates and depreciation, which are not affected by variations in sales activity. Variable costs tend to change in proportion to changes in sales activity. They include items such as the cost of sales, wages and marketing expenses. Figure 10.1 (see page 177) is OSB's 20X1 profit and loss statement divided into fixed and variable costs.

Cost of sales represents the cost of the goods and services that were sold. It has been entered into the variable cost column because it varies in direct proportion to sales activity. Salaries are paid to the permanent staff regardless of the level of sales, so they are a fixed cost. Wages, on the other hand, are paid to the casual and hourly staff, so they are a variable cost. Marketing includes some fixed costs, but since it is predominantly tied

Figure 10.1: Analysis of fixed and variable costs

OUR SMALL BUSINESS
Fixed and variable costs statement
Year ending: 31 March 20X1

	Variable costs $	Fixed costs $	$
SALES			1 000 000
Cost of sales	600 000		
Operating expenses			
Salaries		35 000	
Wages	50 000		
Marketing	100 000		
Occupancy		45 000	
Administration		40 000	
Depreciation		20 000	
Interest		20 000	
TOTAL COSTS	750 000	160 000	910 000
NET PROFIT BEFORE TAX			90 000

to the level of sales activity it has been entered into the variable cost column. Occupancy, administration, depreciation and interest expenses will be the same irrespective of sales activity, so they have each been entered into the fixed cost column. Total fixed costs are $160 000. When sales volume is $1 000 000, variable costs are $750 000.

The separation of fixed and variable costs allows us to isolate the relationship of variable costs to sales. In this example, OSB has $750 000 in variable costs when sales are $1 000 000. The rate of variable cost, therefore, is 75 per cent of sales. Knowing the total fixed cost and the rate of variable cost permits us to determine the profit or loss for any level of sales, as shown in Figure 10.2.

Figure 10.2: Profit/loss at various sales levels

Sales $	Variable cost $	Fixed cost $	Total cost $	Profit (loss) $
0	0	160 000	160 000	(160 000)
500 000	375 000	160 000	535 000	(35 000)
640 000	480 000	160 000	640 000	0
1 000 000	750 000	160 000	910 000	90 000
1 200 000	900 000	160 000	1 060 000	140 000

If there are no sales there will be a loss equal to total fixed costs. The reason is that fixed costs must be met regardless of the level of sales activity. As sales volume increases, the losses decrease. At sales of $640 000, OSB will have neither a profit nor a loss because revenue will exactly equal total cost. This is called the break-even point. As sales increase from $640 000 OSB will show increasing profits.

Contribution margin

A business with no sales will have a loss equal to its fixed costs. Each dollar of sales contributes to a decrease in that loss. The difference between a dollar of sales and the rate of variable cost per dollar of sales is called the contribution margin. OSB's sales are $1 000 000 and its variable costs are $750 000.

$$\text{Contribution margin} = \frac{\text{Sales} - \text{Varible cost}}{\text{Sales}}$$

$$= \frac{\$1\ 000\ 000 - \$750\ 000}{\$1\ 000\ 000} = 25\%$$

The contribution margin is 25 per cent. Once the contribution margin has paid the fixed costs, it becomes the rate at which sales contribute to profit. Profit or loss can be determined at any level of sales using the contribution margin. Increasing sales will decrease the loss until the break-even point is reached. Beyond the break-even point, every dollar of sales will contribute a rate of profit equal to the contribution margin, as shown in Figure 10.3.

Figure 10.3: Contribution margin

Sales $	Contribution margin (25 per cent) $	Fixed cost $	Profit (loss) $
0	0	160 000	(160 000)
500 000	125 000	160 000	(35 000)
640 000	160 000	160 000	0
1 000 000	250 000	160 000	90 000
1 200 000	300 000	160 000	140 000

The contribution margin is one of the most important numbers in business. It represents your efficiency at generating a profit from trading. Know what it should be and monitor it frequently.

Break-even point

The break-even point can be found by dividing the fixed costs by the contribution margin.

$$\text{Break-even point} = \frac{\text{Fixed costs}}{\text{Contribution margin}} = \frac{\$160\ 000}{25\%} = \$640\ 000$$

Using this formula, OSB's break-even point is $640 000. The margin of safety is the difference between the break-even point and the current level of sales. It indicates the extent to which sales may decline before the firm begins to operate at a loss. It is usually expressed as a percentage of current sales.

$$\text{Margin of safety} = \frac{\text{Current sales} - \text{Break-even point}}{\text{Current sales}}$$
$$= \frac{\$1\ 000\ 000 - \$640\ 000}{\$1\ 000\ 000} = 36\%$$

OSB has a margin of safety of 36 per cent. A high margin of safety generally indicates a sound sales and cost position. OSB could absorb a 36 per cent decline in sales before incurring a loss. The break-even point sets your critical sales goal for staying alive. It is good management practice to know what it is, and recalculate it whenever there is a change in fixed costs or gross margin.

Profit-volume chart

A profit-volume chart is a picture of the short-run relationship between sales volume and the contribution margin. Not only does it provide you with a visual presentation of the break-even point, but it also allows you to anticipate the effects of changes in pricing, sales volume, variable costs and fixed costs. Its flexibility makes it a useful tool for analysing profitability. We shall describe how to construct the profit-volume chart in Figure 10.4 using OSB's profit and loss information from Figure 10.1 (see page 180).

In Figure 10.4 sales appear on the horizontal axis and profit and loss appears on the vertical axis. First, plot the fixed costs ($160 000) on the profit-loss axis as a loss. This represents a loss equal to the fixed costs at zero sales. Next, plot net profit before tax ($90 000) on the vertical axis against sales ($1 000 000) on the horizontal axis. Now draw the profit line between the two points. The $640 000 break-even point occurs where the profit line crosses the horizontal axis.

The profit or loss on either side of the break-even point can be read directly from the chart. At zero sales there are no variable costs, so the fixed costs of $160 000 show up as a loss. As sales move to the right towards the break-even point, the losses become smaller. Once past the break-even point, every increase in sales produces increases in profits.

Figure 10.4: Profit-volume chart

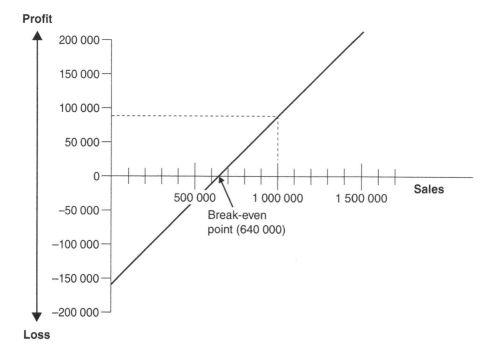

We can analyse the effect of changes in the contribution margin on the slope of the profit line. If OSB can increase the contribution margin, then the slope of the profit line will be steeper. If the contribution margin is reduced, the slope of the profit line will be flatter. As the slope of the profit line increases, the break-even point is reduced and profitability is greater at all levels of sales. As the slope of the profit line decreases, the break-even point is increased and profitability is lower at all levels of sales. In this way, the profit-volume chart can be used to analyse the effect changes in pricing and variable costs will have on profitability at different levels of sales.

We can also analyse the effect of changes in fixed costs on the profit line. If OSB can reduce fixed costs, then the profit line will shift upward in a parallel fashion. Increases in fixed costs have the reverse effect. Changes in fixed costs do not change the contribution margin or the slope of the profit line, but they do change the position of the profit line. A reduction in fixed costs will reduce the break-even point and improve profitability across all levels of sales. Increases in fixed costs will increase the break-even point and lower profitability across all levels of sales. In this way, the profit-volume chart can be used to analyse what effect changes in fixed costs will have upon profitability at different sales levels.

The relationship between fixed and variable costs is called a firm's cost structure.

Two firms with the same break-even point may have entirely different cost structures. One may be a firm with high fixed costs and a high contribution margin that mass produces its product using expensive capital equipment. The other may be a firm with low fixed costs and a low contribution margin in a labour-intensive industry, like many small service businesses.

The high-fixed-cost business has a much greater profit potential when sales are above the break-even point. The high-fixed-cost business also stands to lose proportionally more, however, if sales volume fails to reach the break-even point. It is easy to see why high-fixed-cost businesses tend to be sales-volume conscious, whereas low-fixed-cost businesses tend to be more concerned with keeping down operating costs.

Profit analysis

The techniques of profit analysis can be applied to a wide variety of decision-making and planning situations. Let's look at several applications. Keep in mind that the purpose of these techniques is to help you to exercise your judgement more clearly.

Pricing

Suppose OSB wants to cut its average price by 10 per cent in an effort to stimulate sales. During the past year sales revenue was $1 000 000, variable cost was $750 000, fixed cost was $160 000, and the break-even point was $640 000. What level of sales must OSB achieve to break even at the lower price? A reduction of 10 per cent in the average price will reduce sales to $900 000 and lower the contribution margin.

$$\text{New contribution margin} = \frac{\text{New sales} - \text{Variable cost}}{\text{New sales}}$$

$$= \frac{\$900\ 000 - \$750\ 000}{\$900\ 000} = 16.66\%$$

With the lower contribution margin of 16.66 per cent, the new break-even point increases to $960 000.

$$\text{New break-even point} = \frac{\text{Fixed costs}}{\text{New contribution margin}}$$

$$= \frac{\$160\ 000}{16.66\%} = \$960\ 000$$

A 10 per cent cut in price increases the break-even point from $640 000 to $960 000. This is a 50 per cent increase in the break-even point and OSB will need to make a judgement about whether the price cut will generate enough extra sales to cover this increase.

New investment

OSB wants to invest in new equipment that will add $40 000 in fixed costs per year. OSB's contribution margin is 25 per cent. What increase in sales is necessary to provide sufficient contribution to cover the extra fixed costs?

$$\text{Sales increase} = \frac{\text{Increase in fixed costs}}{\text{Contribution margin}} = \frac{\$40\ 000}{25\%} = \$160\ 000$$

Increasing fixed cost by $40 000 will require extra sales of $160 000, making the total break-even point $800 000. OSB will have to make a judgement about whether the extra fixed costs are feasible.

Cost justification

OSB wants to place advertisements in a magazine that will cost $500 per month. OSB's contribution margin is 25 per cent. What increase in sales must the advertisements generate every month in order to pay for themselves?

$$\text{Sales increase} = \frac{\text{Cost of advertisement}}{\text{Contribution margin}} = \frac{\$500}{25\%} = \$2000$$

OSB will need to generate additional sales of $2000 to pay for each advertisement. It needs to make a judgement about whether the advertisements will stimulate enough additional sales to cover the cost and generate extra profit.

Sales objectives

OSB wants to make a profit of $150 000. The contribution margin is 25 per cent and fixed costs are $160 000. What sales objective is necessary to achieve the desired level of profit?

$$\text{Sales objective} = \frac{\text{Fixed costs} + \text{Profit}}{\text{Contribution margin}}$$

$$= \frac{\$160\ 000 + \$150\ 000}{25\%} = \$1\ 240\ 000$$

OSB needs to make a judgement about its ability to generate a sales increase of $240 000. It should also take into consideration the possibility that a 24 per cent increase in sales may force up some of its fixed costs as well.

Product line analysis

You can analyse the contribution margin and the dollar contribution for each of your product lines. This will tell you which of your product lines is giving you the greatest rate of profit, and which is providing the greatest amount of profit. It will also tell you which product lines are not paying their way and need management attention. For problem lines a price increase, a reduction of direct costs or a combination of both can fix the negative contribution. In some cases the remedy may lie in increased sales because the variable cost proportion may reduce with higher volumes. If none of these remedies is available you may consider eliminating the line taking into account the effect on other product sales. As long as a product line has a positive contribution margin, you can continue to carry it. Your profits will increase if you concentrate on those product lines with the highest contribution margins.

In Figure 10.5 product line A has the greatest contribution margin. Product line B has the greatest dollar contribution. Which product line is more profitable? Don't be confused between dollar contribution and contribution margin. Product line B may have a lower contribution margin, but it clearly has a much higher dollar contribution because of its greater sales volume. Profit is made of dollars, not percentages. Nevertheless, we would be better off if we sold more of product line A than product line B, because its greater contribution margin would generate a greater dollar contribution as well.

Product line C makes no contribution. Total profit would not change whether we kept product line C or not. Profit would improve, however, if we could replace product line C with one that has a positive contribution margin. Product line D is a loser. We could increase total profit if we simply dropped product line D altogether. If product line D is a loss leader, then it should be combined with the product it is designed to promote in order to assess their combined contribution.

Figure 10.5: Product analysis

Product line	Sales $	Variable cost $	Dollar contribution $	Contribution margin per cent
A	500	200	300	60.0
B	1500	800	700	46.7
C	600	600	0	0.0
D	400	500	(100)	(25.0)

Establishing a profit plan

A profit plan is based on estimates. Inevitably, a number of the assumptions will need to be modified because crystal balls become a bit cloudy the further out you forecast. The objective is to keep your plan current so that your profit target remains attainable. A realistic profit plan, established annually and revised as changing conditions require, provides performance guidelines that will help you to maximise your profits with a minimum of uncertainty. OSB's 20X2 profit plan is shown in Figure 10.6 (see page 184).

Forecasting sales

A profit plan begins with a detailed forecast of expected sales. This is not only the most difficult step in profit planning, but also the most important. If you do a really bad job of forecasting sales, the effect will flow through the entire financial planning process. However, it is not necessary to be perfectly accurate. If your sales forecast is within a reasonable range of the eventual outcome, your profit plan will reveal any major problems that need to be addressed.

A sales forecast begins by analysing sales for last year. Divide last year's sales into smaller categories of similar products and services. This makes it easier to examine the factors that affect sales for each category. You will find it easier to measure sales in physical units such as the number of units sold, the number of customers served, or the number of services performed. The physical units can be translated into sales dollars using your pricing schedule.

After sales categories have been selected and last year's sales divided among them,

Figure 10.6: Profit plan

OUR SMALL BUSINESS
Profit plan for year ended 30 June 20X2

	$	$
SALES REVENUE		2 000 000
COST OF SALES		
Beginning stock	100 000	
Purchases	1 150 000	
Less closing stock	(250 000)	1 000 000
GROSS PROFIT (50 per cent)		1 000 000
OPERATING EXPENSES		
Salaries	60 000	
Wages	150 000	
Marketing	250 000	
Occupancy	125 000	
Administration	75 000	
Depreciation	70 000	
Interest	60 000	790 000
NET PROFIT BEFORE TAX		210 000
PROVISION FOR INCOME TAX		63 000
NET PROFIT AFTER TAX		147 000
PROPOSED DIVIDEND		47 000
ADDITION TO RETAINED EARNINGS		100 000

carefully consider the factors that may affect each category next year. The factors that affect sales can be divided into external and internal factors.

External factors

External factors consist of influences outside your business that affect sales. The objective is to identify factors that are working in your favour and those that are not. Here are some examples:

Competition   Technology
Economic and financial conditions   Consumer preferences
Legal and political changes   Population trends
Social and cultural trends.

Internal factors

Internal factors consist of the functions inside your business. They constitute the operating dimensions of your profit plan and they are the result of your strategic decisions. Internal factors affect sales through the following functional areas:

Advertising   Staffing
Promotion   Finance
Product mix   Purchasing
Pricing   Production.

Figure 10.7 (see page 186) represents the 20X2 sales forecast for OSB. First, actual unit sales for 20X1 are divided among profit centres A, B and C. Then total unit sales are multiplied by the 20X1 average price of $10 per unit, resulting in total revenue of $1 000 000. Next, 20X2 unit sales are forecast individually for each profit centre, paying particular attention to the external and internal factors that are important for each category.

OSB has forecast a 5 per cent reduction in unit sales for profit centre A, a 25 per cent increase in unit sales for profit centre B, and a 10 per cent increase in unit sales for profit centre C. OSB has decided to open up two new profit centres and has forecast 25 000 units for profit centre D and 28 000 units for profit centre E. The profit centre forecasts are added together and multiplied by the anticipated 20X2 average unit price of $12.50, resulting in forecast revenue of $2 000 000.

The sales forecast for each category should be supported by a carefully considered marketing action plan. It is simply not realistic to forecast a sales increase without having specific plans to achieve the increase. OSB's marketing strategy is to reposition its products in order to appeal to new market segments. Its new product strategy will consist of a narrow product mix with considerable depth. It will position itself as

Figure 10.7: Sales forecast

OUR SMALL BUSINESS		
Sales forecast for year ended 30 June 20X2		
Profit centre	**20X1 Actual**	**20X2 Forecast**
A		47 500
B		37 500
C	50 000	22 000
D	30 000	25 000
E	20 000	28 000
Total units	100 000	160 000
Average price	$10.00	$12.50
Revenue	$1 000 000	$2 000 000

a specialist, catering primarily to quality-minded customers. It expects to be able to increase its unit volume and charge a higher price by mounting a vigorous marketing thrust. This calls for more marketing staff plus a large increase in the advertising and promotion budget. Moreover, OSB plans to invest heavily in new plant and equipment and expand into additional premises.

OSB's goal is to increase unit sales volume by 60 per cent from 100 000 units in 20X1 to 160 000 units in 20X2. At the same time, it is going to raise their average retail price by 25 per cent from $10 to $12.50 per unit. Combined, the increases in unit volume and price are projected to double sales revenue from $1 000 000 in 20X1 to $2 000 000 in 20X2.

Forecasting cost of sales

Once the volume and mix of expected sales have been estimated, you are in a position to estimate the cost of sales. This consists of costing all the product lines you expect to sell. OSB expects the average cost per unit to increase to $6.25. With sales of 160 000 units, cost of sales will be $1 000 000. This will produce a gross profit of $1 000 000 and a gross profit margin of 50 per cent. The cost-of-sales estimate consists of the following pieces of information:

- The previous year's ending stock becomes the next year's beginning stock. OSB's 20X1 balance sheet shows $100 000 in trading stock so that becomes the 20X2 beginning stock.
- The total cost of sales, based on an expected sales volume of 160 000 units at an average cost of $6.25 per unit, is $1 000 000.
- The 20X2 ending stock is expected to be $250 000.

- By working backwards, we can find the amount of the purchases.

  If cost of sales   = beginning stock + purchases − ending stock

  Then purchases = ending stock + cost of sales − beginning stock

  = $250 000 + $1 000 000 − $100 000

  = $1 150 000

It is important to remember that cost of sales is a variable cost. To the extent that actual sales volume is different from the sales forecast, cost of sales will vary in the same proportion.

Forecasting operating expenses

Some of the operating expenses will be variable and others will remain fixed regardless of the level of sales. Operating expenses are also affected by internal and external factors. The following is a summary of OSB's operating expense forecasts:

- *Salaries* and associated costs will increase from $35 000 to $60 000, to employ a new office assistant.
- *Wages* and associated costs will increase from $50 000 to $150 000, to employ three new sales staff.
- *Marketing* expenses will increase from $100 000 to $250 000, to mount a large advertising and promotion program.
- *Occupancy* expenses will go from $45 000 to $125 000, to move into additional sales premises and warehouse space.
- *Administration* expenses will increase from $40 000 to $75 000.
- *Depreciation* will go from $20 000 to $70 000, reflecting new investment of $150 000 in plant and equipment which will be depreciated over three years.
- *Interest* expenses are expected to rise from $20 000 to $60 000, anticipating about $250 000 in new borrowings.

Total operating expenses are expected to be $790 000 for the year. Therefore, net profit before tax is estimated to be $210 000, and net profit after tax will be $147 000. This represents a 133 per cent increase in net profit before tax over 20X1. If everything goes according to plan, the owners intend to pay themselves a dividend of $47 000, leaving $100 000 to be retained in the business.

Evaluating a profit plan

A satisfactory profit plan is rarely finished on the first attempt. It needs to be reviewed, evaluated and revised until it represents the most realistic, practical profit plan that you can develop. The objective is to fine-tune your profit plan until you have complete confidence in it.

Profit margins

The *gross profit margin* is usually a good indicator of the relationship between your pricing policy and the buying economies of your business. The *net profit margin* is your overall rate of profit after the operating expenses have been recognised. You can evaluate the projected profit margins by making comparisons with three benchmarks:

- Comparisons with objectives permit you to determine how well your plan compares with your original expectations.
- Comparisons with industry averages help you to identify areas where the experience of similar firms can indicate room for improvement.
- Comparisons with performance in prior periods permit you to detect trends.

Figure 10.8 is a series of common-size profit and loss statements that convert dollar figures to percentage of sales. The use of percentages as a basis for comparison and forecasting is particularly helpful when comparing expenses from one period to another, or when comparing expenses with industry averages. Figure 10.8 contains OSB's common-size profit and loss statement for the year 20X0; the planned, actual and industry averages for the year 20X1; and the profit plan for the year 20X2. With this information, we can make the comparisons that enable us to evaluate OSB's projected profit margins for 20X2.

In 20X1 OSB's gross profit margin was 40 per cent of sales. This was an improvement over the 20X0 gross profit margin of 36 per cent and it was better than the 20X1 industry average of 38.5 per cent and OSB's 20X1 profit plan objective of

Figure 10.8: Common-size profit and loss statements (all figures are per cent)

	20X0 actual	20X1 plan	20X1 actual	20X1 industry average	20X2 plan
Sales	100.0	100.0	100.0	100.0	100.0
Cost of sales	64.0	61.5	60.0	61.5	50.0
GROSS PROFIT	36.0	38.5	40.0	38.5	50.0
Operating expenses					
Salaries	4.0	3.0	3.5	3.0	3.0
Wages	5.0	4.5	5.0	4.0	7.5
Marketing	10.0	10.0	10.0	9.0	12.5
Occupancy	5.0	4.5	4.5	4.0	6.25
Administration	4.0	4.0	4.0	4.0	3.75
Depreciation	2.0	2.0	2.0	2.0	3.5
Interest	2.0	2.0	2.0	2.0	3.0
TOTAL	32.0	30.0	31.0	28.0	39.5
NET PROFIT	4.0	8.5	9.0	10.5	10.5

38.5 per cent. OSB's gross profit margin performance has been good, and the 20X2 profit plan calls for a substantial further improvement to 50 per cent.

In 20X1 OSB's net profit margin was 9 per cent of sales. This was an improvement over the 20X0 net profit margin of 4 per cent and was slightly better than the 20X1 profit plan objective of 8.5 per cent. OSB's 20X1 net profit margin, however, was below the industry average. Moreover, the 20X2 profit plan only brings the net profit margin up to the 20X1 industry average.

How can gross profit margin performance be exceptionally good at the same time that net profit margin performance is unimpressive? The answer lies in excessive operating expenses. Operating expenses in 20X1 were 31 per cent of sales compared with an industry average of 28 per cent. The 20X2 profit plan, however, calls for a huge 39.5 per cent in operating expenses. A detailed examination of each individual item would highlight which operating expenses are out of line.

Cost structure

When variable costs are deducted from sales, the result is the contribution margin. In Figure 10.9 we have an analysis of OSB's variable costs and contribution margin.

OSB's contribution margin has improved in 20X1 but it is still slightly below the industry average. The 20X2 profit plan calls for a substantial improvement, despite the fact that wages and marketing expenses are well above the industry average. The projected improvement in the contribution margin is entirely dependent on the 25 per cent price increase. OSB had better be sure that customers will accept the higher prices. If they do not, the entire profit plan will fail.

Fixed costs

Changes in fixed costs should be justified individually and not automatically on the basis of a change in sales. Figure 10.10 (see page 190) is a comparison of OSB's fixed costs in 20X1 with projected fixed costs in 20X2.

Figure 10.9: Common-size variable cost comparison (all figures are per cent)

	20X0 actual	20X1 plan	20X1 actual	Industry average	20X2 plan
Sales	100.0	100.0	100.0	100.0	100.0
Variable costs					
Cost of sales	64.0	61.5	60.0	61.5	50.0
Wages	5.0	4.5	5.0	4.0	7.5
Marketing	10.0	10.0	10.0	9.0	12.5
Total	79.0	76.0	75.0	74.5	70.0
Contribution margin	21.0	24.0	25.0	25.5	30.0

OSB is planning to increase fixed costs by 143 per cent at the same time it is planning for a 100 per cent increase in dollar revenue. The planned increase in unit sales, however, is only 60 per cent. Such a substantial increase in fixed costs should be taken seriously. A comparison of OSB's 20X1 fixed costs with those in the 20X2 profit plan reveals significant increases in every account. Some increases are probably unavoidable, having been dictated by contractual obligations, legal requirements or price increases beyond OSB's control. Others can probably be reduced with closer scrutiny.

Even with the projected improvement in the contribution margin from 25 per cent to 30 per cent the heavy burden of an extra $230 000 in fixed costs is going to push the break-even point out to $1 300 000. Figure 10.11 is a comparison of OSB's break-even point in 20X1 with the implied break-even point in the 20X2 profit plan.

An eight-point plan for higher business performance
A 1 per cent difference in key areas of your business can make a large improvement to your bottom line and return on assets. From the annual accounts take a look at the eight primary drivers of business performance: price, volume, direct costs, indirect costs,

Figure 10.10: Fixed-cost comparison

	20X1 actual $	20X2 projected $	Increase $
Salaries	35 000	60 000	25 000
Occupancy	45 000	125 000	80 000
Administration	40 000	75 000	35 000
Depreciation	20 000	70 000	50 000
Interest	20 000	60 000	40 000
Total	160 000	390 000	230 000

Figure 10.11: Break-even comparison

	20X1	20X2
Fixed costs	$160 000	$390 000
divided by Contribution margin	25 per cent	30 per cent
equals Break-even point	$640 000	$1 300 000

inventory, debtors, non-current assets and creditors. These are the drivers of Earnings Before Interest and Tax (EBIT), and Return On Net Assets (RONA). Other balance sheet factors (shareholder funds, term loans and bank account cash) can all be set aside as they are not part of the trading performance.

In the example below the relationships of these eight, to EBIT and RONA is shown and the power of making only a 1 per cent adjustment to each one reveals why these numbers are such influential drivers of business performance.

Changes of only 1 per cent working in concert with others produce significant improvements in EBIT and RONA. This is something that you can achieve and is an easy project to sell to your staff. Of course you can target bigger than 1 per cent changes and create even more dramatic improvements. Now let's have a look at some of the ways you could make changes to each of the eight key factors.

Price

Price needs to reflect value, so focus on changing the market's perception of value. Work at pricing your product or service at a premium. Innovate around the product and the customers' experience.

Volume

Create innovations in your channels to market using social media and viral marketing. New Zealand companies can double their market overnight by opening distribution into Melbourne—population 4.2 million.

Figure 10.12: Applying 1 per cent change to eight financial drivers

From the profit and loss account			From the balance sheet		
Initial price is $2 and volume is 50 units. The second column shows a 1% increase in both, with a 1% reduction in direct and indirect expenses			On this side each asset value is reduced by 1% while the creditor value is increased by 1%		
Price × Volume	P 2*V 50	P2.02*V50.5	Debtors	+50	49.5
Sales (P*V)	100	102	Stock	+10	9.9
Direct Costs	80	79	NC Assets	+100	99.0
Gross Profit	20	23	Creditors	(40)	40.4
Expenses	10	9.9	Net Assets	120	118
EBIT	10	13.1	RONA	8%	11%
		= 31%	EBIT/Net		= 37.5%
		increase in	Assets		increase in
		EBIT!			RONA!

Direct costs

Get into 'Lean' business methods and tools (see page 279). Redesign your business processes to take advantage of ecommerce and save time and cost in everything you do. Eliminate non-value-adding steps in business processes. For further information on 'Lean' see www.managementsupport.com and refer to Chapter 16.

Indirect costs

'Lean' methods and tools can help here as well. Eliminate waiting time and aggregate similar activities together. Also don't forget to empower and engage your people to gain the synergy and productivity of high-performing teams.

Inventory

Use 'Lean' methods to reduce process cycle time and adopt just-in-time supply and production methods. Reduced process time will automatically reduce inventory and work-in-progress in service companies.

Debtors

Always know who owes you money by producing regular Aged Debtor lists—and then phone them each week to get the cash coming in.

Non-current assets

Measure your asset utilisation rates. Divest non-core assets and rent or hire others that you don't use often.

Creditors

Engage yourself in supply chain management. Actively build relationships with selected suppliers and negotiate more 'friendly' credit terms.

Judgement

There are no magic formulas in profit planning. There are, however, techniques you can use to make the job a little easier. Eventually you will need to exercise your judgement. For example, is this profit plan prudent? Will the gross profit margin hold up? If not, the net profit may become a net loss. Can the excessive operating expenses be temporarily justified in terms of a shift in marketing policy? Are the risks involved in this profit plan realistic? Is it wise to double the break-even point? Would you be prepared to commit the future of your business to this profit plan, or should you re-examine all of the assumptions and try to recast a better one?

Self-development exercise B

The purpose of this exercise is to gain practical skills in cash flow budgeting. Cash flow is the lifeblood of a business. Unless you can anticipate a cash flow crisis, you may end up out of business. To get the most out of this exercise, complete the cash flow budget before you look at the solution. A computer spreadsheet is particularly useful for problems like this one.

Trans-Crash Transport Company

The owners of the Trans-Crash Transport Company have tried without success to sell their business. Now they are offering to let you have the business if you will agree to take over the lease contracts on their two trucks. The combined lease payment for a 2-tonne truck and a 6-tonne truck amounts to $5200 per month.

Income from operations will fluctuate because of the seasonal nature of the goods you will be hauling. All of your customers pay you in cash on delivery. Your expected revenue for the next year is based on the following projections.

Truck	Revenue per kilometre $	km/month (Jul–Dec)	km/month (Jan–Jun)
2-tonne	2.30	12 500	8500
6-tonne	4.00	4300	3000

The truck manufacturer's operating manuals indicate the following variable costs per kilometre of operation for each truck. All of these expenses are paid monthly in cash.

	2-tonne truck (cents/km)	6-tonne truck (cents/km)
Diesel	8.20	29.68
Oil	.56	1.20
Maintenance	2.80	6.40
Road tax	2.44	6.72
Total	14.00	44.00

Other fixed monthly cash expenses

	$	$
Salaries and wages		
Yourself	2500	
Driver no. 1	1900	
Driver no. 2	1800	
Office clerk	1500	
On-costs	1000	8700
Advertising		3500
Lease of premises		2750
Other cash expenses		4850
Total		19 800

Additional information

- The 2-tonne truck will need an overhaul in April at a cost of $5830.
- The 6-tonne truck will need an overhaul in July at a cost of $4425.
- A truck is off the road for the entire month when it is being overhauled and earns no revenue.
- You will have to pay provisional tax instalments of $13 500 each to the IRD in March, July and November.
- Your beginning cash position on 1 January is $835.
- There will be GST payments of $200 in April and $500 in November.

Complete a cash flow budget for the Trans-Crash Transport Company for the next 12 months. Should you take over the business? Can you foresee any difficulties if you become the new owner?

Turn to page 333 for the solution.

Part C
Marketing management

Marketing management seeks to identify and understand the needs and wants of targeted customer groups and then transfer that understanding into specifications for products and services that will deliver superior value. Marketing management's role is to define what 'customer satisfaction' actually means and to have that definition shape the design and delivery of every aspect of business operations. Chapter 11 deals with the concepts of market research, target marketing and creating the right marketing mix. Chapter 12 discusses advertising, selling skills and customer service. Chapter 13 describes the central elements of digital marketing strategies. Chapter 14 examines the opportunities and strategies that underpin export marketing.

11 Marketing strategy

A successful small business is the product of a customer-focused marketing strategy designed to minimise wasted effort and maximise results. Devising a marketing strategy is a process of exploring opportunities, identifying and evaluating options and arriving at a marketing plan to achieve tangible results. Your marketing strategy determines the way in which your business will fit into the competitive environment. Every component of your business strategy should be customer driven.

You begin by gathering enough information about your customers so that you clearly understand what basic motives influence their decision to buy your products and services. Then you segment your customers into groups with different needs. Finally, you zero in on the best market segment by positioning your business to attract these customers like a magnet. The force of your magnet is determined by how well you have shaped your offer to suit the target group and the strength of any competitive advantage you may have. Not only do you need a marketing strategy to get into business, but you also need to continuously evolve your strategy to meet the changing market and stay in business.

Understanding your customers

Understanding your customers begins with identifying their basic buying motives. Customers do not buy goods and services—they buy benefits. For example, when they buy toothpaste, some are buying a pleasant taste, some are buying bright teeth and others are buying protection from tooth decay.

The products and services offered in the marketplace are constantly changing, but basic buying motives such as health, beauty, safety, comfort, convenience, economy and enjoyment change very slowly. For example, what can you do for people who have time to shop only in the evenings and weekends? If your business is open at times that are convenient for them, you offer a benefit that appeals to one of their basic buying motives.

Understanding customers also means gaining an insight into their buying role. The buyer for a one-person household decides what is needed, what will be bought and where it will be purchased. In larger households these roles are often played by different individuals. It helps to anticipate who has the need, who influences the purchase decision, and who actually decides what and where to buy. For example, a teenage daughter wants a party dress for her birthday. Dad has reservations about low necklines and high hemlines and Mum has to decide where to shop and which dress to buy. Each plays a role in the buying process, and you need to be able to satisfy their individual buying motives in order to complete the sale.

Your business strategy will work best when it is squarely aimed at satisfying your customers' basic buying motives. The only things you should be selling are the benefits your customers want to buy. Understanding your customers' basic buying motives pays off in greater sales, lower costs and higher profits.

Market intelligence

In order to understand your customers and your competitors you need market intelligence. Market intelligence means getting the right facts in order to pick a suitable location, select the right products, determine the size and characteristics of your target market, and establish the best ways to promote sales. After your business is established, you will need more facts to decide where to grow, where to cut back or where to change emphasis. Market intelligence does not have to be expensive to be good, but it must focus on your information needs to be effective. Look for answers to the following types of questions.

Who?
- Who uses the product?
- Who decides to purchase the product?
- Who actually makes the purchase?
- Who buys the product from me?
- Who buys the product, but not from me?

Where
- Where is the product used?
- Where do customers seek information about the product?
- Where do customers make the decision to buy the product?
- Where do customers actually buy the product?
- Where are the potential customers located?

What
- What benefits does the customer seek?
- What is the basis of comparison with other products?
- What is the rate of product usage?
- What price are customers willing to pay?
- What is the potential market for the product?

The market-intelligence methods you employ will be determined by the types of questions you ask and the way in which you intend to use the answers:

- Facts are easily obtained by questions that require only a yes or no answer such as 'Do you own a personal computer?' While this information helps you to determine the level of consumption, it yields little information about why the customer bought a personal computer.
- Quasi-facts depend on memory. 'Have you heard of lemon-flavoured mayonnaise?' The answers to this type of question tell us about the customer's product knowledge but they do not help us to understand how the customer feels about purchasing the product.
- Opinions tell us much more about buying motives but they are also more difficult to determine accurately. 'Why do you think margarine tastes better than butter?' We can learn much about customers' preferences with opinion research, but people sometimes express opinions that are different from their actual behaviour.
- Attitudes are the most difficult to determine. 'Would you be satisfied with a self-service hardware store?' People often do not consciously know what their attitudes are to certain goods or services until they are confronted with the decision to buy them. Despite the difficulty in obtaining good attitudinal information, it is the most valuable because it helps us to understand why people buy.

Statistics New Zealand website at www.stats.govt.nz is particularly useful for obtaining demographic data. For example, you can use census data and household expenditure information to compile a profile of your market. You can establish the age distribution of the local population, the ethnic composition, average income, size of family, whether they own or rent their home, whether they have a car, and the number of school-age children.

You can also establish how much the average household spends on a variety of goods and services. Studying this type of information will help you to construct a picture of your target market. For example, the ethnic composition of an area will have a big impact on the types of sales in a delicatessen. Deli products are not popular with Asians, whereas Europeans are big buyers. Home ownership statistics for a particular area are important for a hardware store. People spend more on hardware if they own their home.

You should also contact your trade association to see what information they have already gathered and analysed. For example, if you are starting a tourism venture then the New Zealand Tourism Board website at www.tourismnewzealand.com or the Tourism Industry Association may have just what you are looking for.

The limitation of statistical information is that it is based on historical data. What is more meaningful is recent survey information from the customers themselves. While most of the information you collect will be anonymous, personal information may be gathered as part of the survey and should always be treated as confidential. You should clarify your obligations under the Privacy Act before you undertake a survey. You can contact the Office of the Privacy Commissioner on 0800 803 909 or check the website at www.privacy.org.nz.

One word of caution: market intelligence does not predict the future. What it can do is help you to forecast probable events based on demographic trends and consumer behaviour. It is the best means you have of finding out where you stand and where your business strategy ought to be taking you.

Target marketing

In order to develop a business strategy, you need to aim at a specific target market. Market segmentation is the process of dividing the overall market into groups with similar characteristics. The objective is to select segments that match your strengths and are large enough to support your business. This does not mean you ignore the other market segments. It simply means that a high proportion of your sales will come from the market segments you target. One of the strengths of being small is the ability to play 'nichemanship' in ways that large competitors cannot match. Intelligent target marketing provides you with a way to gain a foothold, an opportunity to be unique and the potential to earn above-average profits. Suppose you are interested in the packaged-food business and you want to create a new approach for this market. You begin by segmenting households according to the dominant way in which meals are chosen, prepared and consumed. For example:

- 'Country cooks' prepare three meals from scratch every day and occasionally make dessert. This market segment is relatively small and it is not interested in packaged food.

- The culinary preferences of 'ethnic eaters' are largely a result of their ethnic identity. Overall, this market segment is declining slowly and it varies a great deal geographically.
- 'Functional feeders' look first for convenience in food preparation, and then for variety and taste. This segment is growing at about the same rate as the population.
- 'Healthy households' place their emphasis on natural food, a balanced diet and fitness. This is the second-fastest-growing market segment.
- 'Grab-it' segments are characterised by people who have an obsession with free time and leisure activities. This is the typical fast-food, frozen-dinner, takeaway eater. It represents the fastest-growing market segment.

Each target market segment represents a different group of customers with different basic buying motives. However, you may be able to target more than one segment if the desire for variety coupled with an increasing emphasis on convenience results in each member of the family wanting to sit down to a completely different and individually tailored meal. You may be able to develop a variety of product strategies such as takeaway franchises, frozen meals for supermarkets and 'restaurant packs' that fulfil the benefits that each market segment seeks. The objective is to identify the target market segment that best matches your competitive advantage.

To segment a market, the characteristics of the segments need to be measurable and the information about them must be available. A market can be segmented according to a variety of criteria such as:

Age	Religious affiliation
Sex	Ethnic identity
Marital status	Lifestyle
Family size	Leisure activity
Occupation	Brand loyalty
Income	Special interest
Home ownership	Education
Geographic location	Shopping style

For example, suppose you want to open a jeans shop. You can segment people who buy jeans into specific target markets. Each one represents a potential niche in which you can specialise.

Market segment	Segment basis	Segment product line
construction workers	occupation	working overalls
children	age	play clothes

| fashion conscious | lifestyle | designer jeans |
| rodeo fans | special interest | cowboy jeans |

In order to develop an effective marketing strategy you need to be able to define clearly the target market segment to which you will appeal, you need to thoroughly understand your customers' basic buying motives, and you need to know exactly how your product or service will provide the benefits they seek.

Creating a competitive advantage

Creating a strong competitive advantage means developing value drivers that are aimed directly at satisfying your customers' basic buying motives. Value drivers are the things your business does particularly well that cannot be easily duplicated by your competitors. Here are some examples:

- Broader/deeper product lines
- Lower costs/prices
- Unique products or services
- Better product quality/availability
- Superior skills/experience
- Superior customer service
- More effective marketing methods
- Better personal networks connected to the target market segment.

It only pays to develop the value drivers that are effective in motivating your customers to make a purchase. For example, you may have the most convenient location in town. If the customer's basic buying motive is lower prices, however, then they may be prepared to drive long distances (away from your business) in order to save money.

It is equally important that a value driver can be effectively advertised and promoted. For example, having lower prices is relatively easy to advertise and promote, but having greater experience is more difficult to explain in terms of its impact on your product or service. Customers not only need to be aware of your value drivers, but they also need to be clear about how these value drivers satisfy their basic buying motives. When you create a competitive advantage, it is your key to survival and prosperity because it acts like a natural magnet, drawing customers to your door. Once your position is established, your competitors will have great difficulty in challenging customers' perceptions about your business.

Marketing mix

The marketing mix refers to the operational components of your marketing strategy. They consist of the five Ps:

- product
- price
- place
- position
- promotion.

Managing the marketing mix is analogous to baking a cake. The marketing strategy is your recipe and the five Ps are your ingredients. When the ingredients are mixed according to the recipe, the result is a cake. Just as there are different varieties of cake to suit different tastes, there are different marketing mixes to suit different marketing objectives. Before we go about creating a marketing mix, we need to have a clear idea about our objectives. There are four types of marketing objectives.

Market penetration

Selling more of existing products and services in an existing market by encouraging greater customer usage or by attracting competitors' customers is an example of good market penetration.

Market development

Selling existing products or services to new customers, such as opening in a second location or advertising in different media to attract new types of customers, is an example of market development.

Product development

Selling a new product or an improved product to existing customers by encouraging them to 'trade up' is an example of product development.

Diversification

Moving into an entirely new line of business with new products and services targeted at new customers is an example of diversification.

The objective you choose is the one that best describes where you want your marketing strategy to take you. If you are a new business you will pursue a market-penetration objective or a market-development objective. If you have a unique product or service, you will be drawn toward a product-development objective. Whatever objective you pursue, it should be the one that capitalises most on your competitive strengths.

Product strategy

The easiest and most profitable products and services to sell are the ones your customers want to buy. Although their buying habits can be influenced through your advertising efforts and your own persuasiveness, the best path to marketing success is to identify your customers' needs and then shape your line of products or services accordingly. For each product line you decide to carry you need to weigh a number of factors, including:

- Availability and terms of supply
- Expected sales volume
- Cost of the initial inventory
- Projected profitability
- Number and types of customers
- Number and types of competitors
- Specific products or services within the line, answering the following questions:
  - Is the product a staple, impulse or luxury item?
  - What range of models, brands, colours or sizes are best?
  - What quality range or price range is best?
- The experience you have in carrying similar goods or services.

Product lines and mix

A *product line* is a group of products that have similar characteristics and uses. For example, the product lines in a camera shop might include cameras, lenses, darkroom supplies, film developing, printing services and portraiture. The product lines that the camera shop actually carries are called its *product mix*. The key to deciding on the best product mix is the consistency with which it conforms to the needs of the target market.

The number of product lines offered by a business is called *product breadth*. If a camera shop carries only cameras and film then its product breadth is narrow. If it carries all the product lines previously listed then its product breadth is wide. The assortment within a product line is called *product depth*. For example, the more models of cameras that the camera shop has for sale, the more depth it has in that product line.

Decisions about product lines, product mix, product breadth and product depth constitute your product strategy. These decisions need to be consistent with the way you have segmented your market. Figure 11.1 (see page 205) demonstrates how a product strategy can vary depending upon different combinations of product mix and market segmentation.

Price strategy

There are three important principles to follow to develop a successful price strategy:

Figure 11.1: Product strategies

	Multiple market segments	Single market segment
Broad product mix	Total market strategy	Market segment strategy
Narrow product mix	Product line strategy	Limited product line strategy
Single product	Product depth strategy	Specialist strategy

- The first pricing principle is not to undervalue your product or service. Profit is the reason that you are in business and profit is what enables you to stay in business.
- The second pricing principle is that price is not only the amount on the price tag, but also other things that influence price such as discounts, allowances and credit terms.
- The third pricing principle is to set your prices in order to maximise profits, not to maximise sales.

The practice of balancing prices of various items is sometimes referred to as *complementary* pricing. The classic example is pricing a popular item below the market average to generate store traffic. You may carry some items that are not profitable because they regularly bring customers into the store. On the other hand, items that you have obtained exclusively will not be subject to price competition and can stand a greater mark-up.

With a new product you need to consider the distinction between a *skimming* price and a *penetration* price. A skimming price is a high price that lasts for a short time to take advantage of early demand. A penetration price is a low price that is intended to rapidly build-up sales volume. The attractive lower price encourages the customer to try it, and if the product is good enough, a large percentage of the initial purchasers become repeat customers.

Basic approaches to pricing

An effective pricing strategy comes with planning and patience. While there is no magic formula that works for all types of businesses, a thorough understanding of your market combined with a knowledge of the five basic approaches to pricing will help to develop a pricing strategy that works for you. Here are the five basic approaches.

Full-cost pricing

This means that the price has to cover labour, materials, a proportion of the overhead costs and a percentage for profit. Few small business operators adhere rigidly to full-cost pricing because they are influenced more by consumer demand and market factors.

Flexible mark-up pricing

It is common practice is to use full costs to establish a reference point to which flexible mark-ups are added within the markets' price tolerance.

Gross-margin pricing

The customary practice in retail firms is to determine price by calculating a mark-up on the wholesale cost of the goods. The aim is to match the mark-ups to consumer demand in an effort to maximise profits.

Going-rate pricing

If you tend to set your prices according to what your opposition is charging, you are practising going-rate pricing.

Suggested pricing

A large number of small business operators prefer not to make their own pricing decisions. If you accept suggested prices, you are accepting the manufacturer's pricing strategy as your own.

Mark-up and mark-down

Mark-up is the amount added to the cost of an item to arrive at its selling price. It is stated as a percentage of the *cost* of the merchandise. Mark-up on cost is straightforward but is sometimes confused with gross margin because it is the same dollar amount but not the same percentage. Consider the following example where the gain is $25.

Price	= cost + mark-up
$125	= $100 + $25
Mark-up is:	$25/$100 or 25% on *cost*
Gross margin is:	$25/$125 or 20% of *price*

There are three occasions when you may wish to hold a sale and to mark down the prices of selected merchandise lines. First, you may wish to run a sale at the beginning of a new selling season in order to introduce your customers to new merchandise. Second, holiday sales are always effective for increasing sales volume by taking advantage of the increased numbers of shoppers. Third, sales to remove slow-moving merchandise should be held regularly. Not only should you be using the shelf space for more marketable merchandise, but a sale will also provide you with the cash you need to buy the new stock.

Meeting price competition

Price is only one element of competition. While there is a tendency to cut prices to meet competition and to increase sales, the usual result is only a cut in your profits. Here are several ways you can meet competition from price cutters without cutting into your own profit margins as well.

Specialisation
Customers usually compare prices for the *same* article. If yours is a bit different and is no longer identical with your competitors', the effects of price competition can be reduced.

Personal selling
The way you and your staff treat customers can make a big difference to your image. Helpful, courteous staff who go about their job with style can help you to create an atmosphere in which customers expect to pay a little more.

Timing
Getting your merchandise on the shelf at the right time as well as at the right price is important. Watch for things like a change in the season to help you to capitalise on new goods coming into fashion and to avoid price reductions for ones that are no longer popular.

Trends
Watch for new trends and adapt your operations to take advantage of them while customers are not price sensitive. Recent examples include do-it-yourself products, video products and natural food products.

Prestige
Attractive displays, imaginative lighting, quiet personal service and quality products combine to create an impression of prestige. This is not the sort of place where customers look for bargains.

Services
Among the most effective means of combating price competition are extra services such as delivery, installation, repair, alterations, and permitting customers to return or exchange goods.

Convenience
People are usually willing to pay a little more when it is easy for them to shop. Convenience generally means handy parking and being open when customers want to shop.

Merchandising
This includes strategies that increase sales turnover such as layout, shelf position and point-of-sale displays. Increased sales turnover decreases your sensitivity to price competition.

Expense control

Look for ways to keep costs down like better record-keeping, controlling stock levels and reducing shrinkage. Lower costs mean greater profit margins, which help to insulate you from the effects of price cutting.

Image

The idea of rendering a useful service rather than simply making a profit is fundamental to creating an image. When you are regarded as part of the community in which you operate, you will enjoy a measure of goodwill and customer loyalty that can offset the effects of price competition.

Place strategy

The location and layout of your premises can make the difference between an average business and one that is spectacularly successful. A poor location can prevent your business from ever getting off the ground by adversely affecting sales and unnecessarily adding to your costs. Similarly, the layout of your premises makes a big difference to the effectiveness and efficiency of your operations.

Retail premises

The major factor in selecting retail premises is the kind of business you want to start and the amount and type of traffic you need to sustain it. Some businesses depend on foot traffic and must be located within walking distance of the people they serve. Other businesses cater to a mobile clientele and can be located some distance from the customer. Cost factors, such as rent and transport, are especially important if you are paying a high occupancy cost for a site that is really not required by the nature of your business.

The size, character and location of surrounding businesses are important. A good retail trading area has a balance of other types of businesses that create extra draw. If they are open during the same hours, that adds to the area's attractiveness. Businesses that are complementary tend to cluster together and draw mutually beneficial trade into the area. Businesses that appeal to totally different types of customers are usually incompatible and lack cumulative drawing power.

Minimum time and effort largely determine the retail trading area that customers will go to first. If the business requires a high volume of traffic, it needs to be highly visible and accessible. Is it easy to enter and exit from the footpath or the street? Is there plenty of handy parking? Is the area a short drive from the customer's home or business? It's important to ask the right questions, and make sure you answer them.

Manufacturing premises

Locating a small manufacturing operation is different from a retail location. Selecting a manufacturing site generally means making a larger capital commitment for a longer period of time. Some of the important considerations include access to your market, access to a workforce, access to transport, access to raw materials and components, the level of community support and the relative costs.

Designing the layout of manufacturing premises begins by identifying the functions that take place and considering the most efficient relationship that each function should have with the others. These functions are generally located in the office, production and assembly area, maintenance area, testing and inspection area, and the receiving, shipping and storage areas.

Positioning strategy

Positioning is the fourth part of the marketing mix. It generally occurs in one of three ways:

- Meeting the competition
- Beating the competition
- Countering the competition.

Meeting the competition is simply a process of copying what they do. The objective is not to create a competitive advantage but to cancel out theirs. Beating the competition is a stronger form of the same tactic, fighting fire with fire, thereby attempting to create some advantage. This strategy runs the risk of further retaliation by your competitor and both of you eventually becoming incinerated. Countering the competition is not only the most effective positioning strategy, but also the most intelligent because it fights fire with water. Countering the competition means that you dictate the grounds on which competition will take place, and those grounds will be the ones in which you have the greatest competitive advantage. The perfect market position is the one that clearly establishes you as the preferred choice in your market niche.

Market position is represented by the image that customers have of your business. When they decide to go shopping, they mentally rate all the businesses that are most likely to carry just what they want and offer the kind of service they prefer. They have developed an image of each business that sums up their feelings about it and they will go first to the business they rate best.

One method of positioning that is particularly useful in retailing is based on shopping style. It segments customers according to the ways in which they approach shopping in order to create a shopping environment that attracts them:

- 'Economic' shoppers are attracted by price, quality, a wide selection and an efficient operation.
- 'Personal' shoppers have plenty of time and are attracted by individual attention and a warm personal relationship.

- 'Indifferent' shoppers see shopping as a necessary nuisance and try to make it as quick and convenient as possible. They are attracted most by location, parking and store hours.
- 'Recreational' shoppers enjoy shopping as a leisure-time activity. They are attracted by things that entertain them such as fashion shows, attractive displays and innovative merchandising techniques.

Every business projects an image, whether it is intentional or not. The decor of the business, the style of the sign outside, and the way in which you dress, answer the telephone and greet customers all express the personality of your business. These impressions tell customers a great deal about your business in the first few seconds. Imagine walking into a restaurant where your waiter is wearing a stained uniform and greets you as 'Luv'. You know all you need to know about this restaurant from your first impression. When you choose an image for your business, make sure that it accurately reflects the basic buying motives of your target market. A number of studies have identified the following factors used by retail customers to form images:

Price	Quality
Assortment	Fashion
Personal selling	Convenience
Parking	Service
Display	Advertising
Atmosphere	Location.

Your overall image depends upon the value placed on each factor by your target market. Since each factor can be controlled or modified, you can emphasise the ones your customers value most so your image represents exactly the benefits they want.

Promotion strategy

Promotion strategy is the fifth component of your marketing mix. The objective is to create an image and to stimulate sales. It consists of the ways in which you communicate with customers, including advertising, publicity, merchandising techniques and personal selling. Determining a promotion strategy consists of a series of six decisions.

Determine your image

What is the image you want to create or support? Establishing an image is important because it will influence everything you do. Selecting an image is like choosing the personality for your business. If the personality is easily recognised and pleasing, your business image is established. For example, if you were to select the image of 'exclusive fashions', all factors must reflect high fashion, including the decor of the store, the window and interior displays, the advertising, packaging materials, the staff, as well as the buying and pricing decisions.

Determine your market area

This should be relatively easy if you have done your market research. A good starting point is to work out a description of the geographical areas within which you do business. People normally go to the biggest place they can get to most easily. Examine the area around your place of business in terms of the ease with which people can get to it and to your competitors. The objective is to draw an approximate sketch of your market area.

Decide what to promote

After deciding on the business image you want to convey and analysing your market area, the next step is to decide what items you want to promote. The goods and services you promote should be the ones your customers want to buy. Combining their wants and your image, you can select items of the right quality and fashion to sell at the right time at the right price. Deciding what to promote means focusing on customers' basic buying motives and developing a promotional theme around them. Here are some of the basic buying motives that customers seek to satisfy when they buy products and services.

Safety

Customers want to protect themselves and their property from harm.

Savings

Customers are not only interested in the initial purchase price but also in long-run savings through less frequent replacement, lower maintenance or lower operating costs.

Health

Customers buy products and services such as exercise bikes, health food, sunglasses and aerobic-exercise classes to protect and maintain their health.

Status

Some customers buy things in order to be recognised. An individual may be more concerned with the designer's name on the label than with the garment itself. A young cricketer may consider the autograph on a cricket bat equally important.

Pleasure

People hire videos, go to football games, eat out at restaurants and buy books to derive personal pleasure.

Convenience

Many products and services are purchased to make the routine chores of life easier. Examples are takeaway food, house-cleaning services and carwashes.

Decide where to promote

Deciding where to promote depends on many factors, such as the nature of the merchandise, how much of it you have for sale, and how much money you believe should be used for promotion. These factors will help to guide you to decide what medium, or combination of media, to use. There are media outside your place of business and inside your place of business. Outside media include the internet, newspapers, magazines, direct mail, handbills, outdoor signs, cinemas, radio and television. Examples of inside media are window displays, interior displays, blow-ups of advertisements, handbills, manufacturers' literature, gift novelties, signs, posters and merchandise attachments such as tags and labels.

Don't forget your principal inside sales tool—your staff. Your staff should be familiar with the advertising and store displays as well as with the merchandise they sell. If goods are moved from their customary location to make room for a special display, your staff should know and understand the reason for it.

Decide when to promote

The number of promotional events depends on the image and reputation of your business. Here are some of the factors that help to determine when to promote.

Climatic factors

You can be prepared ahead of time, for example, by featuring wool jumpers as soon as winter arrives.

Calendar factors

Holidays and special dates such as Christmas, Mother's Day and Easter are easy to plan for in advance.

Special factors

Graduation days, back to school, country shows, community days, and other local affairs are good times for special events.

The right timing is essential. A promotional calendar for the year should include all the dates when various promotional efforts are to begin and end.

Decide how much to spend

Deciding how much to spend on advertising and promotion is not only an important part of your marketing strategy, but also a key element in the cost side of your profit plan. Take a look at your advertising and promotion for last year and see what sales volume it produced. What factors may have changed? What is your sales target for the same period this year? What sort of promotional effort is needed to achieve the sales target and what will it cost? Here are some of the factors you may want to consider.

Age
A new store needs more promotion.

Products
A shoe store needs more promotion than a pastry shop.

Size in a community
A small store in a large community needs proportionally more advertising.

Location
A neighbourhood bookstore needs more promotion than an airport bookstore.

Size of trading area
A farm equipment dealer serves a wider area than a city shoe repair shop and needs wider promotion.

Competition
More promotion may be needed in one situation than in another to counter your competition.

It is important to keep good records so that you know what results you are getting from your sales promotion. By comparing past promotional expenditure with resulting sales it is easier to estimate the amount needed for similar items of display and advertising the next time.

Putting it together
The objective of managing each component of the marketing mix is to create a co-ordinated marketing program that brings your marketing strategy to fruition. It is like adjusting the components in a racing car so they work perfectly together in order to maximise performance. The way in which you combine the components of the marketing mix depends on the way in which you choose to position your business. Here are the components to build a marketing mix best suited to your business.

Exclusive marketing
An *exclusive* market position is usually the sole outlet for a particular product or service. The location need not be highly visible, but inside the atmosphere is plush and

personal. The company is positioned as superior to others in terms of quality and service. Advertising is low-key, refined and never refers to prices. Customers expect many extra services and they are willing to pay higher prices for them.

Specialty marketing

A *specialty* market position depends upon a narrow and very deep product line. The location and premises are distinctively related to the nature of the product. Advertising is primarily based on quality. The business is positioned as being a unique specialist in the field. Customers expect the firm to be expert in its line of business and to offer quality products and services for which they are prepared to pay higher-than-average prices.

Standard marketing

A *standard* market position carries a broad product line but not the depth of a specialty outlet. Location is in a central shopping area where complementary businesses are also found. The company is positioned as being a reliable supplier of value in terms of products and service quality. Regular advertising is based on product availability and sometimes on price. Fewer services are offered and customers expect them to be priced separately. Pricing policy follows suppliers' recommended retail prices with some adjustments for competition.

Discount marketing

In a *discount* market position, customers expect little or no services in favour of the lowest possible prices. The company is positioned as a bargain-priced supplier of reasonable-quality goods. Large amounts of advertising emphasise low prices, broad product lines and convenient hours. Location can be virtually anywhere so long as the premises are extensive and accessible.

Figure 11.2 (see page 215) is an example of how the marketing mix can be managed depending upon the market position chosen.

Internet marketing

Small business operators have to sift through a lot of misinformation about the internet, and it is not always easy to separate the hype from reality. The first step is to determine if the internet genuinely fits your business strategy. If the answer is 'yes', then the next step is to develop a way to fully exploit the marketing power of the internet. Before we examine the nature of internet marketing, we need to dispel some common myths.

Myth number 1

Every small business needs an internet site—website. While many small businesses can benefit from developing and maintaining a website, it is important to recognise that this

Figure 11.2: Managing the marketing mix

Market position	Product strategy	Price strategy	Place strategy	Positioning strategy	Promotion strategy
Exclusive	monopoly	highest	personal	superiority	extensive services
Specialty	narrow & deep	higher	distinctive	uniqueness	quality & expertise
Standard	regular lines	going-rate	central	reliability	product availability
Discount	broad	lowest	accessible & expansive	lowest prices	convenience & price

form of marketing may not apply to all types of businesses. If your customers already buy products or get information via the internet, then you need to be there as well. If, on the other hand, your customers get most of their information from other sources, such as the Yellow Pages, newspapers, magazines or television, you may be better off concentrating your efforts in those media. A website needs to fit into your overall marketing objectives and marketing plan. A successful website that will enhance your business will require constant attention. Can you commit to adding new content every month? Do you have the time and money to support it properly? If you're not willing to do this yourself, can you afford to hire someone to do it for you?

Myth number 2
A website automatically levels the playing field between a small business and its larger competitors. Yes, a professional looking website can make your business appear more substantial than it really is. Unless your website is skilfully implemented, however, it can actually make you look technically and commercially incompetent, resulting in a competitive disadvantage.

Myth number 3
If you put up a website, people will automatically come flocking to it. Don't expect people to find your website on their own. You need to encourage traffic through active promotion on the internet as well as in your traditional marketing media. You need to register your site with all the major search engines, exchange links or banner ads with other sites that have complementary services or products and feature your site in all your marketing literature.

This section has addressed some myths surrounding marketing on the internet. Chapter 13 (see page 234) describes the full range of digital marketing practices from database and email marketing and web page set-up, to guides on the use of social media and mobile marketing.

12 Advertising, sales and customer service

The important communication between a small business and its customers occurs through advertising and promotion, personal selling and customer service. The objective of advertising and promotion is to inform, to persuade and to remind customers about your business and what it offers. The objective of personal selling is to help customers to make a decision by providing them with information and arranging the sale. The objective of customer service is to meet customers' expectations and retain their loyalty.

This chapter begins with a discussion about advertising media and how to go about choosing the ones that best reach your target market. Since the internet and newspaper advertising is important to many small firms, we focus on them in some detail. Personal selling is an activity that does not appeal to some small business operators. We examine a concept called 'relationship selling', which makes personal selling more enjoyable. The chapter concludes with a discussion about customer service and how it contributes to customer loyalty.

Selecting advertising media

It is important to select media that will cover your market and enable you to tell your story effectively. In order to give your marketing communications a clear focus, you need to think about their purpose, target, the message you want to convey and the best medium for that message. You need to ask the following questions:

- What do you want your advertising and promotion to accomplish?
- Who is your advertising and promotion directed at? Trying to communicate with everyone rarely succeeds. Successful marketing communications focus on a specific target market segment.
- What should your advertising and promotion say? Your message should clearly and convincingly speak to your target market explaining the important benefits that you offer.
- How should you deliver your message to your intended audience? No single medium is inherently good or bad. Look for one that fits your goals, reaches your target market efficiently and is cost effective.

Newspapers

Newspapers are a retailer's primary medium because, daily or weekly, they reach the greatest number of consumers. You can be sure that a newspaper's readers are greater than the announced circulation because many copies are seen by more than one reader. A newspaper is a shopping guide in its circulation area. It not only provides information about what is available, where and at what price, but it also reports interesting events and other services that draw people into a trading area such as entertainment, recreation, food and convenience.

Using a local newspaper for advertising will depend on how much of your market area is covered by the newspaper's circulation. If the bulk of your business is drawn from only a small portion of the area that the paper covers, then you will be paying a premium for advertising that is wasted. Very small neighbourhood businesses might consider the possibility of using neighbourhood or shopping papers for advertising within a specified area. Some neighbourhood papers are read with great interest, but others are thrown away or regarded as a nuisance.

You may think you cannot afford to advertise in the newspaper because the volume of your sales will not support the advertising expense. By using only one newspaper and by following a pre-arranged advertising schedule, you may be able to buy regular advertising at a lower rate. You can get a lot of help by working with your news-paper's advertising department.

Getting a good position for your newspaper advertisement is desirable but not always possible. Only rarely can you get a guarantee for a specific location, but you can usually arrange to have it appear on a certain page or in a given section. Occasionally you may find your advertisement at the bottom of the page or next to one of your major competitors. That is why it is important to depend more on layout, design and copy than on a specific location.

Magazines

General consumer magazines are not only an expensive advertising medium, but they have such wide coverage that most of your advertising is wasted. Special-interest magazines are less costly and you can reach people when they are actively thinking about the products they need to pursue their particular interest. Examples include magazines for gardening, photography, skiing, golf, boating, cooking, weddings, fashion and computers. Special-interest magazines are especially useful for small manufacturers, who need to back up their retailers with national advertising, and for mail-order firms that target a national market with a narrow product line. Locally based magazine-type media include visitors' magazines, theatre programs and the newsletters of local organisations.

Radio

Radio advertising is almost entirely local advertising. Some products can be advertised better by voice than in print. Other products benefit from radio advertising as a complement to print advertising. The human voice can establish a rapport with listeners. A woman announcer can impart a feminine character to your message, or you can record your own radio commercials to give them a personal touch. The human voice can also convey a sense of urgency. If you want an instant response, you can ask your listeners to telephone you immediately. However, radio listeners remember messages that are spoken in a conversational manner and repeated frequently.

People must be listening to the radio for the message to get through. That is why choice of station, choice of broadcast times and repetition are important. Use a station that has strong listener-appeal for your type of customer. Each station defines its listening audience by age, musical taste, news and information interest, and geographical market. For example, if your target market is teenagers you would probably select a station that plays contemporary music. Try to get time slots when your customers listen to the radio. For example, commercials for a plant nursery would reach more likely prospects if they run during a gardening program. The non-visual message is short-lived and many radio listeners are 'tuned out'—that is why the key is to repeat your message frequently.

FM broadcasting has better sound quality for certain types of programming while AM broadcasting can be received over a wider area. Your local radio station can provide you with information and assistance. Ask them how you can use radio, what kind of ideas they have for your advertising and how much it will cost.

Television

Television stations have brought the cost of television advertising within the budgets of smaller firms. Spot announcements are becoming popular and television is playing a bigger role in small business advertising and promotion. Sight, sound, colour and motion make this medium the closest thing to personal selling, and it takes place right in the customer's own home. Like radio, you need to be very careful to select the station and the broadcast times that match your target audience. The best time to target men is in the evening and around sporting broadcasts. For women, daytime slots can be more cost effective. For children, Saturday mornings are best. Television is the only medium that can carry motion, so you should capitalise on it. For example, a boat dealer should feature a boat slicing through the water as opposed to a still picture.

Repetition in television advertising is different from radio. It is boring to see the same television commercial repeated too often. Think in terms of short, interchangeable segments that can be mixed and matched to make your television commercials appear different. The beginning and the end of every commercial should consistently identify your business and its image, but the message in the middle can be interchanged for variety and interest.

Brochures

The brochure is an important tool for retail and service businesses and the most economical means of small-volume advertising. Brochures are more readily controlled than other forms of promotion because they are distributed directly by the business doing the advertising and they are cheap to produce. Brochures can be distributed over the specific area that is expected to give the greatest return, and they can also be passed out in the store or inserted in packages and monthly accounts.

Direct mail

Direct mail has many of the advantages of a brochure, and it is also more dignified and personal because it can be directed to an individual customer. Direct mail is more selective than newspaper, radio, television or brochures. To ensure adequate but controlled coverage, use a selective mailing list compiled from your own business records or from commercially available mailing lists. Telephone directories are also useful for this purpose. Direct mail is more expensive than brochure advertising, but there are several reasons why it can give you greater flexibility:

- You can say more.
- You can try novel ideas on selected clients.
- You have a better chance to communicate your business personality.

- You can use a more personal approach and appeal.
- You can save some postage by including direct-mail advertisements with other mail such as monthly accounts.

Yellow Pages

When people turn to the Yellow Pages telephone directory, they are usually ready to buy and they are looking for a supplier. They do not have to be persuaded to buy, they merely have to be persuaded to buy from you. Most small businesses derive a significant proportion of their sales from Yellow Pages advertising. It helps to have the biggest advertisement on the page. It also helps to position the advertisement at the top on an outside edge. Another technique is to list everything that you sell or do. For example, one insurance broker listed every type of insurance sold. Remember, when customers look in the Yellow Pages, they are much more likely to read the entire advertisement, so you can include more copy.

Newsletters

A newsletter can be a potent advertising and promotion tool. Properly executed, it is an effective way to strengthen awareness and keep customers informed about new developments, products and services. Depending on your budget, a newsletter can range from a single-page one-colour format to a 12-page four-colour design. You can have your newsletter written and produced by a professional, or you can do it yourself using a desktop-publishing package on your personal computer. If you are not sure how to plan your newsletter, collect some samples from other businesses. Once you have established the purpose of your newsletter and defined its audience, there are a number of questions that you need to think about.

Content

Newsletter information should reinforce your image. Items commonly found in newsletters include a message from the owner, news about the business, a calendar of events, articles on new services or products and stories about employees. It should be information that is important to the reader. If you are positioning your business as friendly and down to earth, your newsletter should be consistent with that image. If you are positioning your business as a high-tech operation, you want a state-of-the-art publication.

Frequency

A newsletter should be published on a regular basis such as monthly, bi-monthly or quarterly. The schedule should be established with the first issue and readers should know when to expect it.

Design

Your image and your budget are the key elements in choosing a design. Newsletters can be one colour (usually black), two colour (one colour plus black) or four colour (full colour). Typefaces and sizes are also important. Different typefaces can make a newsletter look more formal, more friendly or more modern. Be sure to choose a typeface that is legible. Once you choose a design for the newsletter, keep it consistent from issue to issue.

Photography

Photographs keep a newsletter from looking dull and too dense. Use only professional photos, not snapshots, that are appealing and interesting.

Size and quantity

A newsletter can be just about any size. The number of pages depends on the amount of information you want to communicate. Typically, newsletters are two to four pages in length. The number of copies you produce depends on the size of the audience you want to reach.

Distribution

A newsletter can be a self-mailer or envelopes can be printed. If you have a large volume of newsletters, you may want to use a distribution service or the services offered by New Zealand Post, or consider an e-newsletter. Be sure to keep your mailing list up to date.

Signs

Signs are one of the most affordable and effective forms of advertising. You can place signs outside your business, inside your business and on your vehicles. A sign needs to command attention and to communicate instantaneously. For consistent recognition, your outside signs need to be dominated by your business logo. For instantaneous communication, your signs should carry a simple message using short words and should be legible in terms of colour, size and style.

Studies show that the most legible colour schemes are black on yellow, black on white, yellow on black and white on black. Nevertheless, other colour schemes may be more suitable for your business. For example, children are attracted by bright colours but older people prefer more subtle colours that are restful to the eye.

The size of a sign is determined by the needs of the viewer. The faster motorists are travelling, the larger an outside sign aimed at passing traffic needs to be. Its purpose is usually limited to who you are and what you do. If the outdoor sign is at another location, it needs to indicate where you are and how you can be contacted.

Vehicle signage has become popular among service businesses. Couriers, removalists and home-service operators with distinctive vehicle signage are advertising their services while they are working. Other forms of vehicle signage include buses, taxi boards, magnetic signs and bumper stickers.

Inside signs not only help to promote specific products, but also serve to guide customers through your selling space. Inside signs can be as big as a banner or as small as a price tag. Big signs convey a high-volume, low-cost image, whereas small discreet signs tend to convey a more exclusive image. With new techniques in instant printing and computer graphics, inside signs are no longer drab hand-lettered cards, but colourful and exciting graphic art.

Business cards

Your business card needs to say a lot about your business in a very small space. It needs to contain the important details about who you are, what you do, and how you can be contacted, but it also needs to project your image. A business card is a selling tool, and you need to design it just like an advertisement. Think about paper, colour, typeface and size. Here are some points to consider.

- Most designers prefer a thick paper stock, in either matt or gloss finish. You can use other materials, such as leather or fabric.
- Use a colour that is consistent with the colour scheme for your premises, your vehicles and your stationery.
- Make sure that the print is legible, particularly if it is against coloured paper stock.
- Stick to the traditional size if you want people to keep your business card. Make it bigger if you want to have more immediate impact.
- A gatefold is a double-sized business card that folds in half. It fits into standard cardholders, but it also doubles the amount of information that the card can contain.
- Don't leave the back of your business card blank. Use it to present more information about your products and services.
- Unless a picture is capable of reinforcing your image it may come across as tacky. A logo is usually more effective.

Specialty advertising

Specialty advertising consists of items imprinted with your logo or sales message that are given away free to prospects and customers. It includes items such as hats, pens, T-shirts and calendars. Specialty advertising is a diverse medium that can be adapted for use in different situations. Because it is targeted, your message is delivered directly to your prospects or customers with little waste. Specialty advertising can be a relatively inexpensive way to build and reinforce name recognition. However, its ability to convey lengthy sales messages is limited.

Publicity

Publicity is an important supplement to your advertising. There are a number of important events that can be used to generate publicity, including:

Staff promotions	Staff appointments
Grand openings	Expansion
Remodelling	Launching new product lines
Honours or awards	Community projects
Changing hours of business	Change in ownership
Safety record	Anniversaries.

You can tell all of these stories with paid advertising, but with publicity you get your story before the public for free. The newspaper will publish your story if it is news. What you do makes better news than what you say. It is up to you to write a press release, but lots of badly written press releases end up in the rubbish bin. It may be even worse if a badly written press release is published. The best way to learn about writing press releases is to study the publicity that appears in your newspaper every day.

Sponsorship

Sponsorship consists of underwriting an event such as a community fundraiser, or a school careers expo. Sponsorship support can be in the form of money, in-kind services or products. Event sponsorship can yield a number of marketing opportunities, especially if you work closely with the event organiser to make sure you receive appropriate credit in publicity releases, brochures, advertising, program books, street banners and posters. The key to sponsorship is to match the event you sponsor with the nature of your business. Here are some things to consider.

*   What do you know about the event's audience? Does it fit your demographic?
*   Will there be sponsor clutter? Will your business be seen to dominate the event?
*   What kind of exposure will you receive in terms of signs, event advertising, promotions and public relations?
*   Does the event manager have a good track record? Will the event have credibility and will it enhance your credibility?
*   Are there enough volunteers to run all of the activities effectively? Will it be well organised?
*   Is it the right time to sponsor this event? Will it be popular?

Writing a newspaper advertisement

Pursued with taste, vigour and imagination, newspaper advertising can attract new customers, help you to retain existing customers, and establish your image firmly in the minds of the public. The AIDA model represents the qualities of a good message—the Attention, Interest, Desire, Action model for newspaper advertising:

- It must capture the attention of your target group by being addressed to them in the heading.
- It must develop interest by providing appropriate detail and description.
- It must build desire by appealing to your customers' buying motives.
- It must call for action by making the offer 'time specific'.

There is no single way of creating the perfect newspaper advertisement. There are, however, some simple rules which, with a little experimentation, will help you to create effective newspaper advertisements for your business.

Make it easy to recognise who you are

The secret to immediate recognition is consistency. This can be done with a distinctive logo, a consistent art technique, a certain typeface or a distinctive border. Sometimes, over time, the shape of an advertisement, such as one column width by the full depth of the page, gives you instant recognition.

It is important to choose a technique to make your advertisements easily recognisable, and to do it in a way that reinforces your image. For example, a bold, cluttered border tends to convey an image of low prices while a clean, conservative border tends to suggest quality and service. Using the same border every time you advertise helps to create recognition. People reading your advertisements will associate the border with your business before they begin to read the message.

Use a strong headline to create interest

A good headline says 'This message is for you, so read on'. It is most effective when it promises a benefit that matches the customer's basic buying motive. Here are some of the ways that headlines are used to create interest.

Offer the reader a promise of specific practical information:

- How to Eat and Stay Slim
- How to Invest Your Money
- How to Win at Chess

Offer the reader an answer if they read on:

- Tired of Paying Too Much Tax?
- Would You Like a Free Holiday?
- Are You Sick and Tired of Being Sick and Tired?

Offer the reader a solution to a problem:

- Three Reasons Why You Need a New Pair of Sunglasses
- Why You Will Never Need to Pay for Hot Water Again
- Why I Buy …

Tell the reader to take clear action:

- Buy Your School Clothes Now!
- Come to Our Grand Opening Tomorrow!
- Enter Our Competition Today!

Don't give in to temptation and use the name of your business as the headline. Customers are attracted most by the benefits you offer them. The twelve most persuasive words used in headlines are:

Easy	New
Free	Proven
Guarantee	Safety
Health	Save
Love	You
Money	Win.

Use a simple copy layout

Having gained the reader's attention, the copy layout takes over to help guide the reader through the advertisement. We are accustomed to reading a page from the top left-hand corner to the bottom right-hand corner. The same rules apply to the way the eye moves through an advertisement. Pull the reader's eye across the headline, draw it down through the explanation copy, and finish by reminding the reader who you are, where you are located and when you are open. Use a picture or illustration only if it relates directly to the benefits offered by your product or service, otherwise the artwork may get the reader's attention but it will not direct their buying behaviour.

If a good layout guides readers through your advertisement, it is the body copy that holds them. The body copy builds on the benefit in the headline. Since people are accustomed to reading short sentences in the newspaper, this is usually the best format to use in your body copy. Keep it simple and direct, and try not to use unusual or difficult words. Advertising industry research has shown that readership falls off rapidly as an advertisement approaches 50 words.

Make sure that your body copy is complete. Nothing ruins an advertisement more than the omission of an important fact which the reader needs in order to take action. Be sure to include all the necessary information about what you are selling, where you are, what hours you are open, where customers can conveniently park and which credit cards you accept. A 'just arrived', 'one-day-only', or 'half-price sale' will give your reader a reason not to put off a visit.

Make use of white space

Some people try to cram every bit of advertising space full of print in an attempt to get the most for their advertising dollars. This practice usually leads to advertisements that are not read because they are too 'heavy'. The more white space you leave in your advertisements, the 'lighter' they appear. Light advertisements are easier to read, easier to digest and more pleasing to the eye.

Remember that the reader is reading columns of small type and the white space in your advertisement acts like an oasis where the eyes can pause for a rest. The white space draws the eye as much as a benefit headline or a dominant element. Dark and cluttered advertisements convey an image of low prices, and, sometimes, low quality. Examples can sometimes be found in supermarket and discount-store advertising. Advertisements with plenty of white space, on the other hand, produce a stronger image of quality.

Practise on other advertisements

The key to writing good advertisements is to develop a sense for what works. The next time you pick up a newspaper, study a few advertisements and evaluate their effectiveness using the following checklist as a guide. Ask the following questions:

- Does the advertisement offer merchandise with wide appeal, special features, price appeal and timeliness?
- Is a newspaper the best medium for the advertisement, or would a different medium be more appropriate?
- Is the advertisement located in the best section and position?
- Is the advertisement large enough to do the job expected of it? Does it omit important details, or is it overcrowded with non-essential information?
- Does the headline express the single major idea about the product or service? Remember, the headline should be an informative benefit-statement and not simply a label.
- Does the illustration (if one is used) reinforce the idea that the headline conveys?
- Does the copy contain enough information about the product or service? Does it leave out information that would be important to the reader, such as location, opening hours and telephone?
- Does the layout of the advertisement and the use of white space make it easy to read? Does it stimulate the reader to look at all of the copy?

- Does the advertisement appeal to customers' basic buying motives?
- Does the advertisement have the right approach? Is it written and presented from the customer's point of view?
- Does the advertisement seem honest or is the tone exaggerated and phoney?
- Does the advertisement use a distinctive typeface that is different from those of its competitors? Is the typeface easy to read?
- Does the advertisement stimulate prompt action through devices such as a coupon, statement of limited quantities, announcement of a specific time period for the promotion or an impending event?
- Does the advertisement use a logo or other feature that is always associated with the business and that identifies it at a glance?

Co-operative advertising

Manufacturers advertise nationally in an effort to persuade people to buy products with their brand name. In order to tell people where they can buy these products, manufacturers offer to share the cost of local advertising with the retailers who stock their products. The manufacturer gets more advertising per dollar because the retailer is contributing and the retailer gets more advertising per dollar because the manufacturer is contributing. Think about the length of time a campaign may run, how the cost will be shared, and how payment will be made:

- Co-operative advertising agreements usually last for one year. For special promotions, they may be shorter. They may also be affected by factors such as changes in models or styles, seasonal sales patterns or accounting practices.
- Most co-operative advertising agreements share costs on a 50–50 basis but other arrangements can be used. Some plans also call for cost sharing by wholesalers or distributors.
- The manufacturer sets an amount for each retailer based on a percentage of the retailer's sales of their product. The funds accumulated in this account represent the upper limit on the manufacturer's contribution to the co-operative advertising budget. When you place an advertisement covered by the agreement, you are reimbursed by the manufacturer after you present proof of the advertisement and a copy of the paid invoice. Some manufacturers do not pay you in cash but give you a credit against your next order.

Some small business operators do not take advantage of co-operative advertising plans and others do not advertise up to the limit of the co-operative funds to which they are entitled. Most manufacturers include a provision for co-operative advertising when they set the wholesale price of their product. You have already paid for it. If you want to get it back, you will need to take part in the co-operative advertising plan. If you sell brand name products that have strong national advertising support, you can significantly increase your sales by telling people that you sell these products.

Personal selling

What is it about selling that worries so many people? Some avoid selling because they have a fear of rejection. Others dislike selling because they think it consists of tricking or coercing a customer to buy something that they don't really need. Selling is an essential part of being in business and it can be done in a way that is positive, rewarding and enjoyable. Enhancing personal selling in this way is called *relationship selling*.

Relationship selling is a win/win game. If the product or service offered truly meets the customer's needs, everyone benefits as a result of the sale. It means taking the time to build a relationship with your customer rather than just focusing on making the immediate sale. Although relationship selling may take a little longer to produce the initial results, you will be rewarded long into the future with repeat business and referrals from happy customers. Building trust and really listening to your customers will help build your business.

Trust

Customers want to be served by someone they can trust. Have you ever walked away because you didn't trust a salesperson? On the other hand, do you find yourself going back again and again to someone who is helpful and honest?

How do you build trust? One way is let your customers get to know you. Tell them why you started your business and why you believe in what you are selling. Another way to build trust is to keep your word. From follow-up calls to delivering on time, simply keeping your word is a powerful sales tool. If something unavoidable happens, you can still keep the level of trust intact by telling your customer what has happened and asking what you can do to minimise the inconvenience. When customers know you sincerely care about them, they will feel secure that they are making the right decision to buy from you.

Listening

Something extraordinary happens when you give a customer your undivided attention. This means listening and not interrupting them or impatiently waiting to talk next. If you do all the talking, how will you ever learn anything about your customer? When you listen more than you talk, customers realise that you are genuinely interested in them and you are trying to understand their individual situation. They will become increasingly comfortable with you because they realise you are on their side. Part of listening includes recognising body language. Knowing how to interpret a customer's folded arms or eye contact will give you extra insight into how comfortable they are and whether they are ready to make a purchase decision.

A basic guide to relationship selling

Relationship selling is a way of doing business that is flexible, co-operative and professional. It also enables you to operate as an ethical, considerate and genuinely helpful individual. The following steps are a basic guide to relationship selling.

Step 1: Know your product or service

Before you begin a conversation with a customer, it is essential that you clearly understand your product or service and why people should want to buy it.

Step 2: Make the initial contact

A courteous greeting establishes rapport between you and your customer. The traditional 'May I help you?' often results in an answer like 'Just looking' which fails to get the ball rolling. Simply saying 'Good morning, what may I do for you?' is a more positive greeting. A better approach is to comment on whatever merchandise the customer is examining, such as 'Those new wool jumpers are very popular this winter.' Another alternative is to ask about the customer's reason for shopping such as 'Are you looking for something for yourself or is it a gift for someone special?'

Step 3: Exchange information

This step consists of asking questions, uncovering basic buying motives, giving information, and determining how your product or service will fill the customer's needs. Find out why the customer has an interest in buying a particular product or service. For example, the answer to a question like 'How long have you been playing tennis?' may help you to direct the customer to the right type of tennis racket. The most effective questions are those that are not answered with a simple 'yes' or 'no'. Instead, try using open-ended questions that get the customer talking. These are questions that begin with words like 'Why', 'What' or 'How'.

Step 4: Propose a solution

Once you are comfortable with the relationship you have created, propose how your product or service will solve the customer's problem or fulfil their need. When you describe a product or service, focus on the link between its features and benefits. A feature is a distinctive characteristic of a product or service. A benefit is the way that the customer's basic buying motive is fulfilled by the feature. Customers' buying motives vary widely and different people can buy the same product in order to gain different benefits.

Step 5: Confirm the sale

Rather than focusing on 'closing the sale', a term that indicates the end of the process, confirming the sale means you are reviewing the customer's willingness and ability to make a commitment. It is a natural extension of a sales relationship built on a foundation of trust, respect and rapport.

Step 6: Deliver

Actually delivering the product or service is a very important step. First, if you don't deliver, you haven't completed the sale. Second, during this step you have an excellent opportunity to continue to build trust and to cement your relationship with the customer.

Step 7: Follow up

Now is the time to find out how the customer likes your product or service. It provides you with an opportunity to create repeat business and to ask for referrals to new customers. If there is a problem, you are there to correct it.

One of the main reasons that many small business operators shy away from selling is because they don't like to be rejected. This is a basic and understandable human reaction. A customer will generally say 'no' for one of two reasons. Either they don't trust you or they genuinely do not want to buy what you are offering. If you focus on building a relationship with a customer, you can avoid rejections for the first reason. If you get a 'no' for the second reason, then remember that the customer may return to make the purchase later or refer others to you who do want to make a purchase.

Customer service

The role of customer service is to help build a business in three ways:

* Having more customers
* Having customers shop more often
* Have customers buy more.

The ultimate goal is to keep the customer for life, returning time and time again because they enjoy excellent service. The service objective for any business must be to maximise customer retention through customer satisfaction, and to minimise erosion of the customer base caused by customer disenchantment. A business that is able to continuously deliver excellent service automatically has a competitive advantage. Researchers have identified that from a customer's perspective there are six components of service: reliability, assurance, tangibles, empathy, responsiveness and information. They are expressed in the following ways:

* The ability to perform the promised service dependably and accurately.

- The knowledge and courtesy of employees and their ability to convey trust and confidence.
- The appearance of physical facilities, equipment, personnel and communication materials.
- The caring, individualised attention provided to the customer.
- The willingness to help customers and provide prompt attention.
- The availability and accuracy of information and feedback to customers.

Always remember, you will not get a second chance to make a first impression. An uncaring or negative attitude will be immediately apparent and it destroys any chance of creating a favourable impression. The real test of service quality is how you react when something goes wrong and a customer complains. The key to handling complaints are:

- Settle the complaint quickly. Research indicates that 70 per cent of customers will return if you settle in their favour and this improves to 95 per cent if you settle on the spot.
- Assume automatic legitimacy of the complaint.
- Don't argue. You may win the battle but lose the war.
- Never put the customer in the wrong or make them feel you are going out of your way to fix the complaint. The remedy should be automatic, without the impression that the customer should be grateful.

Sadly, only about 4 per cent of dissatisfied customers actually complain. This means you never hear about much of your customers' dissatisfaction—but they will tell their friends and family. A dissatisfied customer will tell many people about their experience and each of those people is likely to tell others. This can mean that in a very short time a large number of people will think that your business has poor service—but nobody has told you. As is often the case you will be the last to find out.

The quality of your service also helps to retain customers. It costs five to six times as much to attract a new customer as it does to keep an existing customer and customer loyalty reduces the need to run expensive advertising programs to build your business. The best kind of promotion you can get is 'word of mouth'—it is more powerful than any other kind and it costs nothing.

Businesses that provide superior customer service can charge more, realise greater profits and increase their market share. It makes sense, therefore, to build a service-oriented culture in the following ways:

- Go beyond the call of duty—exceed customer expectations.
- Ensure consistency of service quality, any day, any location, anybody.

- Do it right the first time—efficiency impresses.
- Be willing to please at all times, including busy times, break times and closing time.
- Be attentive to customers' needs with urgency, accurate information and respect.
- Strive for excellence—being 'adequate' is not a reason for customers to return.
- Review every aspect of your customer service—and aim to do it better each time.

13 Digital marketing

The economics and practices of marketing have been disrupted by the development of the internet and digital technologies. The processes used, by both consumer and business markets, to find and purchase products and services have changed dramatically. They have moved from responding to company marketing and advertising strategies to actively engaging with others in the market—other buyers, other company offers, even other markets—to find the best way to satisfy their needs. The power of influence in the marketing relationship is moving from the seller to the buyer.

This chapter describes the nature of the new landscape of marketing in the digital age, and the methods and tools that businesses can use to maintain their connection to markets and customers.

Digital reach and influence

Digital marketers have to think differently about how they present themselves to the market. Because the power of influence is moving from business to the people who make up the market, businesses need to find gatekeepers who influence market perceptions, and to build advocates amongst them.

Word-of-mouth influence from existing customers has long been recognised by marketers as a major persuasive force on buyers. Because the internet has become a global network of buyers and sellers who are connected in 'real time' to each other, the word-of-mouth influence in purchase decisions has become a much more powerful world-of-mouth influence. The digital world of marketing is not constrained by geography or distance, campaign cost or market size. It is just as easy to reach a market of thousands in another country as it is to reach one buyer in your own backyard. Instead of finding customers with your marketing strategies and advertising, they will find you (or not!), through their own online searching, or connections to email and/or mobile services.

However, to be noticed in the flood of digital traffic you first need to be present in the digital media. Buyers now connect quickly with multiple brands and offers, and this connection happens outside of the control or knowledge of product manufacturers or distributors. At any time buyers may have several points of engagement open to offers that are available on digital platforms. These connection points include search engines, such as Google or Yahoo!, social media connections such as Facebook, Twitter or YouTube, email clients such as MS Windows Live Mail, Netscape, Hotmail or Gmail, or mobile phone apps such as Yahoo! Upcoming, LinkedIn, or Contacts Journal. This means to get connected to a purchase touch point you need to be present in multiple forms of digital media. This may seem like extra work but the effort to do this can in many cases be automated, and the cost of the market reach to large numbers of buyers is very low.

Engagement with markets has become the new challenge and this happens in a new way. They will do the searching, filtering and evaluation of offers. You need to do all you can to help them find and select you. It is more about shaping and improving perceptions of brand and the customer experience than it is about advertising an actual product or service. Influencing perceptions becomes a publishing job using digital environments. It means frequent publishing of content in the digital media, using blogs, videos, email, discussion threads, and general subject information.

Direct database and email marketing

Database marketing is a form of direct marketing using electronic databases of customer details to generate marketing messages personalised to the names and addresses in the database. Database marketing uses statistical techniques to target and select customers for marketing messages. As a consequence, database marketers rely on efficient database management systems to provide accurate models of consumer segments and their purchasing needs, habits and behaviours.

Email marketing is a form of direct marketing which uses electronic mail as a means of delivering marketing messages to the targeted customer segments. The company builds or buys databases of consumer details that have been collected from previous transactions, loyalty programs, visits to web pages, application forms for free product or contests, product warranty cards, subscription forms and credit application forms.

Direct marketing using both standard or email delivery methods and drawing information from databases has raised ethical issues related to consumer privacy and ownership of consumer information. Further, direct database and email marketing has the potential to generate unwanted 'junk mail' and 'spam'. However, there are some protections against poor email marketing tactics, including the following:

- The Marketing Association of New Zealand outlines good practice, listed below, for both direct and email marketing.
- Spam filters can be added to email systems so that unwanted emails can be blocked.
- The evolution of search engine marketing, social media and mobile marketing has created much more emphasis on consumer-initiated connections to company and product information.
- A way to always send acceptable emails is to provide opt-in email options. Opt-in email advertising uses consent by customers to receiving your email messages. With a foundation of opt-in contacts in the database, promotional materials can be sent out in automated systems that regularly maintain marketing contact with interested customers.

Emailing remains popular with companies and is still enjoying growth because of several advantages, including:

- An exact return on investment can be tracked—email has been proven to produce high results. Email marketing is rated by tracking statistics as second only to search engine marketing as the most effective online marketing method.
- Advertisers can reach substantial numbers of email subscribers who have opted in to receiving emails on subjects of interest to them.
- Over half of internet users check or send emails daily so the connection is frequent and regular.

Guiding principles for direct marketing

To help develop good practice in direct marketing and email marketing the Marketing Association of New Zealand (in accordance with the *Privacy Act 1993*) offers the following six principles for responsible direct marketing:

- Use only legal methods and purposes for the collection of personal information.
- Maintain secure storage of the database of customers' information.

- Individuals must be able to have access to the information held about them.
- Maintain the databases with accurate postal addresses, including correct postcodes.
- Manage the removal or suppression of names from the database. The company should honour requests to have names removed or suppressed to void them from future marketing campaigns
- Check mailing lists for relevance, validity, legal compliance and match them against the Marketing Association's 'Do Not Mail' (DNM) Register containing the names of individuals who do not want to receive unsolicited advertising campaigns. The DNM Register also incorporates the deaths information from public records.

Guiding principles for email marketing

The Marketing Association of New Zealand (in accordance with the Privacy Act and the *Unsolicited Electronic Messages Act 2007*) also offers the following six principles for responsible email marketing.

- Send only relevant offers to consenting recipients.
- Always provide an option to unsubscribe.
- Use open disclosure to show who you are—list company details, physical address, and a genuine reply email address.
- Apply the basic 'truth in advertising' doctrine—do not mislead with false subject lines or misleading advertising.
- Do not abuse the permission embodied in the consent. The respondent should be informed about the purpose for which their email address will be used, and they should be offered a choice of frequency and type of communications.
- Do not harvest email addresses. Harvesting email addresses is forbidden in New Zealand by the Unsolicited Electronic Messages Act and defined by the Act as: 'compiling email addresses through anonymous collection procedures such as via a web spider, through chat rooms or other publically displayed areas listing personal or business email addresses'.

Building a website

There are various ways of implementing a digital marketing strategy and the choice is relevant to your needs and resources. You might decide to start with what you've got by using customer databases and direct marketing linked to an email system. However if you are ready to develop a web presence then you will be considering building a web page and the initial decision is whether to 'make or buy' it.

There are many web page designers and builders to choose from. A Google search on 'New Zealand web page builders' will bring up companies like Enlighten Designs at www. enlighten.co.nz, who for several years have been a leading award-winning company in this field. On the other hand, you may decide to try building your own and in this case there are also many sources of help and advice available online; for example, www.ediy.co.nz, and www.123online.co.nz. You might start with a product like Microsoft Publisher to develop your web page look and feel or use a design-and-build service like the EasySite design tool offered at www.telecombusinesshub.co.nz. EasySite is a service for creating a basic informational website of up to nine pages and is free with Telecom website hosting-plans. Either way, 'make or buy', there are a standard set of steps to building a website whether you do it yourself or work with a consulting service. Here is a basic set of steps to follow:

- Understand your objectives for the site.
- Design a 'look and feel' for the site.
- Develop content for the site.
- Select a development tool (an HTML editor) and build the site.
- Upload your site to a web server that will host your site on the internet.
- Design methods to bring traffic to your site.
- Design ways to measure the performance of your site.

Objectives

Begin the web page design task with clear objectives for the web page performance. What do you want it to do? The objectives commonly range from general public relations and brand or product awareness to making specific product or service sales. At the awareness end of this range the technical and operational issues are more simple, whereas at the sales end the job of the web page becomes much more complex and may involve interaction with your accounting system, credit card facilities at your bank and a dispatch and delivery system.

If your web page objective is to build a network of supporters and advocates then it will need to link with social media sites and contain blog pages that promote discussion streams. If its primary objective is to generate sales then you need to consider issues relating to national versus global sales, currency conversion rates and distribution methods.

Some requirements of the web presence are static and require very little changes to the web page content. Other objectives for the way a web page works may relate to frequently announcing new products, new deals or new events, and this will change the nature of the web page design and the ability to manage changes to the content easily.

Design

As with all interactions with customers a good place to start the design process is to put yourself in their shoes and consider their buying behaviours and preferred processes on the internet. While attractive graphics do enhance the look and feel of a web page, ease of use is a more important criterion.

Connectivity and speed are common issues. People enjoy simplicity and convenience when using the internet. Your web pages should be clear and simple, avoiding the traps of being too complex and too 'clever'. Design the web page functions for ease of navigation and speed of the process. Complex graphics that take a long time to load, search boxes that constantly return irrelevant 'finds', or the lack of 'undo' or 'go back' buttons can frustrate the buyer to the point of them choosing to avoid your web page in the future. The tolerance for poorly designed web pages can be very low, causing the buyer to quickly switch to another supplier because it is so easy to do so.

Another significant issue for the design of your web page is the lines of connectivity to your page and the links from your page to other sites that will support your transactions, including payment systems, alternative options, or further sources of information. Search engine, social media and blogging sites are the catchment tools that can bring traffic to your web page. If you don't design connectivity into your web page that will link these external sites to you, the traffic of interested prospective customers will be severely constrained.

Content

The key to winning engagement with internet markets is great content. Great content is content that is easy to access, relevant to customers and gives excellent supporting information that customers will value. While your connectivity tools may have brought people to your web page they are not necessarily ready to buy. The next task is to hold their interest, enhance their perception and win their trust. The emphasis at this stage is on the intangible values that might reside on your website—values aside from your product or service.

As well as providing easy navigation and simple process steps on your website, providing lots of supporting information for customers is a good way to build the intangible value. Write articles that provide advice, guidance and information for customers about the product or service field—and give it away free. Set up links to other supporting sites, build up your reputation as experts in the field and knowledge leaders. This is the way to recruit advocates for your site and to build traffic of interested potential customers. If the intangible benefits on your website are strong enough you may be able to create 'pre-sold' visitors who are ready to buy because the trust and confidence in you has been created by high-quality content. Keep adding content. As well as attracting many new visitors and generating pre-sold buyers, continually improving the content will encourage customer loyalty to your site and, so, further business.

Choosing a web host

When you have designed and built a great web page it is not available on the internet until it is published. This means you need a host for your page and that requires the service of an internet service provider (ISP). There are many choices of ISP and many plans available from each provider at different costs. To help you choose an ISP you can go to www.ispfind.co.nz, or http://broadband.t5.co.nz to see comparisons on services and costs.

The ISP processes will guide you through the choice of a uniform resource locator (URL) address for your web page and how to upload your page and any other files that go with it, from your hard drive to the ISP server. To do the upload you will need a web browser such as Netscape or Internet Explorer. Once the web page is uploaded you should test the functionality using a different computer from the one you built the page on, to make sure that the files are indeed being provided by the ISP server and not from your own hard drive. You are now ready to go, but need to attract customers to your site.

Building traffic

The previous section on content has emphasised the role of great content in building traffic to your website. However, the market still needs to be aware of your presence on the web and the best way to engage with the people in the market is to meet them in their favourite web places, such as frequently visited search engines, other websites and the full range of social media sites.

Search engines

Search engines allow people to type a word or phrase into a search box which prompts the search engine to find any links to those words on the web. Although search engines such as Google and Yahoo! are well known there are literally hundreds of search engines that could be used to link you to markets. A Wikipedia search on 'search engines' will show you some of them and where they focus their service. Using search engines to bring traffic to your site means registering your URL with one or more search engines and portals. Search engine optimisation (SEO) depends on using carefully selected words in the web page content to help the search engine find your page quickly and hopefully present your link ahead of others. The Marketing Association of New Zealand provides a set of guides for search engine marketing at www.marketing.org.nz.

Links

All of your activities on social media sites should have links to your web page. Also look for sites that complement yours to see if they contain links to other internet sites. If they do, send an email to the webmaster and ask them to include your site in their list of links. Offer to reciprocate by placing their URL on your links page. Your goal is to encourage their visitors to visit you as well. Choose your link targets carefully by making sure their image corresponds to yours and that you share similar customers. You can also seek links with vendors, suppliers and providers of complementary products and services. Your goal is to generate high-quality prospects who will be interested in your site. When you email a webmaster requesting a link, be sure that your email is friendly, informative and includes the following information:

- The name of your site and your complete URL. Use http:// at the beginning of the URL so that it is hotlinked from the email.
- A brief (20-word) description of your site.
- A few key features from your site that will interest users of the site from which you are seeking a link.

Online promotion of your website

You can use the power of the internet itself to promote your site. Here are a few possibilities.

Post an announcement in newsgroups

A newsgroup is an electronic bulletin board where people with shared interests can communicate. Target only those newsgroups that cover topics associated with your products and services. Provide some useful advice, not just an advertisement, and announce that your internet site has more information on the same topic.

Email lists

An email list is like a newsgroup except that the message goes directly to each participant's mailbox. One way to develop an email list is to ask potential and existing customers to submit their email address for a weekly prize draw. The list can be used to announce new features in your internet site.

Run on-site events

Running events is an excellent way to encourage repeat traffic. Examples include contests, games, online interviews, chat sessions and audio broadcasts.

Publish an e-newsletter

Ask site visitors if they would like to sign up for a newsletter that you distribute by email. It can be used to keep visitors up-to-date about changes to your site as well as information about your products and services.

Banner ads

There are many popular internet sites that sell advertising banners. The banner not only advertises your internet site, but it is also a link to your site. Look for banner-ad space on established sites that also cater to your target market. Contact the webmaster at these sites to find out what their ad requirements are, as well as their costs. In general, banner rates are based on the number of times the ad is served. Each time is called an *impression*. The amount you pay per thousand impressions is based on the site's ability to deliver a target audience.

Offline promotion of your website

Tell everyone—customers, prospects, suppliers, business associates, colleagues—that your business is on the internet. Issue a press release. A press release enables you to reach customers through publications that cover your products and services. It needs to be co-ordinated with the launch of your internet site so that it is news.

Put your URL conspicuously on all of your marketing and sales materials including your business cards, stationery, advertisements, brochures, newsletters and product literature. Anything that normally contains your phone number should also contain your URL and your email address.

Monitoring website performance

Traffic-tracking software can provide you with information about who is visiting your website and what's working on the site. This will enable you to improve the content and design of your site. Advice found at www.build-website.com suggests that a good tracking tool provides information including:

*   Where visitors are coming from
*   Which search engines they used to find your site
*   Which words or phrases they searched on
*   Which other sites and URLs are sending traffic to you
*   How visitors navigate through the site
*   Which of your pages is the most and least popular.

Zeald.com suggests a three-stage measurement system for web page performance: the three stages are measure, review, and tune. They suggest you collect data from a minimum of one month's activity, spend a day reviewing the results, and then make adjustments and improvements based on your review. The example web-page dashboard (Table 13.1) provides some interesting data on the sales results of 'new' versus 'returning' customers.

Search engine marketing (SEM)

Good search-engine marketing will help promote your website by increasing its visibility in the result pages of each search engine. That is why it is essential to be listed in the

Table 13.1: A sample web-page dashboard from *www.zeald.com*

Website Success Metrics

Last 30 days: 01 April–01May

Success Metrics	Actual	Budgeted	Variance
Website Visitors	6960	7000	- 40
New	5982		
Returning	978		
Conversion Rate	**2.03%**	**2.00%**	**+ 0.03%**
New Visitors	1.49%		
Returning Visitors	5.32%		
No. of Sales	**141**	**140**	**+ 1**
New Visitors	89		
Returning Visitors	52		
Average Sale	**$148**	**$100**	**+ $48**
New Visitors	$144		
Returning Visitors	$152		
Total Revenue	**$20 720**	**$14 000**	**+ $6720**
New Visitors	$12 816		
Returning Visitors	$7904		
Average Margin	50%	50%	0%
Gross Profit	$10 360	$7000	+ $3360
New Visitors	$6408		
Returning Visitors	$3952		

leading internet search engines. These are the equivalent to the Yellow Pages on the internet. The vast majority of your traffic is likely to come from these search engines. Your first option is to submit your website yourself. Each search engine has its own guidelines for submission, but generally, you only need to list your home page. The search engine then sends out its automated 'spider' to retrieve the other pages from your site and put them in its database.

Search engines vary in the depth to which they catalogue your pages, so you might want to register all of your important pages separately. You can influence how search engines catalogue your site by adding HyperText Mark-up Language (HTML) *title tags*, *meta description tags* and *meta keyword tags*. If you don't know HTML, make sure the person who designs your website includes these tags.

There are alternatives to listing a site yourself. A number of services will submit your URL to major search engines and directories. You fill out an online form that includes your site's title, its URL, keywords, and other information and the service handles the submission process. You can also buy internet promotion software that performs a similar task. While these methods can save you time by automating the registration process, they don't allow much flexibility in terms of how you describe your site or which pages you register.

In addition to the top search engines, list your site in small directories that fit your business profile. These include industry search sites that focus on businesses in a single market, regional directories that list businesses in a specific geographic area, or trade association sites that have searchable member listings. These listings won't generate the same volume of traffic as the large search engines, but they will give you access to a targeted audience for the products and services that you sell.

The term 'Search Engine Marketing' (SEM) covers the spectrum of activities involved in performing Search Engine Optimisation (SEO), managing paid listings at the search engines, submitting sites to directories, and developing online marketing strategies for your business. Wikipedia lists the three largest SEM vendors as Google AdWords, Yahoo! Search Marketing, and Microsoft adCenter. As of 2006, SEM was growing much faster than traditional advertising and even other channels of online marketing, and has become one of the most effective online marketing tools available today.

Adwords

Creating ads and choosing keywords specifically related to your products and services draws traffic to your website. When people search on Google using one of your keywords, your ad may appear next to the search results. Hence you are advertising to an audience that is already interested in you. People can simply click on your ad to be directed to your website and learn about your products and services. Due to cost effectiveness and the quality of traffic generated, Search Engine Advertising is now the fastest-growing method for marketing websites. For example, the Google network reaches 80 per cent of internet users worldwide. With more data on what people are searching for, Google can serve up the most targeted and relevant advertisements alongside the results, drawing more clicks, more leads and more sales. By focusing on SEO and SEM using search engine advertising with, for example, Google AdWords, you can benefit in a number of ways, including:

- Increasing the right traffic by attracting people searching for exactly what you offer.
- Massive market—search engines in combination with mobile technologies dramatically expand your reach.
- Minimise cost of customer acquisition—it is one of the most cost-effective marketing channels.
- Highly measurable—you or your webmaster can constantly track the effectiveness of your online marketing and make changes to increase the conversion rate of visitors to sales.

244

If this seems too much for you, Enlighten Designs at www.enlighten.co.nz provide support and advice on SEO and SEM activities. Their view is that search engine optimisation (unpaid search) and search engine advertising (paid search) will build significant internet traffic to your site over time. Typically, search engine advertising will dominate initially, but as the SEO process kicks in, paid search can be scaled back in favour of the more sustainable, natural search traffic.

Guiding principles for search engine marketing

The Marketing Association of New Zealand provides six guiding principles for responsible marketing activities on the web. While the Association is concerned with developing industry-wide standards of best practice and ethical conduct in the use of SEM in New Zealand, their principles tend to support the material provided in this chapter. Their six principles are:

- *Target relevant keywords*. Keywords should direct search engines and users to pages that relate directly to their point of interest.
- *Avoid unnecessary repetition and duplication*. Too much repetition of a keyword can be construed by the search engine as a gaming tactic and can result in penalties.
- *Create useful, information-rich content for both visitors and search engines*. While it is acceptable for marketers to include content that is overtly sales-oriented, it is not acceptable to create pages with the sole purpose of lifting the search engine rankings and then directing the searcher to other gateway pages.
- *Don't conceal, manipulate, or over-optimise content*. All web page content should be clearly visible to the visitor and not concealed in the coded language of the page or obscured; for example, by using tiny font sizes or by writing white text on a white background.
- *Links should be relevant and achieved legitimately*. While it is good practice to negotiate trading reciprocal links with other websites so that the users of both sites can find material that is relevant and useful, it is not acceptable to participate in 'link farms' or participate in black-market link trading for the purpose of gaming the page-rank algorithm.
- *Follow the rules*. Don't infringe copyright or trade mark law. Don't create deceptive or misleading advertising; and don't create spamming tools. (If in doubt, Google and Yahoo! also provide advice on acceptable practice to web page developers.)

Social media

The world of social media is a rapidly evolving landscape and it is taking an increasingly important role in consumer's digital lives. Brands that want to engage with consumers in this environment need to understand how, where and why they are using the many different platforms that enable content creation and sharing. Increasingly, people are using social media sites to communicate, find and share information, engage in discussions about products and services, and to find solutions to their needs. Universal McCann's Social Media Tracker report from 2010 shows 1.5 billion global visits to social networks per day with 47 per cent of the users joining brand communities and 30 per cent of them accessing social media via mobile devices. In their surveys of almost 38 000 respondents in 53 international markets they found that around 70 per cent were engaged in creating and/or using social media material. Social media is changing the role of the internet. 'It is no longer just a place for information seeking and shopping but a platform where connections are made, friendships formed and information and opinion exchanged' (Universal McCann). The characteristics of this change produce disruptive influences on traditional marketing in the following ways:

- The marketing power is moving from business to the consumer.
- The market finds and evaluates you immediately—you lose the power of marketing persuasion and enticement.
- The media *becomes* the market.
- It's about moving your online presence and messages to where the main traffic is—to where interested consumers hang out in increasing volumes discussing brands, products and services.

The range of popular social media sites, such as YouTube, Facebook, LinkedIn, Myspace and Twitter, has exploded to include hundreds of new sites. This explosion in the use and influence of social media cannot be ignored by modern marketing strategy. A digital marketing strategy will include the use of blogs, microblogs (tweets), video sites, forum/message boards, instant messaging, and social networks. An excellent source of information, advice and direction on the use of social media can be found at www.mashable.com.

Five ways to use social media

- *Branding*: Enlight Photo used a series of YouTube clips to promote their brand by featuring videos of someone demonstrating how their Orbis Ring Flash takes shadowless photographs.
- *E-commerce*: Enlight's YouTube links to their web page were then supported by blogs and tweets that drove interested traffic to the interactive website where transactions could be completed in real time.
- *Research*: Some companies use their social media as a vehicle to deliver and manage formal market-research surveys, or they use blogs to encourage feedback which can then be analysed to gain vital customer opinion data on products and services.

- *Customer retention*: By engaging in the flow of communication between and with customers in the social webspace, companies can counter misinformation, solve customer problems, deliver rapid service recovery and turn dissatisfied customers into advocates. Perhaps more importantly, talking directly with customers allows a company to develop personality, humanity and attitude. Innovative business owners can use the technology aspect of digital marketing to reintroduce the personal touch and enhance connectivity with customers.
- *Lead generation*: The traffic to your page created by your social media presence is already full of prospective buyers. If you have loaded great content onto your website these prospects can be turned into strong sales leads or, even, immediate sales.

Five habits of good social media practice

- *Continuously point users to your content*: This again emphasises the importance of creating and regularly adding great content to your website. It is the content that displays your competence and gives assurance to prospective buyers.
- *Promote your social presence with social links*: Generate reciprocal traffic. On your website show links to your social media sites so that search engine visitors can be directed to your videos, blogs, and tweets. Use all of your traditional promotional material such as business cards and letterheads to display links to your social media sites.
- *Monitor conversations about your brand and your competitors*: Over 70 per cent of Universal McCann's 2010 respondents said they had joined a brand community to share consumer opinion, access free content and get advance news on products. This brand-related traffic on social media sites is a rich source of market information for you and, if you participate in the conversations, a great way to engage directly with your customers. You can make special offers, lead potential customers to your own sites, fix individual complaints and counter misinformation that might be generated.
- *Respond to customer questions and feedback*: Try to respond to every review and engage in dialogue with customers. Act promptly to answer customer questions and carry out service recovery quickly if something has gone wrong with a particular customer's experience. If you want to improve your service and product quality, customer reviews are the best source of ideas on what needs to be fixed.
- *Support your social media strategy with traditional publicity activity*: Meet people through joining business organisations and speaking at business events. Build relationships and talk about your products, and tell people about your social media sites and addresses.

An overview of the social media landscape in relation to your webpage and digital marketing is shown in Figure 13.2.

Figure 13.2: Overview of the social media landscape

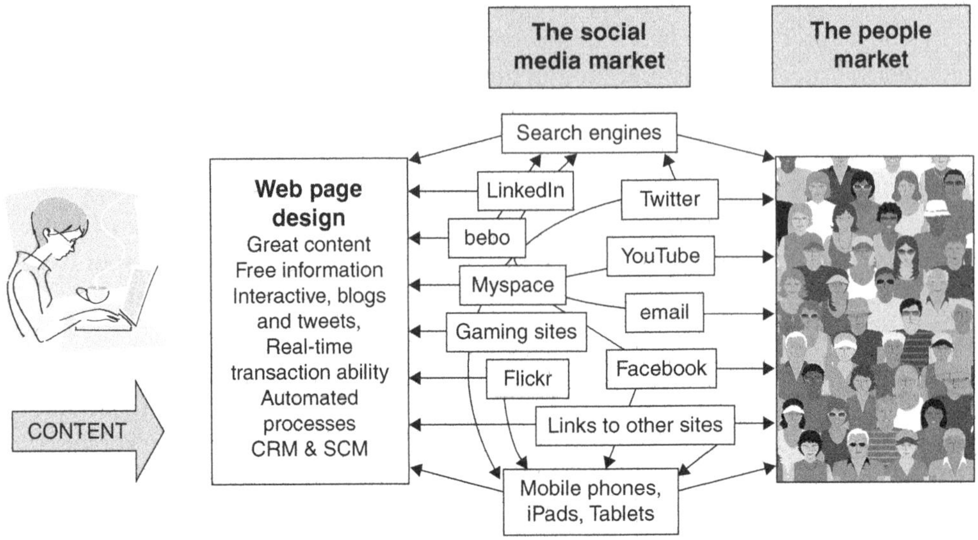

Blogging

Blogs are an integral part of the small business digital-marketing strategy. Hubspot. com is a site offering a digital-marketing software platform with impressive records of increasing SME web traffic and customer-base volume while reducing the cost per lead generated. The operators of HubSpot tell us that sites with blogs generate an average of 67 per cent more leads than those sites that don't have them. The reasons are related to the nature of blogs versus the nature of standard web content.

Blogs are personal. They display the knowledge, opinions and insight of the blogger rather than just static information. Adding a face and personality to the company marketing communications can build credibility, trust and following. The personal touch extends to the editorial freedom in the content of what is written. The 'blog and response' environment can develop its own thread of discussion and allows the writer to move easily into complementary topics that are of interest to customers. A further benefit from the personal nature of blogs over standard web content is that blogs are likely to initiate a *conversation* between the company blogger and potential customers. The conversation gives the opportunity to 'soft sell' by answering questions, overcoming objections and positively affecting the perceptions of the blog traffic.

Rich Site Summary (RSS)

RSS is a format for delivering regularly changing web content. Many news-related sites, bloggers and other online publishers syndicate their content as an RSS feed to whoever wants it. The benefit for the blogger is ongoing connection to interested parties. RSS allows social networkers to stay connected and informed by retrieving the latest blog content from the sites they are interested in. The number of sites offering RSS feeds is growing rapidly and includes big names like Yahoo! News. The following seven points (paraphrased from Mark Evans' blog at www.blog.sysomos.com) summarise the reasons why it's good to have a company blog.

* A blog can link to target audiences in a way that holds their interest, enhances their perception and wins their trust in your competency.
* Blog content can be distributed widely at low cost and shared in a way that engages large audiences.
* Constantly evolving blogs can seed further development of web content, newsletters and other sales materials.
* Blog traffic can give your company competitive advantage over competitors who don't blog, and enable greater conversions of prospective interest into firm sales.
* Blogs are dynamic and can change to stay in line with current market, company and product developments. Changing blogs attract frequent return visits by product and company followers.
* Search engines respond well to fresh content. A blog can be an effective and low cost way to optimise search-engine activity.
* In the technology-dominated digital business environment, blogs provide the softer personal face to your company, and provide a 'soft sales' environment that can pre-sell social media traffic.

Mobile marketing

Universal McCann's research suggests the most significant shift in social media over the last few years has been the ability of users to engage in social media via mobile appliances, especially smart phones such as the iPhone and the Android contemporaries.

The power of mobile marketing is in the expansion of 'reach'. The adoption of mobile devices is far outpacing the earlier adoption rates of desktop and internet technologies. The rapid adoption rate means that you can reach a greatly expanded number of users with your digital marketing. The mobile devices provide constant connectivity. They are convenient to carry and are powerful and easy to use. Not only can you reach a lot more people, you can reach them continuously as long as the device is switched on. Downloadable apps turn the phone into a source of mobile intelligence never enjoyed before. For users they provide the ability to access social media sites and websites, find bus timetables, order show tickets and find geographic locations with GPS maps. They can hold databases of product details, personal contacts, and digital business cards, as well as take photos, record videos and memo notes, make credit card payments and read barcodes. All this can lead to impulse purchasing.

Impulse purchases

Mobile marketing campaigns can work through emails and text messages, offers made directly to the device or site links to the internet search engines, social media sites and websites. Location-based services enable users to recommend their favourite restaurants and shops, and group buying sites; for example, www.1-day.co.nz can aggregate orders for quick social purchases at heavily discounted prices and Groupon at www.grouponnz.co.nz aggregates orders geographically so marketing offers can be made to selected cities. Mobile payment options enable a purchase, based on peer recommendations, to be made immediately without going to a web page or noting it for later consideration. Mobile digital marketing can capture impulse buying with a few clicks, enabling customers to buy your product the instant they want it. If you are a mobile vendor, apps are available in the US that attach to iPhones, iPads and Android phones. For example, using the device offered by Square at www.squareup.com and GoPayment at www.gopayment.com vendors in the US can get paid with Visa, MasterCard, American Express and Discover. Payments are deposited daily into the vendor's bank account less a small transaction fee. You can make enquiries with your bank about the availability of these payment methods in New Zealand.

Quick response (QR) Codes

QR codes can be scanned by smartphones and barcode readers. They may contain text, URL or other data and take people immediately from an offline environment to online sites and information sources. You can place QR codes on business cards, flyers, brochures and company stationery. They can also be placed on storefront windows. The QR code can link the phone holder to a variety of online sites. They can be directed to YouTube videos, Flickr photosets, Facebook pages, Twitter, blogs and mobile-friendly web pages.

Although a new concept to users, QR codes can prompt purchases by instantly providing extra product information and ways to buy. You can also use them as a promotional tool by giving discounts or giveaways that are exclusive to QR code users.

Business networking

Being connected in mobile networks of customers, colleagues and associates, and working with 'real-time' technology gives small businesses new marketing power. A variety of mobile applications help you to get the most out of this networking power. Here are some of the most popular:

- Yahoo! Upcoming provides a social events calendar system to supply nearby events data.
- iPhone apps like Bento and Contacts Journal allow you to organise contacts, track projects, plan events, and manage things—all in one easy-to-use iPhone personal database.

- LinkedIn gives you the ability to connect with over 60 million professionals world-wide. You can invite contacts, accept invitations, read and respond to messages and keep up to date with your contacts' developments.
- MeetMe by Basara LLC is an iPhone app that provides a quick and easy way to select a meeting point between two locations (yours and theirs). Set points A and B. The app allows you to select a location from a list of options between points A and B, send an email with directions and get on your way.
- Apps like ABBYY Business Card Reader enable you to scan business cards directly into a contacts database with an iPhone or Android smart phone.

In summary, mobile marketing uses the high reach of mobile phones for managing networks, and for promoting and selling products and services in real time. You have the ability to create and run your own text-message marketing campaigns, offer discount coupons and specials, run promotional contests, or provide other specialised content. These can be supported by a variety of mobile apps, the use of QR codes and immediate short-term deal sites like www.1-Day.co.nz. However, the need to fit your campaigns to the needs and preferences of customers still remains true. Steve Strauss from the Strauss Group, writing in www.openforum.com, gives four pieces of advice for mobile beginners:

- *Consider your audience*: The mobile audience is different from the audience for TV, newspapers and magazines. The message must exploit the immediacy of mobile media. Use QR codes, solutions for 'need it now' issues and short-life product offers that make the most of impulse-buying behaviour.
- *Don't spam*: It's a mistake to send unsolicited SMS (text) messages. When people receive messages they don't want they resent the intrusion and the mobile phone charges associated with the message. It is always better to allow people to 'opt-in' to accepting text messages. They may be encouraged to do this by the offer of exclusive offers and sale events, or early alerts to new product launches.
- *Choose the right service*: Some services simply allow a batch of SMS messages for a set fee, while others provide an expanded service that might include campaign software, dashboard reports, customer databases and the ability to issue coupons for discounts.
- *Create a campaign that fits the mobile culture*: Your campaign has to fit in with the culture of the mobile phone. It should be quick and easy to use and blend with the social flow of connected users. Contests, polls, sweepstakes, games and real-time promotions work best.

14 Export marketing

Exporting offers many opportunities for small business operators in New Zealand. For some, it is the obvious way to grow their business; for others exporting provides the scope and volumes that give economies of scale and higher utilisation of production capacity. Just because a business is small does not mean it cannot operate successfully in overseas markets. The key to small business exporting is finding a market niche rather than pursuing market share. The purpose of this chapter is to examine ways in which you can evaluate your export potential, identify export opportunities and develop an export strategy. How a typical export transaction takes place and sources of export information and assistance are also explained.

Evaluating your export potential

The first step in evaluating your export potential is to examine your competitive profile in the New Zealand marketplace. This amounts to a SWOT analysis of your strengths, weaknesses, opportunities and threats with a view to identifying your competitive advantages and disadvantages. A strong domestic operation generally forms the basis for entry into international markets and increases the chance of success. New firms that depend on export sales to survive from the outset represent a higher risk of failure. If you are not making a go of it in New Zealand, then think carefully before you attempt to crack the tough export markets.

Here is a three-step plan to help you evaluate the export potential of your business.

Step 1: Look at your current operation

Can you see any opportunities to make use of excess manufacturing or distribution capacity? Are there any opportunities to employ unused capacity in the off-season? Can you extend the life of a product by exporting into a less technically developed part of the world?

Step 2: Identify your resources

What resources can you use to enter the export field without a large additional outlay of time and money? Here are some examples for you to consider:

- Experience and skills in research and development, manufacturing, services or marketing
- Experience in dealing with distant or different types of markets or in reaching these markets through distributors or agents
- Managerial expertise and capacity
- Technology
- Availability of capital
- Location of facilities
- Knowledge of particular overseas markets
- Technical services or maintenance services
- Advisory expertise.

Step 3: Review your products and services

How might you position your business in overseas markets? Just because your products and services have been successful in New Zealand does not mean they will automatically have the same success in overseas markets. Some very successful products and services in New Zealand actually failed overseas because they did not match the needs of a different customer base. Here are some things to think about:

- Are consumers' habits, customs and practices for products or services similar to yours in overseas markets?
- What functions and features could be used to differentiate your product in overseas markets?
- What impact do things like taste, style, customs, religious practice and government regulations have on choices of quality, packaging, size, colour, shape, taste or ingredients in overseas markets?

Finally, evaluating your export potential is a combination of investigation and judgement. You will be in a position to decide if it is worthwhile investing the time and effort to identify an export opportunity when you can answer these questions:

- What forces operating in your domestic business are likely to make export attractive?
- What stresses and strains will export activity create for your business and how can they be met?
- What kind of customers is your product or service likely to appeal to in overseas markets?
- What features of the products or services that you currently sell in New Zealand provide a competitive advantage in overseas markets?
- What alterations will need to be made to your products or services before they can be sold in overseas markets?

Identifying export opportunities

If you are convinced that you have export potential, the next step is to identify an export opportunity. In addition to government agencies, there are others who may be able to help you including customers, suppliers, freight forwarders, carriers and bankers. There is always the temptation to engage a consulting firm to identify export opportunities for you. Be cautious if this is your intention because some firms that claim to conduct international market research actually do little more than assemble material that is generally available.

The following procedure is one way to conduct a survey on a country-by-country basis. The objective is to identify and rank countries that represent significant export opportunities for you. You may also want to collect similar information for the New Zealand market to use as a basis for comparison.

Step 1: Look at economic and social characteristics

You can get a feel for a country by assembling information on significant economic, political and social factors. What is the standard of living? How important are imports? Is it easy or difficult to do business? You are looking for signs of a healthy economic environment, a favourable political climate and a social structure that is compatible with your exporting objectives. This may lead you to eliminate some countries at this stage.

Examples of economic information include rates of growth in different sectors, levels of disposable income, imports and exports, inflation, unemployment, interest rates, exchange rates and the degree of industrialisation. Examples of political information include trade policies and controls, bilateral and multilateral trade agreements, stability of government, the degree of government involvement in business activities, taxation and other fiscal policies, and relations with New Zealand. Examples of social structure information include population size and rate of growth, class structure, ethnic groupings, rural versus urban distribution, education and training, and consumer habits.

Step 2: Look at trade statistics

Trade statistics report the flows of various products and services, either by quantities or by their monetary value. They reveal which countries import significant amounts of products or services like yours and, therefore, represent possible market opportunities. They also indicate which countries export products or services like yours and represent your competition in the international marketplace.

A market that is served primarily by imported goods is an encouraging sign. First, it means that customers are buying the product or service. Second, local producers are probably not so well established that they can exclude outsiders. And third, there appear to be no restrictions on these products or services being imported into this market.

Step 3: Look at export entry methods

What methods are available for marketing, delivering and, perhaps, servicing your product? You are looking for countries in which the export entry methods offer the least amount of resistance, are within your resources and best match how much you want to be involved.

Countries with the fewest trade restrictions represent more accessible markets. The most frequently encountered trade restrictions include tariffs, quotas, import licences and exchange permits. A tariff is a tax assessed by a foreign government on products imported into its country. Quotas are limitations placed on the amount of a product that may be imported from specific countries or from anywhere in the world. Licences are import permits that are used to distribute a quota amongst a number of exporters.

There are direct entry methods in which you can retain responsibility for sales negotiations, shipping the product and final distribution. You may decide to use foreign manufacturer's representatives who will contact buyers, negotiate sales and give you marketing advice while you handle shipping, financing and advertising. Alternatively, you may use distributors who purchase your product or take it on consignment for resale to customers.

There are also indirect entry methods in which an intermediary in New Zealand will assume responsibility for all phases of the export operation. You can use buying agents who work in New Zealand on commission to find products in response to foreign demand. An alternative is export merchants who purchase products for resale abroad, sometimes under their own label.

Developing an export strategy

Once you have made a judgement about the offshore opportunities for your product or service, you are in a position to focus on an export strategy. Developing an export strategy is like developing your domestic business strategy. It is based on understanding your customers, doing your market research, targeting a market niche and positioning yourself among your competitors. The objective in developing an export strategy is to formulate an operational plan for each component of the marketing mix. Special attention needs to be given to packaging and packing, distribution, advertising and promotion, pricing, paperwork and visiting overseas markets.

Packaging and packing

Packaging is an important product variable in export marketing. Will it be tough enough to withstand the stresses and strains of rough handling and still arrive in saleable condition? Will the colours and design appeal to your export customers? Is the packaging correctly labelled and in accordance with local laws and regulations? Be sure that you avoid any name, image or colour that is offensive to people in your export market. The export services advisers at New Zealand Trade and Enterprise can help you with advice about marking, labelling and packing for export. You can find more information at www.nzte.govt.nz and www.marketnewzealand.com.

One way to solve many export packing problems is to use a standard-sized steel freight container. It does not advertise its contents, it is far too heavy to be moved by hand and it is sealed or locked from the beginning to the end of its journey. These features are all defences against pilferage and theft. Port workers are accustomed to handling standard-sized containers, and freight rates favour containers because they simplify the transport process for the carriers and freight forwarders.

Distribution

The easiest way to distribute your product to export markets is by selling to an export merchant located in New Zealand. An export merchant is like a domestic wholesaler, except they resell your products overseas. However, you will not have control over how your products are marketed and distributed overseas by an export merchant.

Alternatively, direct exporting means you deal directly with your export customers or distributors. This can be done by establishing a sales office abroad, employing travelling sales representatives or by appointing foreign firms as your representatives. Direct exporting is more complex and requires a greater investment than indirect exporting, but it also means you retain greater control over your export-marketing effort.

Advertising and promotion

If advertising and promotion are important for the sale of your products and services in New Zealand then this activity is likely to be even more important overseas where customers are unfamiliar with your business and what you offer. Your advertising and promotion strategy will be influenced not only by the regulations and restrictions in overseas markets, but also by the local availability and use of advertising media and promotional methods. New Zealand advertising agencies and marketing consultants that have overseas offices are in a good position to offer information, advice and referrals to overseas advertising and promotion experts.

Pricing

Export pricing is more complicated than domestic pricing. In addition to your domestic price, there are export costs that need to be recovered for packaging, loading charges, freight, insurance, customs duties and export agents' fees. The way in which export prices are quoted depends upon which expenses you are going to pay and which expenses the buyer is going to pay. These terms are standardised in international trade and are known as incoterms.

In most cases the domestic price is used as a base to which the export costs are added. However, this may result in a price that is not competitive against local producers or other exporters. An alternative approach is marginal-cost pricing, in which only the direct incremental costs of producing and selling for export are considered in establishing a minimum-price floor. Prices above the floor may be more competitive and will contribute to profits because your overhead costs are already covered by your domestic operation. This approach only works if you have unused production capacity—it is not valid if you need to increase capacity for export production.

Charging lower prices overseas than you charge in New Zealand may be considered 'dumping' and you should check with New Zealand Trade and Enterprise before you adopt this strategy. However, a third approach involves modifying the product or service to bring its cost down so that it can be exported at a more competitive price. This strategy often works when your product or service is more elaborate than export customers demand.

Be prepared to adjust prices as foreign currency exchange rates vary. You may have to lower your price if the New Zealand dollar appreciates, but you may be able to raise your price if the dollar declines. Some exporters establish exchange rate variation points at which they adjust their prices. Other exporters assume all or part of the exchange rate risk as part of their export package.

Paperwork

One of the big differences between selling your product in New Zealand and selling it overseas is the amount of paperwork. The magnitude and complexity of export documentation can become a nightmare if you do not plan for it. Every export transaction involves a number of documents that must be meticulously correct. Mistakes and omissions can mean even bigger headaches if the goods cannot clear customs or the bank cannot make payment until the paperwork is corrected. Most small exporters use a freight forwarder to handle the paperwork for them.

There are a number of ways in which you can arrange for payment from your export customers. The method you choose will depend on how much risk you are prepared to take and what your customers will accept. Here are some examples.

- *Prepayment* before shipment involves no risk to you, but it is not usually acceptable to export customers because they have no guarantee of delivery.
- *Credit card payments* are possible when an exporter has a merchant agreement with an international credit card company. Merchant accounts dealing in non-New Zealand currency depend on the exporter having an account with the participating bank in the country of settlement.
- A *documentary letter of credit* is a guarantee from the export customer's bank to make payment when they receive documents proving that the goods have been shipped.
- *Documents against payment* release goods that have arrived overseas when payment is received.
- *Documents against acceptance* release goods before payment but only after the customer signs a bill of exchange that provides for future payment.
- *Discounting of export bills* is a service from banks whereby they buy the export draft or bill from you at a discounted rate and then collect the full amount of the payment when it falls due. Note that the exporter is still responsible for non-payment.
- *Open account* simply means that you are extending credit to your export customer without any letter of credit or other documentary requirements. This is the riskiest form of payment arrangement.

You should get advice from your bank, export consultant or New Zealand Trade and Enterprise before you agree to payment arrangements. They will also be able to advise you about your exposure to foreign-exchange fluctuations and how you can protect yourself against this risk. Credit insurance is available for some markets, and for major or well-known clients in most markets.

Visiting overseas markets

If you are serious about developing an export strategy there is no substitute for gaining first-hand experience by making an overseas visit. You will be able to verify the results of your market research, make your own observations of the marketplace, and establish personal contacts with agents and distributors. Since an overseas visit involves expense, time and effort, you need to plan for it. You need to have a clear idea about what it is you want to accomplish while you are overseas and you need a well-planned itinerary. New Zealand Trade and Enterprise or your Chamber of Commerce can help you with arranging an itinerary, introductions and appointments.

Do not underestimate the importance of cultural differences. There are many stories of negotiations going badly because of an accidental improper word, an inadvertent gesture or some other unintended behaviour. Although your overseas customers may be familiar with New Zealand customs, it is in your interest to learn about their cultural traditions and to respect them. Find out about the negotiating practices in the host country. There are books on the subject and New Zealand Trade and Enterprise is a good source of information. It can also recommend qualified local interpreters. You need to know whether haggling is expected or not, if a 'best and final offer' is really what it says, and what gifts and hospitality are appropriate.

A typical transaction

Completing an export transaction is more complicated than doing business in New Zealand. There are more players involved and the process of completing the transaction involves some extra steps. The more complicated the transaction, the more specialist assistance you will need.

The transaction process

Suppose you are a New Zealand manufacturer and you have received an inquiry from a Japanese agent for 100 'robokits'. A typical export transaction would proceed through the following steps.

Step 1

First, you furnish the price, product description and packaging information to your freight forwarder, who quotes packing, shipping and insurance costs from your plant to an airport or seaport in Japan nearest the importer.

Step 2

You notify your bank of the inquiry and obtain advice about the method and terms of payment. You decide to request payment by an irrevocable letter of credit, confirmed and to be paid by your bank.

Step 3

You check with the New Zealand Customs Service about any possible export licensing requirements for robokits. You also contact New Zealand Trade and Enterprise for an update on relevant import regulations in Japan.

Step 4

You combine information about the product, pricing, delivery and payment terms into a pro forma invoice, which you send to the importer. You clearly specify an incoterm together with the applicable price. You also include an expiration date for your offer in the pro forma invoice.

Step 5

The importer accepts your quotation and terms of delivery to a particular Japanese airport. The importer opens an irrevocable letter of credit in your favour at a Japanese bank, and you are notified of it by your bank as the confirming and paying bank.

Step 6

You review the letter of credit to ensure that you can comply with all of its terms, including the latest shipping date. It is acceptable and you schedule the production of the robokits. If there had been a problem with the letter of credit you would have proposed a suitable amendment to the importer.

Step 7

You inform your freight forwarder to book the international transport to meet the required shipping date. You stay in touch with all parties to provide reassurance while the robokits are being manufactured.

Step 8

When the robokits are ready the freight forwarder has them picked up at your factory and shipped by air to Japan. The freight forwarder prepares the shipping documents, including an air waybill, and has them executed by the carrier. As your agent, the freight forwarder clears the robokits for export with the New Zealand Customs Service. Finally, the freight forwarder takes the paperwork, including a commercial invoice that you have prepared using the pro forma as a guide, to your bank and requests that payment be released.

Step 9

The bank inspects the documentation to ensure that shipment of the goods requested has been made, that it was within the time allowed, and that all other letter-of-credit terms have been met. The bank keeps the paperwork and pays you the amount in the letter of credit, less the bank's fees. You pay the freight forwarder.

Step 10

At the time you are paid your bank sends the documentation on to the Japanese bank so they can complete the transaction with the importer. As a courtesy, you contact the importer to let them know the robokits are on their way.

Information and assistance

There are many sources of exporting information and assistance, including the New Zealand Trade Centre, Export New Zealand, New Zealand Trade and Enterprise, the New Zealand Customs Service, the Chamber of Commerce, the Employers and Manufacturers Association, and independent export consultants and international freight forwarders.

The New Zealand Trade Centre

The New Zealand Trade Centre is a permanent exhibition of over 2000 New Zealand products for export. The centre maintains information on markets, events, trade fairs, grants and funding, exchange rates and international directories. It also provides links to other export websites from its site at www.nztc.co.nz. The New Zealand Trade Centre is located at 38 Albert Street in downtown Auckland and is endorsed by New Zealand Trade and Enterprise. Exporters who would like information about having their products on display can contact the centre by phone on 09 929 1180, or through the website.

Export New Zealand

Export New Zealand is a private-sector organisation devoted to encouraging exporting through exporter education, communication, motivation and information. The institute's main activities are:

* *Monthly fee-based networking* meetings with accompanying presentations on exporting given by exporters and others with hands-on experience in specific markets
* *Educational programs* in exporting skills, including a series of seminars on 'First Steps to Exporting'
* *Advocacy* for exporters with government and other trade-related organisations to ensure that exporters' needs are fully understood and seriously considered.

You can find more information at www.exportnz.org.nz.

New Zealand Trade and Enterprise (NZTE)

In September 2002 the New Zealand government decided to integrate the services provided by Trade New Zealand and Industry New Zealand. New Zealand Trade and Enterprise is the result of that merger. Ten regional centres throughout New Zealand help exporters and companies preparing to export by:

* Assisting with market selection
* Advising on export procedures
* Assisting with business planning for export
* Assisting market research
* Identifying contacts and channels to the market

- Helping companies into their first export market
- Providing referrals to outside agencies
- Providing information and advice
- Organising missions to export markets
- Providing advice on trade shows
- Conducting education programs, seminars and workshops for exporters.

The New Zealand Trade and Enterprise website at www.nzte.govt.nz offers a wide range of services to educate and support exporters and people thinking of becoming exporters under the headings:

- Get ready to export
- Develop knowledge & expertise
- Access international networks
- Explore export markets
- Find funding assistance
- Features & commentary.

There is a wealth of information on this site, including:

- Under 'Develop knowledge & expertise' there are business-mentoring and business-training services.
- Under 'Explore export markets' there is detailed information and analysis of the markets in individual countries and a function that enables you to compare countries.
- Under 'Access international networks' there is information about the Beachheads Programme that provides mentoring to high-growth New Zealand companies that want to improve their international business connections.

The New Zealand Customs Service

The New Zealand Customs Service is responsible for clearing all goods for import or export, as well as collecting customs duties, sales taxes and excise taxes. Customs prefers that you use the services of a *customs broker* for exporting. A customs broker is licensed by the Customs Service to provide a variety of specialist services, including determining the proper classification and dutiable value of goods, and ensuring compliance with clearance regulations. Check with the New Zealand Customs Service for a list of licensed customs brokers. You can contact the New Zealand Customs Service by phone on 0800 428 786, email to feedback@customs.govt.nz, or at www.customs.govt.nz.

The New Zealand Chambers of Commerce

Your local Chamber of Commerce is linked through the New Zealand Chambers of Commerce to a worldwide network of 20 000 chambers. They are a contact point for many overseas businesses wanting to do business with New Zealand companies. The Chambers of Commerce in New Zealand also offer training and publications in all aspects of business, including export trade. The following services and advice are available from the Chamber of Commerce:

- Export strategy
- Market research
- Export production preparation
- Making contacts
- Selling overseas
- Pricing quotations and terms
- Financing the sale
- Getting paid.

Links to your local Chamber of Commerce are available at www.newzealandchambers. co.nz.

The Employers and Manufacturers Association (EMA)

The EMA has 5000 members from all sectors and sizes of business, including local and central government, Maori enterprises, incorporated societies, associations, charities, hospitals and educational institutes. The association provides a wide range of advocacy, advice, learning and networking services. The Member Service Centre is the gateway to all EMA services. It is a free telephone information service for members with problems or enquiries on employment or business matters. This includes advice on employment matters, training, trade and exporting. Find contact details for your local office at www.ema.co.nz.

Independent export consultants

Some consultants specialise in export information and services. Many have expertise in a particular industry sector or a particular export market. Export consulting services can be expensive, so make sure you cannot get the same services at a lower cost from government agencies such as New Zealand Trade and Enterprise. Some export consultants are prepared to arrange their fee structure on a performance basis.

An independent export consultant may have special expertise or overseas contacts that you cannot obtain elsewhere. They can save you a lot of time in evaluating your export potential, identifying export opportunities and entering export markets. They can also provide valuable help in guiding you through the labyrinth of rules and regulations associated with government assistance schemes.

International freight forwarders

International freight forwarders have a network of offices or agents who will handle the shipment of your products to export markets. They can give you a quote for freight, insurance, documentation, packing, customs duty and other fees. They can schedule the shipment, pack the product, arrange insurance, complete the documentation, monitor the shipment and clear the goods through customs. They can advise you on the most cost-effective way to get your product into an export market and identify and correct problems that inevitably arise with export activity. Since they are in the business of exporting they can also help you with market information and introductions to overseas contacts.

Self-development exercise C

Are you ready to export? The following Export Assessment Guide has been designed to help you make a realistic evaluation of your strengths and weaknesses and assess your capability to take that first step. You will discover whether your company has what it takes to be successful overseas. It can also show you which areas you will need to work on in order to prepare your business for exporting.

		Points	Your score
1	**Does your company already have product available for export?**		
	It is currently in production.	10	
	It is at prototype stage.	2	
	It is an idea only.	0	
2	**Is your product selling on the New Zealand market?**		
	It is selling and market share is growing.	10	
	It is selling but market share is low.	2	
	It is not selling.	0	
3	**Are you selling product in more than one of the three main centres (Auckland, Wellington, Christchurch)?**		
	My business is selling in more than three cities.	10	
	My business is selling in more than one city.	5	
	My business is selling in only one city.	0	
4	**Have you already achieved export sales for your product?**		
	Yes	10	
	No	0	
5	**Does your company already have surplus production capacity available for export orders?**		
	Yes	10	
	No	0	

		Points	Your score
6	**Do you have finance available for export marketing and product development?**		
	Yes	10	
	No	0	
7	**Describe the management of your company.**	**Yes No**	
	You have experience in exporting.	2 0	
	You are committed to a sustained export effort.	5 0	
	You have the full support of your senior team.	5 0	
	One of your senior team has export experience.	2 0	
	Your team has a good track record in meeting deadlines.	6 0	
8	**Do you have promotional materials such as product brochures or videos available?**		
	Yes	5	
	We are in the process of preparing material.	3	
	No	0	
9	**Has your company calculated FOB (free on board) and CIF (cost insurance freight) prices for export products?**		
	Yes	5	
	No	0	
10	**Has your company undertaken research into overseas markets?**		
	We have undertaken detailed research including visit(s) to the market(s).	5	
		3	
	We have done some research.	0	
	No		
	Your Total Score		

Turn to page 334 to analyse your assessment summary and find your export diagnosis.

Part D

Operations management

Operations management is concerned with productivity and efficiency in products and services to ensure your business delivers customer satisfaction. To achieve the first goal operations management seeks to minimise waste caused by under-utilised assets, long process-cycle times, unproductive labour time and poor quality. To achieve the second goal it focuses on excelling in a mix of the five competitive priorities: low cost, high quality, flexibility, on-time delivery and high-value-added service. Chapter 15 describes operations management for retail and service businesses. Chapter 16 describes operations management for manufacturing businesses. Chapter 17 covers employment issues, including recruiting, retaining and managing staff. Chapter 18 focuses on the use of computer information systems for small businesses. Chapter 19 examines the tools for troubleshooting and recovery if you happen to get into trouble.

15 Retail and service operations

Retail and service businesses account for about two-thirds of the small business sector. The nature of these businesses, however, varies tremendously. Some sell a product with accompanying services to enhance the product's appeal; for example, personal computer retailers. Some sell a service with accompanying products to enhance the appeal of the service; for example, beauticians. And some businesses sell a pure service, such as child-minding. Even a pure-service business, however, can be equipment intensive, like a video repairer, or people intensive, like a marriage counsellor.

Retailers will tell you that their businesses are constantly changing. The retailer with a competitive advantage is one who is prepared to innovate. The challenge for small retailers is trying to keep up with the big ones. Changing customer behaviour is also creating changes in retail outlets.

Service businesses are beginning to dominate the small business sector. Information services and corporate outsourcing are the main factors underlying the growth in business services. Growth in personal services has been fuelled by an ageing population, increasing leisure time and increasing numbers of working women. The key to a competitive advantage in services is productivity and reliability. The purpose of this chapter is to examine some of the principles that underpin effective retail and service operations.

Buying merchandise

In most retail businesses the largest cost is the merchandise purchased for resale to customers. Not only do you need to control this cost, but clever purchasing is also important for maximising sales. The purchasing cycle is a systematic approach for buying the right merchandise, of the right quality, in the right quantity, at the right price and at the right time. The purchasing cycle consists of four stages.

Stage 1: Determine your merchandise needs

Various categories of merchandise call for different approaches to determining what and how much to buy. Some lines are staples, which are always in demand with no change in model or style, so determining what you need merely involves looking at your current stock and your current rate of sales. Other lines may be seasonal, perishable, or affected by style changes. For these categories you have to make risky decisions about which styles to select and how much of each to buy. You don't want to get stuck with a lot of old stock when a particular style is no longer popular. The goal is to maintain them at the lowest level possible and still have a sufficient variety of colours, sizes or models available from which customers can choose.

Stage 2: Select your suppliers

Some merchandise can be bought from only one supplier. In this case your only decision is whether or not to carry the line. For most merchandise lines, however, there are usually several suppliers. You can contact them through their marketing representatives, trade magazines, trade directories, trade shows and the Yellow Pages. You not only need to evaluate their prices, but also pay attention to other things such as reliability of supply and delivery, attention to problems and product support, help in emergencies, credit terms and any other forms of assistance you may require.

Stage 3: Negotiate purchases

Find out what lines and quantity discounts are available from other vendors, and what kinds of deals your supplier has been doing with your competitors. Make the supplier's representative work for you, even if you are fully prepared to buy from them anyway. Negotiation involves not only the purchase price, but also quantities, delivery dates, whether you want a single or multiple shipments, freight and packing expenses, guarantees on quality, promotion and advertising allowances, and special deals on end-of-line sellouts.

Stage 4: Follow up

Review your relationship with each vendor on a regular basis. Keep yourself informed by regularly searching for alternative suppliers who may be able to do a better job for you.

Look for ways to improve the selection of merchandise and look for clues to help you time changes in your merchandise lines.

Merchandise control

There are many technological solutions to help you control merchandise and the merchandising process.

Maintaining stock

Employ a practical system for maintaining stocks that is designed to determine the correct quantities and assortments, simplify buying, assist in selecting items for special promotion and expedite the liquidation of slow-moving items. The following four-step system will help you to control your merchandise.

Step 1: Divide your merchandise into three basic groups:

- *Maintained reorder items* are usually of a staple nature and are consistently available from your supplier. They do not change styles or models often and variations in your stock position can be adjusted gradually.
- *Maintained selection items* normally come in a variety of styles, colours and sizes. Whenever an order is placed, the entire customer selection needs to be carefully reviewed. You need to shift slow-moving items because stock won't sell once it loses its popularity.
- *Fast-turning selection items* are usually the least predictable but the most profitable stock. Merchandise planning for these items needs to be very flexible and set up to change rapidly. Over-buying is costly because mistakes cannot be reduced gradually and severe price reductions may be necessary to move merchandise that is no longer marketable.

Step 2: Determine how far in advance merchandise should be planned

Each category will have its own buying period, which is determined by the frequency of stock reviews (order review period), and the time it takes to receive goods once they are ordered (delivery period). For example, if you review a certain line once each week and delivery takes three weeks, then the buying period becomes four weeks and sales for this line are planned four weeks ahead.

Step 3: Determine the total amount of stock to be provided

Here is a working example. Assume that the average rate of sales is six units per week. If the buying period is four weeks, then we must have stock for *planned sales* of 24 units. In addition, let us carry a *basic stock* of four units, which means keeping enough merchandise on hand to be sure that we can offer any one customer an adequate selection. Finally, let's carry another three units as *cushion stock* to take care of any unexpected increase in sales volume or delays in delivery. In total, we will need to provide 31 units for the buying period.

Planned sales	24
Basic stock	4
Cushion stock	3
Total to be provided	31

Open-to-buy means that we look at the amount of stock to be provided and subtract the amount that we are already holding and the amount that we have already ordered. Therefore, if we are holding 11 units in stock and we have an unfilled order for 5 more, it leaves us with 15 units open-to-buy. This is the amount we should order now.

Total to be provided	31
Less: Held in stock	−11
On order	−5
Open-to-buy	15

Step 4: Establish a system for accumulating and recording sales information
There are four main systems to think about:

- *Rotated* systems use physical stocktakes on a rotated or staggered basis. They are often used for maintained reorder stocks.
- *Perpetual* systems use current information about individual lines by adding purchases and subtracting sales on a continuous basis. These systems are used for maintained and fast-turning selection stocks.
- *Visual* systems can expedite reordering and simplify record-keeping for certain types of merchandise. Visual systems include bin-ticket systems that specify minimum and maximum stock levels for each stock item, a two-bin system whereby the emptying of one bin triggers the replenishment order for a bin-lot quantity, visual forward stocks and colour coding.
- *Computer-based* systems use various methods to capture stock information in the process of carrying out the book-keeping for the buying and selling functions. Computer-based systems can also be used to monitor your stock position for each line and to provide you with exception reports for those items that are outside the guidelines you have established.

Stocktaking
A physical stocktake needs to be conducted periodically to ensure that the actual quantities on hand are equal to those shown on the stock records. Unless this information is

correct, your merchandise control system will not work. If *shrinkage* becomes a serious problem, you need to be able to detect it as soon as possible.

One common reason for shrinkage is shoplifting. Other reasons can be more subtle but equally damaging. For example, if you do not check the actual quantities of merchandise received against the vendor's packing slip, your records will be out by any differences. You may also be paying for merchandise that you did not receive. Through oversight or carelessness, merchandise may be sold without being billed. In this case, the records will show more stock on hand than really exists. What is worse, you will suffer a loss equal to the cost of the goods as well as forgoing the profit you should have earned on the sale.

Any of these factors can result in discrepancies in your merchandise control system and impair your merchandising effectiveness. While most small businesses take precautions against theft, few adopt serious procedures for protection from stock shortages caused by poor receiving procedures or careless billing practices.

Merchandising technology

Technology has enhanced the merchandising and selling processes in ways that give faster response to consumer demand and more convenience for shoppers. Today's small business owner needs to stay in touch with developments in technology and its role in retail operations.

Electronic Funds Transfer at Point of Sale (EFTPOS) is expected at all retail outlets. The use of Universal Product Coding (UPC barcoding) in combination with barcode scanners to register sales is spreading from the supermarket into many other types of retailing. Sometimes product sales can be linked into a reorder system with your suppliers to reduce the supply-cycle time, reduce transaction costs in the supply chain, reduce inventory carrying costs and help you to make sure you are always in stock.

As the commercial world moves rapidly into the electronic and digital era, new methods of marketing, transacting business and supplying goods to markets are evolving. This produces both threats and opportunities for small businesses, which need to be well informed and proactive in adopting changes that enhance the customer's perception of value and meet their expectations of service.

Retail sales management

Successful retail operations depend on the selection, training and motivation of the staff. If you have a small retail operation you have a unique advantage over larger competitors because you and your staff have a close personal relationship with your customers. In fact, you and your staff are a major reason why customers choose to come to your business. Your staff add another element to the marketing mix by the way in which they reinforce your product, place, price, positioning and promotion strategies.

Select your staff so they match your customers in the same way as the other elements of your marketing mix. Customers enjoy doing business with people who share their interests and with whom they feel comfortable. A health-food store needs staff who are committed to health and nutrition. A music store needs staff who are mad about music. A sporting-goods store needs staff who are really into sports.

Sales report systems, personal observation, customers' letters, complaints and customer surveys will enable you to evaluate the performance of your sales staff and to provide rewards where they are deserved—or to provide extra training and support where it is needed. Incentives in the form of sales meetings and contests, and sales awards or prizes can be highly motivating but never forget the power of personal praise and the magic words 'thank you'.

Service operations

A service business relies on expert knowledge, skills and experience. There are some unique operational issues that apply to service operations.

- Services are intangible. They cannot be seen, tasted, felt, heard or smelled before they are bought.
- Services are inseparable from the customer's point of view. The person *is* the service and so the person and the service become one inseparable unit.
- Services are variable. Service quality may vary depending on the person, time, location and circumstances.
- Services are perishable. Services are produced and consumed at the same time and cannot be stored in readiness for peaks in demand.
- Services usually involve the customer in the delivery, which adds an uncontrollable element of variation and perceived service quality.

Service businesses can range from a simple, standardised operation to a highly flexible, complex operation and they can approach their target market with a variety of different strategies. You need to define your service objectives and the customers you serve before deciding which of the four main strategies to use. You may want to use more than one strategy:

- *Simplicity* is a specialisation strategy that lends itself to distribution and control.
- *Standardisation* is a strategy that reduces costs, improves productivity and produces a uniform service.
- *Flexibility* is a strategy aimed at providing a broad range of customised services.
- *Complexity* is a penetration strategy designed to offer more services to an existing customer base.

Positioning a service

You can position a service business in ways that create a competitive advantage. Service customers' basic buying motives are price, value and quality. Therefore, you need to identify service differences that are highly valued and affordable, superior in quality, and capable of being effectively advertised and promoted. Research has shown that the following key areas influence customers' perception of service quality:

- The appearance of physical facilities, equipment and staff
- The ability to perform the promised service dependably, accurately and consistently
- A consistent willingness to perform promptly
- An empathy for the customer that results in caring individualised attention
- Knowledge and courtesy that gives assurance and instils trust and confidence
- Availability and accuracy of information relating to the service before, during and after the service delivery.

Quality assurance

To maintain service quality you can develop your own system of quality assurance. Quality assurance systems document and communicate your quality standards and procedures, and provide for checks, measures and corrective actions to keep the service performance up to the established standards.

Advertising and promoting services

Advertising and promoting services is based on the same principles that are used for manufactured goods. However, you also need to be sensitive to the differences between tangible goods and intangible services. Here are some suggestions for advertising and promoting services:

- Provide tangible elements within advertising and promotions to compensate for the intangible nature of a service.
- Services need greater explanation in order to make the nature of the service fully understood.
- Promise only what you can deliver.
- Maintain a continuous presence with advertising and promotion.
- Ensure continuity of theme and style—they are important for developing an image and positioning a service business.

One of the distinctive characteristics of service businesses is the importance of personal referrals and word-of-mouth recommendations. Customers personally experience the nature and quality of a service. They form an opinion that will be sought by others who are interested in buying the same service. Research indicates that a word-of-mouth recommendation is one of the most potent sources of new customer information and it outweighs all other forms of advertising and promotion. On the other hand, dissatisfied customers tell many more people about their experience and they can severely damage a service business. That is why you must only promise what you can deliver, and then you need to deliver on time every time.

Pricing services

When customers buy a product, the price is usually clearly stated and they can evaluate the tangible benefits that the product offers. When they purchase a service, however, they tend to underestimate its value. Customers generally equate the price for services with what they think is a fair wage for the labour involved. They do not think of overheads, equipment, materials and profit margins.

It is important to have a standard pricing policy in order to avoid unnecessary customer squabbles over prices. Nothing destroys a service business faster than for customers to get together and compare prices only to find out that they paid different prices for the same service. Wherever possible, published prices should be used to calculate charges. Even if customers believe the prices are high, they find comfort in the fact that they are being charged the same price as others for the same service. One approach to setting prices is to construct a comparison schedule using your competitors' published price lists. Use the price comparison schedule in conjunction with your cost base to determine a pricing policy that is consistent with your marketing strategy.

Some service businesses do not lend themselves to standardised pricing because there is considerable variation from one job to another. In these cases, you need to evaluate each job individually and prepare a bid price. The trick to bidding competitively is to bid the job, not the market. Each job needs diligent research and a full examination of all the contingencies that might affect the cost of doing the job. Winning a bid that results in a loss is no win at all.

Consumer credit

Consumer credit is a mixed blessing in retail and service businesses. Although it attracts new customers and enables existing customers to purchase from you more easily, it can also result in potential collection problems and credit losses. There are two ways to grant consumer credit. You can accept one or more of the established credit cards, or you can grant credit directly.

Which credit cards to accept depends on your business. The more cards you accept, the more paperwork you create. The discount is usually a fair price to pay for not having to worry about collections or bad debts and avoiding the investment in working capital that results when you grant credit directly. Accepting credit cards, however, limits your credit policy to whatever the credit card issuer requires.

Sometimes it is necessary to offer direct credit. If it is industry practice to offer credit, then refusing to do so will probably result in customers going elsewhere. If your customers are large companies or government organisations, they automatically expect to be offered credit services. If your customers make many small purchases, it may be practical for both of you to do business 'on account'.

There are two ways to grant credit directly:

- The first is based on a credit period that you allow customers before you expect payment. No finance charges are levied. In fact, a discount may be offered for prompt payment.
- The second is a revolving credit arrangement whereby charges are accumulated and the customer is expected to pay a minimum amount each month. A finance charge is levied on the outstanding balance.

When you grant credit directly you will need to have a good system of record-keeping and you will need to monitor customer accounts regularly. You should also be aware of the impact that granting direct credit will have on your cash flow and working capital—when you sell for cash, your sales and collections are equal, but when you offer credit, you will not receive payment until some time later. Therefore, you need to anticipate the effects that your credit policy will have on your cash flow.

The cost of providing credit will depend on whether you accept credit cards or offer credit directly. The cost associated with accepting credit cards generally consists of how much you pay in discounts. The costs associated with providing credit directly can include a number of items such as extra book-keeping, producing and mailing invoices and statements, credit checks, and chasing slow payers and bad debts.

16 Manufacturing operations

Manufacturing, wholesale and construction operations account for about one-third of the small business sector. They differ from service and retail businesses because they are primarily concerned with making and distributing physical goods.

The key to success is knowing what is important to your customers and then becoming excellent at providing what they want. The purpose of this chapter is to focus on manufacturing operations by examining the important elements including productivity, product and process design, plant layout, production planning and scheduling, stock control and quality.

Gaining competitive advantage

Competitive advantages in operating a manufacturing business are essentially driven by:

- *Low unit cost*—the sum of direct labour costs, material costs and overhead costs that are applied to a product
- *Quality*—the percentage of product shipped that meets design and customer specifications
- The average of time between receiving an order and completing delivery

- *Delivery reliability*—the percentage of complete and correct deliveries made by the date promised
- *Flexibility*—the ability to offer a wide variety of products to the market without affecting cost, quality or delivery performance
- *New products*—the ability to develop new products and get them into production and out to the market quickly.

Order qualifiers are features of your business that enable you to meet customers' minimum requirements. Order winners, however, are those features that positively differentiate you from your competitors and enable you to capture the order ahead of your competitors.

Drivers of productivity

One of the primary concerns of operations management is the productivity of time and assets. Time productivity can be thought of as *cycle time*, asset productivity as *capacity utilisation*, and the productivity of both as *waste elimination*. Elimination of waste of time and resources is the focus of 'Lean' practices and the main concepts are outlined in the sections that follow. Visit www.managementsupport.com for a full summary of 'Lean' concepts.

Cycle time

Cycle times occur in many ways. There is a cycle time for debtor turns, stock turns, invoice processing, service delivery and production of products. A large number of these relate to the operations function in a business because it is usually the manner in which a process has been designed that regulates the cycle time. Cycle-time reduction is an excellent strategy for reducing cost and improving customer satisfaction. Cycle time in manufacturing has five components:

- Move time
- Queue time
- Set-up time
- Wait time
- Run time.

Of these, queue time usually explains the largest part of the cycle. One recent study of New Zealand manufacturers found the following percentages for times in the production cycle:

Move time	3%
Queue time	85%

Set-up time	3%
Wait time	1%
Run time	8%

Product and process design, production planning, lot sizes and the range of products all have an impact on the cycle time and each should be investigated for potential rationalisation and standardisation. Long queue times and shifting bottlenecks in the flow of production can usually be traced to a dysfunctional system of production planning and control rather than physical capacity constraints of machinery. Reducing cycle times reduces direct labour costs and automatically reduces raw material, work-in-process and finished-goods stocks. At the same time it enables improved delivery performance and greater flexibility because short cycle times allow greater variety to be included in the production mix without creating delays.

Capacity utilisation

Capacity is represented in fixed assets (including buildings, plant and machinery) and the people employed in the production area. Because the cost of capacity accounts for a large part of the funds invested in a business and all of the direct labour cost, it is critically important to keep both physical and human assets productive. The basic rule is to restrain the investment in assets without affecting the ability to increase sales volume. High capacity utilisation means that assets are lean and hard working, asset turns are improved and pressure to fund growth is reduced.

Small market size and highly variable demand make it difficult to keep manufacturing units fully productive and many run for only 10 hours a day or less. Export markets sometimes generate enough production volume to achieve higher capacity utilisation. Other strategies include working with flexible capacity by using outsourcing, short-term equipment rental and flexible staff in terms of both skills and working hours.

Achieving a high rate of capacity utilisation and keeping customers satisfied are often in conflict. Whereas the customer wants variety and immediate delivery, the production team wants fewer products and longer production runs. The answer to this dilemma lies in the efficiency of the production planning system and shortened cycle times. Much of the loss of capacity is due to random bottlenecks forming in the flow of materials. These blockages starve downstream machines of work while upstream machines have to slow down or even stop producing. Random, shifting bottlenecks are a telltale sign of problems in the production planning system. Here are some other tips for getting the best out of your capacity:

- Reduce set-up times.
- Use layouts and technology that allow one worker to run several machines.

- Allocate production people to what they do best.
- Optimise the sequence of tasks.
- Simplify and standardise the product designs.
- Use early demand indicators to feed into the production planning system.
- Aggregate orders as much as possible without creating delivery dates that are too far out into the future.
- Carry out aggregate planning to balance demand and capacity across jobs, machines and people.
- Use capacity cushions in planning so you can be sure of producing to plan and maintaining stability for workers on the shop floor.
- Maintain equipment regularly to avoid having breakdowns in the middle of a production run.

Waste elimination

Waste is the hidden enemy of productivity. To eliminate waste the first task is to identify and measure it. In some cases waste such as scrap may be visible in the production area but the majority of the cost will be hidden in unnecessary or non-value-adding activities. Some of the more common forms of non-value-adding activity include:

- Moving product or people around the production area—this adds cost but does not add value. Reduce distances wherever possible.
- Scrap may be caused by operator error. However, most scrap problems come from poor integration between product design and the size of raw materials, resulting in low yields in initial cutting and trimming of components.
- Having to rework material that wasn't processed correctly the first time may recover the materials but it increases the labour and overhead cost because of the extra handling.
- Errors in calculating quantities or setting specifications will create wasted time and production inefficiency.
- Seek out activities that don't need to be done. Sometimes design and technology changes or changes in customer requirements make some processes redundant, but they persist through habit or because no one told the operators about the changes in requirements.
- Product that is returned for any reason creates cost. The product has to be physically handled and stored awaiting further action and there are costs associated with issuing credit notes and ordering replacements.
- Complaints about product failure or lack of performance may require an onsite visit to recover a customer's goodwill.

Product and process design

Innovation in both products and production processes can create a competitive advantage if it is rapid, cost-effective and results in products that match customer expectations.

The product

Product design is both a marketing issue and a manufacturing issue. Concept development starts with ideas for new products. However, manufacturing issues need to be included from the beginning. It may be a great idea but how do you make it? What are the implications for manufacturing capacity, equipment and people? What problems will you have with machining tolerances, raw material supplies or operator skills?

Design for the customer means not only giving customers a voice in the development process but also anticipating product designs and features that will excite them. Customers will seldom be able to tell you exactly what they want, so the responsibility for creativity and innovation always remains with you and your manufacturing team.

Design for manufacturing and assembly involves design principles that make the product easier to manufacture, less susceptible to variations in the production environment and easier to assemble. These principles are:

* Design for *wider tolerances* in the parts specifications
* *Simplification* to remove manufacturing complexities
* *Combine* parts into one piece to reduce the number of parts
* *Standardisation* of components so that one component can be used in several products.

When market testing and production trials produce satisfactory results, you are ready to go into production. Production capacity and material purchasing can be ramped up for the first commercial production run. In your marketing and administration areas, sales promotion needs to be organised and order-entry systems set-up to receive and process orders.

The process

The manufacturing process you select is driven by the nature of your products and markets. If you make one-off sheet-metal ventilation ducts then your process will be a *project or job shop process* with a jumbled flow of materials, low volumes and low standardisation of parts and products. At the other end of the range, if you manufacture paint you will have a *continuous flow process* with tightly linked process-stages and high volumes of a standard product. During the life cycle of products and processes there is often a trend to move away from project or job shop manufacturing methods toward processes that have more standardisation and flowing production lines.

Factory layout

The *focused factory* is the natural domain of small business manufacturing where focus and specialisation become strengths. The focused factory uses many 'design for manufacturing and assembly' and 'capacity utilisation' techniques to leverage its specialisation into a competitive advantage in a niche market.

There are two essential elements in the layout of a production and assembly area. The first is the space requirement for each machine and the efficiency of its arrangement. The second element is the relationship of the machines to each other and the efficiency of the overall production and assembly operation. The layout of a production and assembly area can be described as a process-type layout or a product-type layout:

- A *process-type* layout is particularly suited to job-lot manufacturing because of its flexibility in producing a variety of products with the same equipment. New products can be introduced without changing the plant layout.
- A *product-type* layout is best suited to manufacturing a limited variety of items in which the same sequence of operations is required. In these circumstances, it is more economical to have the machines arranged in the order of their use so that materials move directly from one stage to the next.

Production planning

Production planning consists of issuing work assignments to the production units and co-ordinating the materials flow between production areas. The goal is to optimise capacity utilisation on the one hand, and meet customer delivery expectations on the other. Production planning is like carrying out rehearsals before a stage play. All of the scripts, actors' movements, props and stage sets have to be co-ordinated and practised before the event so that on opening night the show goes on without a hitch. In manufacturing, the rehearsal occurs in the planning system before the event occurs on the shop floor. Figure 16.1 (see page 284) is a flow chart for a small manufacturing business that has 14 machines on the shop floor grouped into five production units.

The flow between the production units is indicated by the heavy arrows and the flow between machines is represented by the light arrows. In between the production units there are stores that act as checkpoints in the flow. Stores may exist physically to balance or buffer the flow or they can be 'virtual' stores that exist only in the planning system as a point where output from a production unit can be measured.

Scheduling

There are a number of tools that can be used to simplify production scheduling, including routing tickets, network diagrams and bar charts. Some can be done manually, but most lend themselves to computer applications.

Figure 16.1: Flow of materials

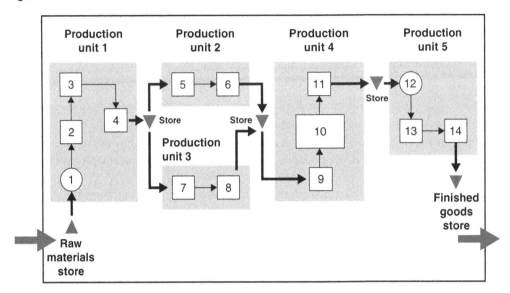

One method of scheduling work and materials is to use routing tickets. When an order is received, a ticket is filled out containing information about the operations to be performed, the dates when they need to be completed, and the assignment of machines and people for each operation. Routing tickets tell each person what they are supposed to do, when the work needs to be finished, and where the job goes next. This helps in ordering materials and getting a job done on time. Routing tickets are limited, however, when it comes to planning and scheduling complicated work because they do not provide an overall picture of a production operation.

Scheduling charts are useful because they help to visualise the load that is being placed on people and equipment. One type of chart is the bar chart and the Gantt chart, in particular, is a type of bar chart that gives an overview of the workload and specific schedules for people and equipment working on a specific project. A Gantt chart shows which jobs are in progress and the amount of time scheduled for completion of each. Other resource information such as the components and materials required, and the people and equipment assigned to each job, can also be added. Another type of chart is the critical path method (CPM) algorithm to create a network diagram that shows the relationship between the different stages of a job. While bar charts are more useful for routine production, network diagrams are better for complicated activities and projects. Computer programs are available that automatically produce the graphics and reports once the data has been entered. Microsoft 'Project' is the software that is dominant in this field.

Stock control

Stock control applies to raw materials, components, work-in-progress and finished goods. It includes knowing when to order and how much to purchase. If you keep too few raw materials and components you run the risk of shutdowns in production caused by shortages. If you keep too few finished goods you run the risk of lost sales to customers who are unwilling to wait for delivery. On the other hand, if you purchase or produce too much stock you will have extra costs. The purpose of controlling stock is to provide maximum service to your customers at the lowest cost to your business. Your aim should be to achieve a rapid turnover of stock without running out. The less money and space you have tied up in raw materials, components, work-in-process and finished goods, the better.

ABC classification system

The ABC classification system divides stock into three basic categories:

- Category A requires careful control
- Category B requires some monitoring
- Category C requires a minimum of control.

Here are criteria for establishing the category into which a particular stock item falls.

- Cost per unit—high-value items require more careful attention than low-value items.
- Lead/delivery time—long or irregular delivery times require more careful attention than short or highly predictable ones because of the increased possibility of a stockout.
- Amount used—items used in large quantities throughout the year should be watched carefully because they represent a large proportion of the investment in stock.
- Contribution margin—items with high contribution margins are the foundation of profitability and need to be managed regularly to avoid stockouts.
- Patterns of use—irregular use can result in either a stockout or an oversupply, and seasonal items should be watched carefully to avoid an oversupply at the end of a season.
- Size and weight—heavy and bulky material should be monitored carefully because it is costly to handle and occupies a large amount of space.
- Obsolescence and spoilage—fad or fashion items, fragile material and perishable goods are a big source of stock loss and should be carefully controlled.

The items in category A need to be kept under very tight control. Some items may need to be reviewed every day or every week depending on changes to production schedules, customer demand and supplier dependability. Frequent reviews provide very good control, but it is time-consuming and expensive. Its use should be limited to those items that are critical to your operation.

The items in category B require less attention. They can be controlled by a perpetual control system that combines the principles of the bin system with more accurate written records. First, the amount of safety stock should be determined for each item. Instead of setting aside the safety stock in a bin, however, either manual stock cards or computer-based records that include all the relevant stock control information are kept for each item.

The items in category C are low volume, low margin, inexpensive, sturdy and non-spoiling with predictable delivery times. They can be controlled with a minimum of attention by using the bin control method which consists of setting aside enough safety stock to last through the time it takes to receive a new order. This amount can be sealed and labelled with a note that says 'reorder when this stock is opened'. When the new shipment arrives, the same amount is set aside again.

Just In Time (JIT) systems

'Just in time' is a manufacturing philosophy that aims at high-volume production while maintaining minimal quantities of raw materials, work in process and finished goods. Production is *pulled* through the manufacturing unit by demand from the front end as opposed to work orders being loaded or *pushed* into the production system from the back. Under a JIT system, nothing is ordered or processed until it is needed. Final assembly is triggered by customer orders—work at the last production station is triggered by an order from assembly and so on back to raw material supply, which arrives just in time for the next period of production.

Quality management

Quality management means having systems in place to ensure you can meet your customers' expectations the first time and every time thereafter. 'Total quality management' (TQM) is a philosophy based on maximising your competitive advantages with a solid focus on your customers. It is a program of continuous improvement in which you keep examining your operations, your strengths and weaknesses, your position in the marketplace and the ways in which you produce and deliver your goods and services.

TQM results in the reduction of waste and errors in processes and systems, making it possible for you to offer improved products and services and to better satisfy your customers' expectations. Effective quality improvement includes lower manufacturing costs from cycle-time reduction and reduced errors and defects that create waste. In addition, improved capacity utilisation of both machines and people reduces the direct operating cost in production areas by eliminating non-value-adding activities and down time. At the same time, sales can be increased through better on-time delivery, more competitive pricing and higher reliability.

Quality management is important for every business, but *Quality Assurance Certification* (such as ISO) is critical for businesses that intend to export or tender for some government contracts. Firms that want to export need to keep in mind that many overseas markets demand quality assurance certification. Over 50 countries have adopted ISO quality assurance as national standards. Quality-assurance systems do not actually specify product or service quality. Their role is to ensure that you conform to the practices specified in your quality systems. Minimum documentation will include the quality policy, departmental procedures and responsibilities, work instructions and machine instructions, and a process for managing forms, records and other documents. Internal and external audits check that your business is operating according to its stated quality policies.

17 Employing staff

It is one thing to be self-employed, but it is quite another thing to be an employer. The employment environment generally makes employing staff a difficult proposition for many small business operators. Before you commit yourself to employing people, think carefully about the consequences. You will need to be prepared to devote a great deal of time, effort and money in order to cope with the government legislation that comes with being an employer. Moreover, the people in today's workforce may not share your ideals about quality, productivity or employer loyalty. The total cost of employing an individual is much greater than their pay packet, so you need to be hard-nosed in comparing the high cost of employing people compared with the value of their contribution.

But sooner or later you will probably find that you cannot be everywhere at once, nor will you be able to do everything yourself. If you want your business to grow and develop then you will need to employ staff. From this point on, the greatest asset in your business will be the people who work for you. Unless you can find, attract and develop people who will work in a productive and co-operative manner your business is unlikely to reach its potential. The purpose of this chapter is to introduce skills that you will find useful in employing staff.

Designing a job

Getting your staffing needs right begins with designing the jobs you want to fill. Designing a job consists of analysing the tasks you want to be done and then specifying the qualities you want to see in the people who will do them.

Task analysis

Task analysis is a method for setting out your requirements and helping you to sort out the necessary tasks from the unnecessary ones. Then you can group related tasks together to make up a job. Here are some questions to guide your analysis:

- What physical and mental tasks need to be accomplished? Examples are grinding and cleaning, and planning and directing.
- How is the task done? Describe the methods and equipment used. Examples include using a metal lathe to shape parts and writing out dockets and ringing them up on a cash register.
- Why is the task done? This explains the purpose and responsibilities of the task, which will also help relate it to other tasks. An example is writing up the daily sales sheet so the manager can balance the cashbook.
- What qualifications are needed for the task? These are the knowledge, skills and personal characteristics required for a person to be able to do the task well. Examples include knowledge of a foreign language, a licence to drive a truck, or being capable of lifting 40 kilograms.

Tasks tend to fall into related groups. Each group constitutes a job. The quantity of work to be done indicates how many positions you need to fill for each type of job.

Job description

A job description is a concise outline of the dimensions of a job based on the information obtained from the task analysis. Writing it down helps you to clarify your thinking about the work that needs to be done and the kind of person you need to do it. A job description usually includes the following items:

- Job title—keep in mind that titles can be important to some people.
- Work to be performed—provide a brief summary of its general nature.
- Major job duties—include responsibilities for quality and quantity of work, the supervision and safety of others, equipment to be used and schedules to be met.
- Minor job duties—these are duties performed only occasionally.
- Relationship of the job to other jobs—say if the person will supervise others and to whom they are responsible.

A job description serves more than one purpose. The obvious one is to outline the important functions of a job. When you evaluate applicants, you have a measure against which to match their attitudes, skills, education and experience. Job descriptions can also help you with other functions:

- Recruiting—a job description makes it easier for you to write advertisements or notices announcing a job opening.
- Interviewing—since a job description provides an outline of the duties and requirements for a job, it can be used as a guideline for conducting an interview.
- Training—a job description makes it easier for you to determine what knowledge and skills have to be taught, and it helps you to see that important skills are learned first and the training is comprehensive.
- Co-ordination—job descriptions help your staff know what is expected of them and how their activities are related.
- Wages—a job description gives you some perspective on the relative wage rates associated with the work performed and the qualifications needed.
- Employee relations—a record of the job description should mean fewer misunderstandings between you and your staff about the respective duties and responsibilities of various positions.

Describing the person

Job descriptions and personal qualifications are different. A job description sets forth duties, whereas personal qualifications are the sum of an individual's talents and experience. In trying to match the two, you need to translate the job description into qualifications for the job. Qualifications can be grouped into skills, education and experience.

Skills

What specific duties and functions must a prospective employee perform? What skills are needed? Should they know how to run special equipment? Will they need to know the techniques of retail selling? You need to carefully spell out the skills that the job needs and decide beforehand whether the applicant must have these skills before being employed or if you can teach them on the job. Remember that the tasks you give to an employee need to be within a reasonable range of their abilities.

Education

What level and type of education is necessary? Do they need to have specific training in book-keeping or typing, or do they need to be a qualified tradesperson in carpentry or plumbing? An untrained person in a position requiring specific knowledge is a liability to your business and a source of future expense when you have to replace them or compensate a customer for substandard work. Filling a job with an over-trained person, however, can also be a waste of talent and money, as well as a likely source of personal frustration to the employee.

Experience

Skills and education are important, but you may also need staff who have had practical experience at putting them to use. Just as a medical doctor must serve an internship and a bricklayer must serve an apprenticeship, you may need staff who have demonstrated that they are capable of doing the job without supervision. On the other hand, you may be prepared to accept an employee who can work under supervision while gaining necessary experience.

Hiring new staff

Hiring a new employee can be the beginning of a productive and mutually rewarding relationship. Getting the right person depends on how well you recruit, interview and select. However, there are also clear legal obligations governing the nature of the employer–employee agreement, the framework of the relationship, and the ways it may be terminated. These legal issues are covered by the *Employment Relations Act 2000* and the 2004 amendments.

Recruiting

When there are many people with the skills you need looking for work, recruiting is easy. When suitable staff are in short supply, you will need to find ways to attract applicants. Here are some pointers:

- If the position represents a promotion, ask your existing staff if any of them would like to apply.
- Ask your staff if they know someone who is qualified and might be interested.
- Contact former employees and ask if they are available for work again.
- Advertise in the newspaper. If you place a 'blind' advertisement, one in which the name of your firm is not given, be sure to tell your employees first to avoid possible embarrassment.
- Run spot ads on the local radio station.
- Post announcements on bulletin boards in places such as the local shopping centre.
- Advertise in the journal of your trade association.
- Lure staff away from your competitors.
- List your job with the Department of Work and Income.
- List your job with an employment agency.

Conducting the interview

The best method for choosing a new employee is a personal interview. In addition to facts, an interview can also tell you something about the applicant's personality and character. To evaluate these less-tangible qualities you need to be skilful, observant and objective. Plan for the interviews by having a checklist of questions to ask each applicant. Here are some suggestions on how to conduct an interview:

- Put the applicant at ease. Job applicants are usually tense and they will relax more quickly in an informal discussion.
- Provide the applicant with a copy of the job description and discuss it with them. Give the applicant plenty of opportunity to ask questions.
- Let the applicant do most of the talking while you guide the conversation with open questions such as 'Tell me a bit about yourself' or 'Tell me about your last employer'.
- Review the written application and probe the accuracy of the information contained in it. Pay particular attention to the reasons for leaving previous positions. Test the applicant's knowledge and skills required for the position.
- Determine whether the applicant has the personal characteristics required for the job. What are their aspirations and goals? Are they willing to accept the responsibilities of the job? Are they emotionally stable? Would they make a loyal employee? Do they demonstrate an ability to learn and to develop in your business?
- Ask the applicant how they feel about the position and note carefully any comments. Be sure that the financial rewards of the job are understood.
- Immediately schedule a second interview to hold a qualified candidate while you continue to interview the others.
- Write down your impressions of the applicant immediately after the interview.

People who feel that they have always worked for poor supervisors and unfair managers will probably find you to be the same. Those who tell you that they have enjoyed working with interesting people in their previous jobs are more likely to find them in your business, too. The interview is a good way to discover their attitudes towards supervision, workmates and the whole idea of co-operation.

Selecting the best applicant

References should be checked for those applicants who appear to be best qualified for the job. New Zealand's privacy legislation prevents you from collecting information without the applicant's knowledge, so ask them to provide a list of people you can contact. Using the telephone has several advantages. It is quicker than using a letter and it sometimes turns up facts that were not presented at the interview. Ask specific questions rather than general ones. This is an instance when a few minutes of caution can save you a lot of grief. The information you get should be considered with judgement. Always evaluate the person from whom it comes and do not blindly accept either severe criticism or bountiful praise.

Review your interview notes in conjunction with the information you have obtained from the applicant's references. If a clear preference does not emerge, try to narrow the field to two or three and then ask them to come in for a second interview. Accept the fact that, in the final analysis, the selection process is a judgement about human nature. There are times when you may make a mistake and you will be faced with repairing the damage. Nevertheless, with a bit of experience, you will learn to recognise those applicants who represent the best fit with the needs of your business.

Wages

Your staff expect their pay to reflect the skills and energy they put into your business. If you want to attract and keep good staff, match the rates paid and the fringe benefits offered for comparable work by other firms like yours. The dividing line between 'compensation' and 'fringe benefit' is blurred. Yesterday's benefit has become today's compensation. Whatever the name, the expense is part of the total cost of hiring and keeping good staff.

Wages should reflect an employee's contribution to your firm, and they should be consistent within the firm. Job classifications enable you to establish a normal wage for each job and a regular scale for merit increases, and increases based on length of service. Don't forget about the various government regulations when you set your wage rates. For more information about employment legislation refer to Chapter 4.

Training

Give some thought to how you will bring new staff on board. On their first day show them around your business, introduce them to the rest of the staff, give them an overall view of the entire operation, and explain exactly how their job fits into the total picture. These small gestures require little effort and they can save you time and money in the long run.

Even when you do a good job choosing a new employee, you need to back it up with training. Every new employee, even those with previous experience, needs training in your particular ways of doing things. Decide who is to do the training—yourself or one of your staff. Doing it yourself, if time permits, will give you an opportunity to get better acquainted. The following steps will help you to get them started.

Step 1: Prepare new staff

Purpose:
- Relieve tension.
- Establish a training base.
- Arouse interest.
- Give them confidence.

Method:
- Put them at ease.
- Find out what they already know about the task.
- Explain the relationship of the task to the business.
- Tie the task to their previous experience.
- Ensure that they are in a comfortable position to see you perform the task clearly.

Step 2: Present the task

Purpose:
- Be sure they understand what to do and why.
- Ensure retention.
- Avoid giving too much information too soon—more than they can grasp.

Method:
- Tell, show, illustrate and question the newest staff member patiently.
- Stress key points.
- Instruct clearly and completely, one step at a time.
- Keep your words to a minimum and stress action words.

Step 3: Let them try the task

Purpose:
- Be sure they have learned the correct methods.
- Prevent bad habits from forming.
- Be sure they know what they are doing and why.
- Test their knowledge.
- Avoid putting them on the job prematurely.

Method:
- Have them perform the task but do not ask them to explain what they are doing the first time through. If they make a mistake, assume the blame yourself and go back to Step 2.
- Once they have performed the task correctly, have them do it again. This time ask them to explain the steps and the key points.
- Continue until you know that they know.

Step 4: Follow up

Purpose:
- Give them confidence.
- Be sure they do not take chances and that they know they have not been left alone.
- Be sure they stay on the right track.
- Show your trust in them.

Method:
- Give them a little praise.
- Encourage questions and tell them where they can get help.

- Check frequently at first.
- Gradually reduce the amount of checking and put them on their own.

Formal apprenticeship training is run by some industry training organisations. However, apprenticeship training can also be informal. For instance, some firms hire people on the understanding that they will first familiarise them with the support operations of the business. Another method of training that is particularly appropriate for a small business is job rotation. Staff are moved about for training in jobs requiring greater skill or responsibility. When they are trained in various jobs you stand to gain in at least three ways. You have a more flexible workforce. You can more easily fill openings if experienced staff leave. You are able to demonstrate to your staff that they are being prepared to move ahead to better positions.

Building motivation and loyalty

Luckily, a small business has some built-in advantages for developing employee motivation and loyalty. Perhaps the most important is the close relationship between you and your staff. Working together facilitates communication, which is the key to teamwork. Your deeds and your attitudes are also important and only a continuous working relationship can properly reflect them. There are key motivating factors that engender a deep commitment to job performance, including:

- The work itself—to what extent is the work meaningful and worthwhile?
- Achievement—is there an opportunity to undertake tasks that are a reasonable challenge?
- Responsibility—is there the authority and trustworthiness to carry out a significant function?
- Recognition—do your staff know how highly their contribution to the business is valued?
- Advancement—is there genuine opportunity for promotion?

Managing people on the job means fulfilling their personal needs so they are motivated towards fulfilling your objectives. They will feel that their work is satisfying if they enjoy it and regard it as purposeful and worthwhile. A sensible approach aimed at recognising how job satisfaction contributes towards fulfilling basic individual needs is the key to building employee motivation and loyalty. It will lead to higher morale, greater output, lower turnover, and better use of each employee's ability. These practical suggestions may give you some ideas:

- Establish confidence and trust with your staff through open communication and demonstrated sensitivity to their needs.

- Allow and encourage staff participation in the decision-making that directly affects them.
- As much as you can, permit your staff to set their own work methods and work goals.
- Express appreciation publicly for jobs well done—offer criticism privately in the form of constructive suggestions for improvement.
- Look for ways to restructure jobs so that they are more challenging and interesting.
- Give increased responsibility, independence and authority to those who can handle it.
- Be firm, but be fair.

Despite your best efforts to motivate staff, your expectations may not always be met. Try to find out why. Identify the problem to see if there is something you can do about it. For some problems, the solution will lie in changes to the working environment or the work procedures. For other problems, the solution will lie in your approach to human behaviour. Here are some examples.

- Fatigue and illness—people lose motivation when they exceed their physical capacity. It could be a result of working overtime, inadequate rest, work beyond their ability, or attempting to work when they are sick or not fully recovered from an illness or injury.
- Inadequate skill or training—when a person is doing a job for which they have inadequate skills or training they are likely to lose confidence and become dispirited.
- Routine tasks create boredom, especially when there is little or infrequent action required of the operator. Boredom can also occur in simple repetitive tasks, particularly where the job is paced by a machine.
- Inadequate working conditions slow down productivity and impede quality performance.
- It has often been said that a good worker never blames their tools. Nevertheless, if the necessary tools are inadequate or unavailable, productivity and quality are going to suffer.
- People can only act on information to the best of their understanding. Errors occur if they are given the wrong information or if they misunderstand the information because it was unclear.
- When staff are rewarded for the quantity rather than the quality of their work, carelessness tends to creep into their performance. Careless errors can also result from 'don't care' or 'she'll be right' attitudes on the part of staff who are not interested in their work.
- Occasionally an employee may make a deliberate error in anger or as a means of revenge. If the problem cannot be resolved, and it can be shown conclusively that the

error was not accidental, then the employee should be dismissed before any further damage is done. There are specific procedures for dismissal under the *Employment Relations Act 2000* and the *Employment Relations Amendment Act 2004*. These need to be followed carefully. Your solicitor will be able to advise you.

Evaluating your staff

Staff development is a continuing process and you need to stand back occasionally to see what you have accomplished and what remains to be done. An evaluation checklist is a helpful tool for assessing how well your staff are doing the work outlined in their job descriptions. It is especially useful when you want to reward improvement and it is a good device for keeping your evaluations objective. An evaluation checklist is designed to help you recognise an individual's strengths, show you where more training and counselling may be needed, point out promotional possibilities or justify a pay increase. A good evaluation process also allows the employee to give you feedback on how they feel about their job.

In the following checklist the factors have been kept to a minimum and the phrases describing the levels of achievement have been chosen to apply to most types of jobs. Disregard your general impressions and concentrate on one factor at a time. Read all four specifications for each factor before deciding which one best fits your employee. Make judgements on events that occur frequently and not by isolated instances that are not typical of their work.

Factor 1: Quality of work

Poor   Often does unacceptable work, is careless, requires constant supervision
Fair   Needs supervision and frequent checking
Good   Makes only occasional mistakes, requires little supervision
Excellent   Rarely makes mistakes, needs no supervision.

Factor 2: Efficiency of work

Slow   Almost never finishes a job in the time required
Erratic   Sometimes quick and efficient, other times slow and inefficient
Steady   Works consistently and occasionally exceeds expectations
Exceptional   Works quickly and does extra work to stay busy.

Factor 3: Flexibility

Poor   Does not adapt readily to new situations, instructions need to be repeated frequently
Adequate   Requires thorough, complete instructions before taking up a new function

Quick	Learns new assignments quickly with some instruction
Adaptable	Self-starter, independently meets the needs of a new situation.

Factor 4: Job knowledge

Poor	Limited job knowledge, shows little desire to improve
Passable	Functional, but needs frequent instruction and continuing supervision
Adequate	Needs occasional instruction or assistance
Superior	Able to proceed alone on almost all work.

Factor 5: Responsibility

Irresponsible	Seldom carries out duties without being prodded
Variable	Occasionally needs reminders to do work assigned
Good	Reliable most of the time
Excellent	Can always be depended upon.

Factor 6: Housekeeping and safety

Poor	Never cleans working area, is reckless in behaviour
Inconsistent	Cleans work area occasionally, is sometimes forgetful about safety
Good	Keeps work area clean and is generally careful about safety
Excellent	Keeps work area spotless and is always careful about safety.

Factor 7: Attitude

Unhelpful	Often complains and is disruptive
Indifferent	Does not seem to care about the job or workmates
Good	Attentive to the job and gets along with other staff
Exceptional	Very interested in the job, always attentive, helpful and considerate.

Staff turnover

All businesses lose staff and have to replace them. Some quit, some are dismissed, others may become ill, start a family, or retire. For whatever reason, they leave your employment and you will need to replace them. Meanwhile you have a job that is not filled that you must cover by working overtime and generally limping along. The vacancy may last for only a few days or it can stretch out into weeks and even months. Finally, when you do get that new employee, they are likely to be untrained for your particular job, or at least your way of doing it. Losing one employee may not seem too serious, but losing three or four at once can be disastrous. Sometimes the causes of staff turnover are not immediately apparent: it can take some digging to put your finger on the problem. The causes of staff turnover usually fall into one of the following categories:

- Poor placement—different jobs call for different aptitudes and skills. Misplaced people can cause problems for themselves and you. In jobs for which they are unsuited, staff may eventually quit or have to be let go.
- Poor orientation—a good orientation program seeks to make new employees feel at home and to tell them what they want to know about your business. If the orientation is mishandled, either by neglect or by doing it poorly, it may eventually result in turnover.
- Low wages—do your wage rates compare well with other firms in your community? If not, expect dissatisfaction and turnover. Can your staff move up to a better job? If ot, they will think of their job as a dead end.
- Some firms fail to maintain a good working environment. Employee dissatisfaction with their surroundings can result in turnover.
- Poor supervision is a major cause of poor work quality and staff quitting. It is not always easy to find the soft spots and correct them, but look for unfairness, favouritism and erratic discipline.
- Lack of training—people need some training on any new job. Even if they have done the work before, your ways are probably a little different. If they have not done the work before, then training is imperative. If they move on, it could be because the training they received was unsatisfactory.

Dismissal

While the emphasis is generally on minimising employee turnover, there may be occasions when you will be compelled to dismiss an individual. No one likes it, but sometimes you have no alternative for the good of others and for the good of your business. When you suspect that you may be forced to dismiss an employee, check with your solicitor to ensure that you comply with the procedures and conditions for dismissal prescribed by legislation. The Department of Labour lists the following general principles in relation to dismissals.

- Any relevant provisions in the employment agreement must be followed.
- If an employment agreement does not have a notice period, then reasonable notice must be given. What is reasonable depends on the circumstances.
- Employees have the right to be told what the problem is and that dismissal or other disciplinary action is a possibility. Employees must then be given a genuine opportunity to tell their side of the story before the employer decides what to do.
- The employer should investigate any allegations of misconduct thoroughly and without prejudice.
- Unless there has been misconduct so serious that it warrants instant dismissal, the employee should be given clear standards to aim for and a genuine opportunity to

improve. The sort of conduct that warrants instant dismissal may be set out in the employment agreement.

- The employer should treat all employees in the same circumstances in the same way, or be prepared to justify the difference.

First, try to salvage the situation. Ask the employee to discuss your dissatisfaction. Review the cause of the problem as you see it and let the employee tell you the cause of the problem as they see it. Ask if there is a way you can help them to do a better job. Be helpful but firm. Give yourselves a reasonable length of time to work for improvement. Be sure that the employee knows this is a formal warning and that failure to resolve the problem will result in dismissal. It is generally appropriate to give two warnings but in some circumstances a third and final warning may be used. If your warnings and attempts at counselling have no effect, and you must dismiss the employee, then get on with it. Perhaps the following suggestions will make your task a little easier:

- Choose the right time and place. Privacy and freedom from interruption are important. Plan to spend enough time so that the individual has plenty of opportunity to express their feelings and opinions.
- Discuss the problem only. Never comment on an individual's personality or character unless it is directly related to the problem.
- Make the meeting final. Be firm, calm and reasonable.
- Permit the individual to let off steam. Their reaction may not be logical, but don't argue with them.
- Have a face-saving approach in mind such as offering to let them resign. Do not humiliate them in front of their workmates.
- When it is all over, ask yourself how you might improve your methods for recruiting, selection, training and team-building in order to avoid this problem in the future.

Under the Employment Relations Act the employee has the right, for up to 60 days after the dismissal, to receive a written statement of the reasons for dismissal. The dismissal process that you use may be the basis of a personal grievance case for unjustifiable dismissal. It is therefore good practice to put all warnings in writing and to document all meetings and actions leading up to the dismissal so that the Employment Court can see that you have followed the correct procedures.

18 Information systems for small business

Small business operators who ignore computer technology are making a big mistake because it has become an indispensable tool. The purpose of this chapter is to outline the nature of small business information systems, the benefits they offer, and how you can make your own judgement about using computers in your business.

Computer equipment

Most small business applications run on IBM-compatible personal computers (PCs). There are many brands to choose from and performance factors are critical in choosing the right computer for your needs. In today's internet-connected world your computer system can be accessible to unwelcome visitors and viruses. When planning your investment in hardware—the many physical components that make up your computer network—and software—the applications and programs that make up your operating system—you also need to consider the best protection for your system in terms of firewall, antivirus, and anti-spyware software. Protective software is part of good risk management for your business.

Hardware

The power of the computer is its ability to process information in a fraction of a second with absolute accuracy. This function is done by the *processor*. The new generation of processors are smaller, cheaper and more powerful than ever. Rather than getting bogged down in technical specifications, let's look at the factors you can evaluate without much technical background:

- The speed of a processor is measured in gigahertz (GHz).
- The capacity of the processor's working memory (also called *RAM*) is measured in *bytes* and this is a critical factor when you are choosing software packages. RAM is rated in multiples of one million bytes called *megabytes*.

You need to be certain that you have more than enough working memory to run your operating system and several application programs simultaneously. If you are going to be a serious computer user, don't settle for less than a 2GHz processor with 1 gigabyte of RAM and 160 gigabytes of hard disk storage.

Printers

There are different levels of printing capability and your choice will be largely determined by the following considerations:

Speed	Noise
Workload	Waste
Print quality	Cost
Graphics.	

Inkjet printers

An *inkjet* printer literally sprays the image onto the paper. It is ideal for a home office or a small business that does not do a large amount of printing. Its chief advantage is that it is quiet and produces reasonably good-quality output. It prints about three to four pages per minute and is capable of accommodating different types and sizes of fonts, graphics and colours.

Laser printers

A *laser* printer produces the best-quality output and performs best for flexibility, speed and quiet operation. To select a laser printer that matches your needs, you need to make choices about print resolution, speed, and printer memory.

Colour laser printers are expensive but worthwhile if you plan to do a large volume of high-quality colour printing. If you need occasional colour printing it may be more cost-effective to buy a black and white laser printer and a colour inkjet printer. Laser printers are also found in multi-function devices in which a printer can be combined with a photocopier, a scanner and a fax in the one machine. A telephone and answering machine can also be included.

Modems

A modem is a device that translates signals between the digital format used in computers and the analogue format used to transmit sound in the telephone system. You will need a modem if you want to link up remote locations in your business or if you want to access online computer services, send faxes or email from your computer or use the internet. Modems are designed to operate at different speeds called bits per second (bps). For modern internet use you will need at least a 2mbps unit to do the job. However, other types of modem connections are available with higher speeds and capacity. The commonly used connection methods are:

- A 56kbps dial-up connection will provide the slowest connectivity.
- A broadband connection will provide high-speed connectivity.
- A cable modem connection will provide medium–high speed 'always available' connectivity.
- A wi-fi or wireless connection will provide convenience in connecting laptops and printers to the system.

Portable computers

Laptop computers and notebook computers have become increasingly popular because you can take them wherever you go. However, portability also costs more. Some small business operators use a portable computer at work in conjunction with a *docking station* so that it doubles as a desktop computer. After work they pull the portable out of the docking station and take it home. Two important considerations with a portable computer are battery life and the built-in screen.

Battery life is a problem for portable computers. Depending on the type of battery used and the applications you are running, run time ranges from three hours up to six hours. Battery life is limited by current battery technology, so most portables employ sophisticated power management systems. Since portables can be plugged into a power supply, this is only important if you must use the battery.

The built-in screens that come with portable computers produce a similar quality image to a desktop monitor. Screens on portable computers have also become larger, which is a welcome relief. If you are going to spend many hours peering into a screen, however, you can always attach an external desktop screen to your portable for better quality and comfort.

Mobile work tools provide workers with access to enhanced productivity. The ability to effectively conduct business from anywhere, at any time and with anyone has become critical. Hi-tech portable technologies (smartphones and tablets) are becoming the information tools of choice for business. While tablets have less capacity and functionality in comparison to portable laptops, their lightness and convenience make them attractive for carrying your information system with you.

Smartphones are showing an even more dramatic pattern of usage in business. Although the small size of the screens and keypads are a constraint, 79 per cent of American users cite the smartphone as the phone they used the most to conduct business, as compared to an office phone or home phone (Ring Central survey 2010, found at www.ringcentral.com). Smartphones are encroaching on computers as well, with 34 per cent of respondents using the smartphone more than the computer for business. According to the survey, the smartphone has become the focal point of communications for business professionals.

Software

Computer software consists of programs that give instructions to the computer equipment so that it will perform its functions. Computer software is divided into *application* software and *operating system* software.

Application software

Application software is the key to getting the most out of a computer system. Word processing, stock control programs and payroll programs are examples of application software. The successful operation of your computer system, and in some cases the successful operation of your business, is directly related to the quality and suitability of the application software you choose.

Standard software packages for the applications common to most small businesses have been the key to the success of small business computer systems. They are available for a variety of applications such as accounting, sales and manufacturing, and some are designed for particular types of businesses, such as contractors, dentists, newsagents or travel agents. Prices range from a few hundred dollars for a single application up to a few thousand dollars for a fully integrated business-management system designed for your particular type of business. Quality packaged application software is reliable and well documented because it has been proven in thousands of other businesses.

Operating system software

Operating system software works like an orchestra conductor. It monitors, co-ordinates and controls the various components of the computer system to ensure that each is doing its part properly. Operating system software is supplied by the computer manufacturer along with the computer equipment. It is essential that the computer equipment you buy has an operating system that drives the application software you want to run.

For small business computer systems running on IBM-compatible PCs, the latest operating system is *Microsoft Windows 7 Professional* with *Internet Explorer 9.0* as the web browser. If you have multiple computer work stations you might invest in an internal server such as *Windows Small Business Server 2011*.

Microsoft Windows operating systems incorporate a graphical user interface that allows you to 'point and click' without the need to learn operating system commands. They also provide a standard format for accessing different applications such as a word processor, spreadsheet and database. This feature makes it easy for you to move from one application to another. The vast majority of small business application software has been written for the Microsoft Windows operating system.

Small business applications

The only justification for installing a small business computer system is to maximise your profits. A computer system can help you to increase your sales, reduce your costs, improve your operational efficiency and obtain more accurate and timely information for planning and control. Some of the ways in which computers are used to achieve these objectives include high-volume applications, control applications, problem-solving applications, word processing, spreadsheets, databases and electronic data interchange.

High-volume applications

The applications that are usually installed first are those involving the greatest volume of score-keeping information. The need for these applications tends to be critical because the burden of paperwork is high. They can be implemented quickly and they pay back the initial investment in a relatively short time. Here are some examples of high-volume applications.

Order processing	Sales commission accounting
Accounts receivable	Inventory accounting
Accounts payable	General ledger accounting
Payroll	Mailing lists.

It is a good idea to keep financial records in a computerised format that is compatible with the system your accountant uses. This enables your accountant to easily access your information in order to prepare financial reports and it eliminates the costly and time-consuming process of having to re-enter information. Also see page 310 on cloud computing.

Control applications

Control applications help you to manage the operating areas in your business. Their purpose is to direct your attention to ways of achieving greater efficiency and productivity by making important information readily available. Here are some examples of the tasks control applications can be set up for:

Inventory control	Barcoding
Back-order control	Materials cost control
Credit control	Labour cost control
Production control	Cash flow budgeting.

Problem-solving applications

Problem-solving applications are designed to help you make planning decisions. They usually require information from a number of other applications. For example, a comprehensive purchasing application needs order information, on-hand inventory information and vendor information. Problem-solving applications do not offer the quick payback of the high-volume applications but their long-term impact is more significant. Sometimes it is difficult to locate suitable problem-solving software, but you can often develop your own models using a standard spreadsheet package. Here are some examples of the tasks problem-solving applications can be set up for:

Sales forecasting	Materials planning
Marketing research	Machine scheduling
Purchases planning	Shift scheduling
Financial planning	Strategic planning.

Word processing

A word processor creates and stores documents such as letters, reports, catalogues, mailing labels and operating manuals. Its many features include a spellchecker, thesaurus, grammar checker, mail merge and graphics. If your business requires written documents that are constantly revised (such as contracts, price lists, quotes or proposals) then word processing can mean tremendous efficiencies in the time it takes to produce the final documents. You can also use word processing to generate customised mailings and process your day-to-day correspondence.

Spreadsheets

A spreadsheet is like a big sheet of paper divided into rows and columns. It does calculations for budgets, business plans, cash flow analysis, statistical analysis and 'what-if' analysis. It consists of a matrix of cells in which you can store text, numbers or instructions. A spreadsheet enables you to 'model' a problem by manipulating the cells. Spreadsheets are versatile, easy to use and include a number of inbuilt special functions.

Databases

A database stores information about customers, suppliers, or inventory, and database software organises, sorts and updates the information for use in reports, catalogues, invoices, statements or form letters. Using a modem, it is also possible to access and search databases on other computers.

Management information system

A management information system is built on business information held in databases. The databases could be on printed paper but it is much more practical and powerful to use electronic computer files stored in databases. The databases might be developed especially for your business using a common database product such as Microsoft Access, or they could be standard application software packages such as a small business accounting package. Figure 18.1 is a framework for a management information system using computer databases and report-writer software.

Figure 18.1: Management information system

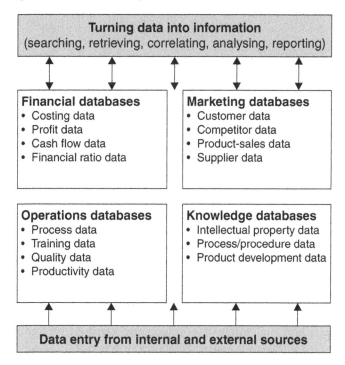

The internet

Most small business operators in New Zealand are connected to the internet. The majority of small businesses use the internet to explore for information and to send email messages. However, the real potential of the internet is its use as a marketing tool and as a method of automating transactions between suppliers and customers.

The internet is an enormous network of computers around the world. Literally millions of computers are linked together using the international telephone system. Host computers are permanently connected to the internet while most users only log on for a visit. Any computer in the system can communicate with any other computer quickly and inexpensively. Now, the internet is used for communications, recreation, research, education and business.

To connect to the internet you need an account with an *internet service provider* (ISP). You can find ISPs in the Yellow Pages and in specialist internet magazines, such as the *New Zealand NetGuide*. An ISP will sell you access to a host computer. You simply dial the ISP's local telephone number and connect your computer via a modem. Some of the software you need to use on the internet comes with your computer, your ISP may provide you with more, and anything else you need can be downloaded once you are connected. Most ISPs base their charges on a joining fee and the amount of time that you are connected. However, not all ISPs provide the same quality of service, so it pays to do your homework and to shop around.

The World Wide Web

The most popular small business application on the internet is exploring for information using a system called the *world wide web* or simply the web. It is a system for displaying information containing text, illustrations, sound or animation. To get on to the web you need a *web browser* program. Most web users access the internet with some version of Mozilla Firefox or Microsoft's Internet Explorer. Each website has a unique address (URL) that you type into the browser to gain access to the site. Every URL begins with the letters http://www, which tells the browser to use *hypertext transfer protocol* (http) and to search the world wide web (www). Because every URL begins with the same group of 10 characters, website addresses are now commonly written without http://www.

The best way to find sites that contain information on a specific topic is to use a *search engine* which is a continually updated index of the content on the web. You type in the key words you are looking for and click on the *search* button. The search engine will tell you how many matches it found and display addresses of the first 10 or 20. If you see a site that interests you, you can click on its hypertext address and jump to it. To access a search engine you simply type its internet address into your browser. Some are better than others for particular purposes. Here are a number of search engine addresses:

Google	www.google.co.nz
Yahoo!	www.yahoo.com
MSN/Bing	www.nz.bing.com
Search NZ	www.searchnz.co.nz

As you surf the web you will find sites to which you will want to return. You can use the *bookmarks* or *favourites* option in your browser to save these addresses so that you can find them again quickly. To get you started, here are a few internet addresses that contain useful information on small business topics.

Small business management	www.business.govt.nz
Franchise New Zealand magazine	www.franchise.co.nz
Export advice	www.exportnz.org.nz
Entrepreneur magazine	www.entrepreneur.com
Government funding	www.msi.govt.nz

Electronic commerce

Electronic commerce—also known as e-commerce—enables buyers and sellers to transact business in real time using the internet. This revolution in business may involve process redesign and the implementation of new working methods depending on the nature of the business and the extent of connectivity and system integration between participants. Here are some examples.

Customer relationship management (CRM)

CRM software objectives are to enable market segmentation down to multiple and flexible individual offers. Business-to-customer connectivity allows real-time matching of customer information to company resources and company knowledge. This in turn enables a business to select and target opportunities to grow their business through retention and development of revenue by connecting with profit-generating customers.

Supply chain relationships

Business-to-business connectivity enables shared stock files, direct order-entry and order tracking, direct account enquiries, electronic invoicing and electronic funds transfer.

Knowledge management

Document management software enable a firm's entire documented production information and knowledge to be collected, coded and classified, and made instantly available to any staff member with authorised access.

Manufacturing processes

Flexible manufacturing systems, equipment and technology can be integrated with other databases to create links between order entry, production planning and scheduling.

Stock management and forecasting

Barcoding systems that record stock movements in and out of production and distribution areas, and shared stock files between suppliers and distributors, enable accurate information on stock levels and stock movements throughout the whole distribution chain.

Distribution channels

Business-to-customer transactions on the internet can make the role of traditional agents and distributors redundant. Interactive web pages operating on secure servers enable customers to shop and pay for anything, anywhere, at any time. Systems that integrate all of your applications into one system are called Enterprise Resource Planning (ERP) systems. An ERP system can include software for manufacturing, order entry, accounting, purchasing, warehousing, customer-relationship management and human resources. The internet has enabled ERP systems to extend out of your company and along the supply chain, to connect with suppliers; for example, for inventory planning or to improve customer service by allowing customers to track the progress of their orders.

Cloud computing

Cloud computing describes the outsourcing of computer applications and server capacity to external providers via the internet. The benefits of cloud computing are well suited to small business because they give small business access to increased software functionality at a lower cost. In particular cloud computing offers:

*   Ease and speed of set-up
*   Little or no start-up costs
*   Reduced need to invest capital in hardware or software
*   Charge by usage—you only pay for what you need and use
*   Two-way scalability—as your business grows or shrinks, needing more or less computing power and capacity, you can increase or reduce your usage at any time
*   Real-time access to updated and upgraded software and hardware.

Getting started

To get started many businesses will begin by using just a few software applications from a cloud provider. However because scalability is one of the main advantages, the selection of a cloud provider should be based on their ability to provide more extensive services in the future. The range of services that are available on the cloud fit into three main types:

- *Software as a service*—there are various types of business software packages, including CRM packages such as Salesforce.com, accounting packages at xero.com and quickbooks.intuit.com, and email, calendar and office tool sets as offered by Google Apps at google.com/apps.
- *Infrastructure as a service*—there are web services that offer server and data storage systems for flexible, private computer networks, including Amazon's Elastic Compute Cloud (Amazon EC2) and Simple Storage Service (Amazon S3) at http://aws.amazon.com and Dropbox at www.dropbox.com.
- *Platforms as a service*—there are computer and mobile operating systems hosted by an outsourced service provider, including Force at force.com and Windows Azure platform at www.microsoft.com/windowsazure.

Risks

The cloud news is not all positive. There are risks involved if you move your computing system to the cloud. Top of the list are issues to do with privacy and security of your information that is held in a cloud-based system. Cloud supporters counter this by pointing out that the risks are no greater than with an in-house system—hackers can break through security walls, staff can steal intellectual property and sensitive information, and hard drives can fail causing loss of data. Other risks relate to the reliability and usability of the cloud provider's system:

- Will it always be available and working when you need it?
- Can you export data in standard formats and share it between other cloud services?
- Can you get all your data back if you decide to leave?

General advice

The general advice on moving to cloud computing is straightforward:

- Start small but seek scalability.
- Ensure you can export data in standard formats.
- Evaluate providers carefully and look for user recommendations.
- Experiment with innovations in business-model and business-process design to capture the full promise of the cloud.

Protecting your information

Regardless of whether your system is in-house or outsourced, protecting your business information is critically important. A hard drive crash, infection by a virus, a fire or a natural disaster could result in the total loss of all of your business records and your marketing and operational knowledge. If you don't continuously back-up your business information, a crisis could put you out of business. Back-up files should be regularly maintained so you can restore critical business information on your computers if disaster strikes.

The first step in designing a back-up system is to identify the data that needs to be saved. Software programs such as word processing or spreadsheet programs can be re-installed from their original disks. What you need to back up are all the data files that you have created within the programs including:

- Databases, such as customer data, supplier data and stock records
- Financial data files, such as accounts receivable, accounts payable and general ledger data files
- Documents, such as procedures manuals, quality records, staff records and any important correspondence
- Email, especially messages that relate to contractual obligations, sales orders, employment and any legal issues
- Any other data that would create a significant problem if it were lost.

The key is to identify the data in your system that is critical to the operation of your business and to have that data regularly saved into a separate back-up system. The back-up system should hold the data in a remote location away from the main business site as a further precaution against losses from fire or natural disaster. Your data is only as secure as your last back-up so it is important to stick to a regular schedule such as daily, weekly, or as determined by particular events or stages in your business operations.

Modern integrated information systems create opportunities for small businesses to compete in new ways. Collaborative industry alliances and innovative process design working with advanced information systems can enable your business to be both small and large at the same time and have immediate access to global markets. In this new e-commerce trading world, systems assets will be more valuable than tangible assets and connectivity more important than cash flow. For further information on business solutions software and ERP systems refer to iStart Ltd at www.istart.co.nz, an information technology and communications (ITC) research hub for technology in business. For more specific information and comments on cloud computing go to www.pcworld.com/businesscenter and search on 'cloud computing', and www.smallbiztrends.com.

19 Troubleshooting and recovery

Small businesses have a high failure rate in New Zealand, with only 60 per cent surviving the first three years. The overwhelming cause of failure is lack of management skills. Researchers have identified the important management skills that are essential for success and grouped them into financial skills, marketing skills and operations skills:

- Key financial skills include managing your cash flow in order to maintain liquidity and managing your operating and financing decisions in order to maximise profitability. Financial management skills are described in Part B.
- Key marketing skills include finding a market opportunity, understanding your customers and creating a competitive advantage by the way in which you design your marketing mix. Marketing management skills are described in Part C.
- Key operations skills vary tremendously depending upon the type of business you have decided to enter. However, this usually means developing explicit operating goals and strategies to achieve them. Operations management skills are described in Part D.

Despite your best efforts, you may nevertheless find yourself in difficulty. Perhaps there was an inherent weakness in the start-up plan, perhaps you lacked important management skills or perhaps you did not anticipate the effects of rapid growth. The purpose of this chapter is to identify the factors that can lead to problems in order to help you avoid them in the first place. We provide recommendations for early-stage troubleshooting and correction. The chapter closes with short-term 'life saving' steps for a firm that finds itself in serious danger of failure.

Troubleshooting

A firm that is running into trouble shows signs of distress. Typically, the owner does not control events but is controlled by them and spends most of the time 'putting out fires'. There is usually little management information available. The time to correct problems is early, before they become a serious threat to your business. Don't miss the warning signs.

Warning signs

Case studies of business failure show that, in general, there are three stages of decline and each stage has a different set of warning signs. Make sure you know what to look for.

Early warning signs

Include production inefficiencies, slow deliveries and rising stock levels relative to sales. Operating profit margins are eroded, payments to creditors go a little beyond normal, and cash balances are dropping.

Intermediate-stage warning signs

Production problems becoming more acute. There are material shortages and quality problems. Gross margins begin to fall and working capital is limited. Suppliers are demanding payment before extending further credit and some are demanding COD payment terms. Cash balances are low and meeting staff wages becomes a weekly challenge. The bank is showing concern. Employee morale is dropping and some staff leave the firm.

Final-stage warning signs

Only prioritised orders are shipped, production is in chaos, and there are many quality problems. The business suffers chronic material shortages, and payments from customers are slow due to dissatisfaction with the product and service. Supply terms are COD with all vendors, or even COD plus part of the past debt. Covering the overdraft becomes the major focus and very little management time is spent in other areas. The bank is discussing recovery action and most of the staff are looking for a new job. Collapse is imminent.

Causes of business failure

The reasons why things have gone wrong can be inside the business—called internal causes—or outside the business—called external causes.

Business studies have identified the primary *internal causes* as:

- Lack of planning and lack of forecast budgets
- Allowing excessive credit to customers
- Allowing stocks to build up to excessive levels
- Expanding sales too rapidly in relation to the working capital available
- Fluctuations in cash flow due to seasonal factors or trade cycles
- Investing too much equity capital in fixed assets and not enough in working capital
- Taking excess credit from suppliers and coming under pressure to pay
- Failing to meet market expectations
- Lack of management information and poor financial reporting
- Lack of productivity in the operational systems.

Most of the internal causes you can act to change. On the other hand, *external causes* are generally beyond your control. You need to monitor them and take defensive action if any develop into a threat to your business. Things to look out for include:

- Changes in industry conditions—e-commerce and the internet will dramatically change the supply-chain structure of some industries and may even wipe out the need for some agents and retailers.
- General economic conditions—if the economy drops your sales will probably drop, too.
- Regulatory conditions—new laws can create greater costs and less flexibility to operate.
- Foreign competition—new strong entrants can suddenly dominate your market, especially through the internet.
- Technology risks—in the past 50 years there have been many products and services which have become redundant in the face of new technologies.
- Shifting consumer preferences—it's important to stay close to your customers and anticipate changes in their wants and needs.

Indicators of poor health

When you are a one-person business, first-hand knowledge of your profitability and cash flow is easy. As your business grows, however, the signals get blurred by delays between cause and effect and the complexity of managing a wider range of activities, people and events. Management reporting becomes important and you need to ensure that you pay attention to the following indicators of impending poor health:

- Increasing debt to equity ratio—a high debt to equity ratio (low ownership ratio) indicates the business is becoming more highly leveraged. If this constitutes too much borrowing, it is a sign of poor health.
- Low current ratio—a low current ratio means you may not be able to pay your bills as they become due. Some current assets, such as stock, are not always easy to convert into cash so the liquid ratio may be used instead.
- Increased ageing of debtors—an increase in the average number of days of outstanding debtors either indicates poor cash collections or the deteriorating credit worthiness of your customers.
- Increased ageing of creditors—an increase in the average number of days of outstanding creditors is usually associated with a low current ratio and poor cash flow resulting in slow payments.
- Paying for long-term assets with short-term finance—this practice suggests either reckless financial management or an inability to obtain long-term finance. If a firm is unable to regularly refinance its short-term credit, both working capital and the long-term assets are at high risk.
- Slowing stock turns—apart from the fact that rising stocks consume cash, this situation may suggest a more serious underlying problem. Increasing stocks may indicate obsolescence, lack of production planning, lack of stock-control systems, congested manufacturing, returns of poor-quality stock, lack of sales analysis or slow production cycles.
- Declining gross margin—in a manufacturing business it indicates inefficiencies in production or incorrect costing and pricing practices. In a retailing firm it indicates errors in pricing or loss of stock. Gross margin is the profit engine of a business.
- Declining net profits—a declining gross margin will certainly result in declining net profit but it is also possible to have a stable gross margin while profits decline. In this case it is usually increases in administration, selling, or interest costs that is causing a fall in profitability.
- Declining sales—internal causes include poor alignment of the product to the market, lack of product innovation, prices that are too high, poor quality, poor customer service and slow deliveries. External causes include increased competition and a drop in overall demand in the economy.
- Declining unit prices—dollar sales can be maintained artificially by discounted prices, but margins will be eroded and declining profitability will set in.

Potential for a turnaround

If you find yourself heading for trouble, there are a number of things you can look at to bring your business back on track. Pay particular attention to your profit and loss account, balance sheet, cash flow, marketing strategy, production planning and how you manage staff.

Profit and loss account

There are a number of key questions to ask.

Can you reverse a declining sales trend?

Get closer to your customers and re-evaluate the marketing strategy. Can you change the product mix, the product design, the location, or your selling and promotion methods and skills?

Can you improve a poor gross profit margin?

Can you eliminate waste in a production area, improve capacity utilisation or reduce cycle times? Check that everything is invoiced correctly and that delivery dockets for materials coming in match the delivered items. Check your costing systems. Mind your stock and cash security. Know your margins for each product and look for ways to build sales in high-margin products. High labour costs indicate low productivity. High material costs indicate excessive purchase prices, wastage or theft. Can you reduce distance or movement, improve staff skills, combine or eliminate steps in the production process? Can you redesign products for faster processing and redesign layouts to give a better flow of materials? Can you increase checks and balances to avoid stock losses?

Can you reduce your salary?

Your salary should be in line with market rates for the scope of responsibility and difficulty of the tasks involved in the management of your particular firm. Are you paying yourself too much?

Can you improve earnings before interest and tax (EBIT)?

EBIT indicates how efficient you are at managing operational costs relative to sales. Can you reduce any of your overhead costs, especially the two big ones—rent and wages?

Can you improve retained earnings?

Profits can be paid out as dividends or held in the firm as retained earnings. Retained earnings sustain working capital, owner's equity and growth. Dividends paid to shareholders reduce the capital available for the business.

Balance sheet

There are a number of key questions to ask:

Can you improve the structure of the balance sheet?

Are long-term assets being funded by long-term finance and short-term assets funded by short-term finance? Long-term assets funded by short-term finance is an immediate sign of asset vulnerability and you need to rearrange your financing to match long-lived assets with long-term money.

Can you improve shareholder funds?

Is lack of profits destroying shareholder funds? You need retained earnings or injections of new capital to improve your equity position.

Can you improve the return on owner's equity (ROE)?

ROE is driven by return on assets (ROA) and the ownership ratio. ROA can be improved by increasing profits or reducing assets. Can you maintain current sales with fewer assets by increasing capacity utilisation and reducing cycle times?

Can you improve the debt to equity ratio?

If equity is too low can you put some more equity into the business by rearranging your personal finances, including your mortgages and loans? You can talk to your bank about restructuring all of your borrowings to arrive at a better overall position.

Can you improve the current ratio?

As a rough rule of thumb a current ratio of at least 2:1 is desirable. The surplus of current assets over current liabilities is your working capital. If too much of your equity is tied up funding fixed assets, then working capital will be starved. Can you rearrange your financing to free-up equity for current assets?

Can you improve stock turns and debtor ageing?

Low stock turns indicate poor stock control, lack of sales analysis and operational inefficiency. An increase in the average age of debtors indicates poor credit control and collections. If stock turns are falling, you probably have dead stock that needs to move off the shelves. If debtors' ageing is increasing, you need to put more effort into collections. Then you can reinvest the freed up cash into fast-moving lines and working capital.

Cash flow

There are a number of key questions to ask.

Can you improve your cash flow forecasting and reporting?

Cash flow forecasts provide you with a monitoring tool and by measuring actuals against forecasts you have an early warning system.

Can you improve debtor collections?

An increase in the number of days that accounts receivable are outstanding indicates a deteriorating debt collection rate, and an increasing investment in debtors with the accompanying strain on cash flow.

Can you shorten the production cycle?

Long lead times on material supplies and slow production cycles result in unnecessarily high inventories of raw materials and work in progress. Long production cycles usually are caused by inefficient production control or a product range that is too extensive.

Can any component of wages expense be renegotiated into commission or subcontract arrangements?

By making wages a variable cost instead of a fixed overhead cost, you can lower your break-even point and enjoy better profits.

Marketing strategy

There are a number of key questions to ask.

Can you delete old product lines and liquidate obsolete stock?

Obsolete or slow-selling stock can be blocking your cash flow. You need to identify and eliminate it with clearance sales and discounts.

Can you sharpen the focus on your target market?

Focus your precious resources as accurately as possible into market segments that produce results. Target the most attractive segments on the basis of fit, access and profitability. Lack of segmentation and targeting often explains low sales figures.

Can you realign your product or service design closer to the market's needs?

Good marketing practice involves continuously aligning your offer with the customers' needs and wants.

Production planning

There are a number of key questions to ask.

Can you reduce cycle times?

Long cycle times incur high inventory costs, reduce the productivity of equipment and people, and reduce customer satisfaction. Internet systems connecting suppliers and customers into your system can greatly reduce order-entry and supplier lead times. Long internal cycle times tend to be caused by poor production planning and control methods. Can you fix this problem by hiring some specialised skills or by finding a suitable software solution?

Can you reduce the levels of raw material, work in process and finished goods?

High raw material stocks point to poor performance by suppliers and undesirable lead times. High levels of work in progress may be caused by an excessive product range and poor planning, but also by inefficient production processes. High finished-goods stocks may also result from an excessive product range but it is often caused by a make-to-stock mentality driven by the lack of a good production planning and control system.

Can you adopt just-in-time in parts of your production system?

Just-in-time systems and short planning periods can reduce the total inventory to 24–48 hours' worth of stock in many businesses. Even part progress towards just-in-time in combination with efficient production planning and control will significantly reduce stocks.

Can you improve your quality?

Improved quality produces increased profitability. The prevention of problems reduces manufacturing costs and servicing costs. Improved quality also improves reputation and develops market share, enabling you to command higher prices. Higher prices, in combination with lower costs, produces increased profits.

Managing staff

There are a number of key questions to ask.

Can you improve the 'culture' of the firm?

Your values and beliefs will be reflected in the attitudes and behaviour of your employees. Teamwork and a strong spirit will only grow through careful cultivation, whereas a lack of good spirit will be accompanied by low morale, high staff turnover and low productivity.

Can you improve the systems of communication?

Good communication systems are essential for good organisation and management. Information must be available to staff so that they can perform their tasks. Shared information and experience should be 'networked' within the team.

Can you improve your leadership of the team?

What levels of leadership, motivation and training are present in your business? Your staff can be your competitive advantage. This requires skill in leading and motivating people, and providing support for teamwork so that synergies are achieved.

Can you improve the reward system?

People are motivated by intrinsic factors such as job satisfaction and being included in the decision-making process. If the reward system fails to motivate staff, productivity drops.

Crisis recovery

Recovering from a business crisis is similar to giving first aid at an accident site. First you check for signs of life, then ensure airflow by giving mouth-to-mouth resuscitation, if necessary, and stop any bleeding. When the breathing is normalised and the bleeding is stopped you ask for help—call for an ambulance and seek medical assistance. Once the victim is in medical care the injuries can be diagnosed and a treatment plan put into action.

Check for signs of life

Some businesses cannot be saved. The first task is to see if it is worth an attempt. If the current assets have good realisable value and the current liabilities are not too overpowering in value or in age then there is a chance of recovery. The chance is significantly improved if there are strong fixed assets on the balance sheet, such as land and buildings.

Ensure airflow

Cash flow in a business is like airflow is to life—we need air to breathe. The immediate need is to maximise positive cash flow in whatever way possible. The survival of a business often depends on how decisively you take action. All possible sources of cash must be explored including:

- Selling off stock
- Encouraging cash sales
- Collecting from your debtors (accounts receivable)
- Selling off any surplus equipment
- Leasing rather than owning equipment where possible.

Although asset sales will bring in cash, take care not to handicap the firm's ability to continue to produce and create revenue. If you have no more funds to put into the business, unencumbered assets may be used as collateral to secure further debt finance. The costs must be evaluated along with the reaction of existing creditors to the fact that you are taking on further debt. The types of property that can be pledged to secure financing include:

- Tangible property (equipment and inventory)
- Intangible property (accounts receivable and other convertible investments)
- Land and buildings.

If you cannot borrow more cash, or if the amount you can borrow is not enough, then you will need to look for sources of new equity. It is not easy to interest an equity investor in a troubled firm. In some cases, a creditor may be willing to exchange their debt position for an equity position, thus reducing the need to service that portion of the existing debt. There are turnaround investors who are experienced at seeking out and investing in financially troubled firms. They look for a high return in the future and when the turnaround is successful they can resell their equity in your firm.

Stop any bleeding

Immediately stop all non-critical payments in order to reduce the flow of money out of the business. You may need to take drastic action:

- Cancel unnecessary expenses that are not essential to immediate survival.
- Staff that are not immediately needed should be released. You should involve the staff as much as possible in the crisis decisions and treat people fairly, giving help where possible to find other jobs or to resolve other personal situations. It is essential that remaining staff feel motivated and part of the team if your business is to pull out of trouble and this may depend on how you handle any redundancies.
- Reduce wages and salaries.
- Reduce insurance to a prudent minimum.
- Sublease any surplus space.

Ask for help

Ironically, the only people who can really help are your creditors. The only way to survive a serious business crisis is with the co-operation of the people to whom you owe money, so you need to include them in your recovery plan. Making special arrangements with creditors means being open and honest with them because you need their trust. Supply must continue, even if it is on a cash-on-delivery (COD) basis. Past debt cannot be paid out of current sales, but must wait for profits generated by a successful turnaround. A common process is to 'park' all past debt in a number two account and for the situation to be reviewed in six months. Creditor negotiation is critical to recovery. If creditors press for full payment, it will probably result in the business going into receivership and then everyone loses. A 13-week business plan with cash flow projections can be used in negotiation with creditors and other stakeholders to buy time. Your creditors need to have confidence that you have a workable recovery plan and that you will stick to it.

Diagnosis and treatment

If the business is going to recover fully it may need corrective surgery. If you have been able to negotiate time in which to implement a recovery plan for the business, review the situation to discover what went wrong. If the fundamental cause of the crisis was a lack of sales, then you may need to redesign the marketing mix. Accept that something may have been wrong with your initial ideas for the business and try a different approach based on what you have learned.

Other forms of treatment may include a new management information system, improved production planning and control system, installing a stock control system, correcting production inefficiencies, and installing 'just in time' and 'total quality management' systems. Any work on new product development should be done only if you are certain that immediate extra sales will result.

Self-development exercise D

The accounting information that follows is from a building supplies company that has a number of problems. Read the information and develop a turnaround plan for the next 12 months. Detail the actions you would take and the financial effects of each action. Make sure your recommendations are realistic for a 12-month time frame.

Puhoi Building Supplies Ltd (PBS)

PBS is a family owned building supplies business that trades under its own brand and is not associated with any of the dominant trade and retail building-supplies groups. A family trust owns the land and buildings and the company pays rent to the family trust. Dave Gordon, the owner-manager, is in his late 50s and is hoping to sell the business within the next few years and retire on the proceeds of the sale. The business was started in 1960 by Dave's father and traded profitably until the mid-1990s when competition from Auckland-based suppliers began to take market share away from PBS. Unfortunately, the current poor financial performance is destroying the value of the business and Dave is unlikely to realise a worthwhile sale price for his business.

Customer profiles

Trade and rural customers are strongly driven by cost, quality and delivery performance, while the retail and DIY customers seek a wide range of product choice and high levels of service and convenience. Analysis of the PBS customers shows that sales are dominated by trade customers at 72 per cent, with DIY customers accounting for 17 per cent and rural customers providing the balance of 11 per cent. Only 5 per cent of PBS customers are women.

Supplier relationships

The strategic emphasis in this industry is on building long-term relationships with suppliers based on trust, quality and value. PBS currently deal with a large number of suppliers. The number of suppliers creates some redundant or duplicated supply arrangements and limited purchases with any one supplier, leading to a lack of close relationships with any of the key suppliers.

Competitors

The national building supplies market is very competitive and dominated by a small number of major organisations. Market share is always vulnerable to existing competition, new entrants, competing product innovations, and new channels of distribution such as the internet. Currently PBS has no significant building supplies competitor in the Puhoi district but a number of builders are using out-of-district suppliers for their main requirements. Also a new garden centre has opened recently which has curtailed the small amount of garden product sales that PBS previously enjoyed.

Products and services

PBS specialises in a range of products and services including:

Timber	Plumbing and electrical products
Building products and materials	Building plant and equipment hire
Building tools and electrical equipment	Garden products
Hardware and paint	Homeware

Industry benchmarks and operational details

Industry gross margin	25–30%
Industry occupancy cost	4–6%
Industry staff cost	9–12%
Yard area m²	7000
Building area m²	1000
Staff (ftes)	10
Total annual invoices	15 000

PBS Annual Accounts			
PROFIT/LOSS ACCOUNT		**BALANCE SHEET**	
SALES (20% cash)	2 500 000	Owner's Equity	300 000
Opening Stock	380 000		
Purchases	1 980 000		
Closing Stock	(420 000)	Current Assets (stock)	420 000
Cost of Sales	1 940 000	(debtors)	420 000
		Fixed Assets	350 000
GROSS PROFIT	**560 000**	Intangible Assets	100 000
Less Expenses		Total Assets	1 290 000
Acc Levy	2500		
Accounting	3500	Current Liabilities	
Advertising	7000	Creditors	540 000
Bank Charges	2000	Bank OD	50 000
Cleaning & Rubbish	4000	Total	590 000
Electricity	8000		
Entertainment	0	Term Liabilities	400 000
Fringe Benefit Tax	0		
General	2000	**Total Liabilities**	**990 000**
Hire Purchase & Lease	0		
Insurance	6000	**Net Assets**	**300 000**
Licences & Registration	700		
Legal & Consultancy	800		
Marketing Fee	7200		
Motor Vehicle Expenses	1500		
Occupancy Costs	150 000		
Packaging	2000		
Repairs & Maintenance	10 000		
Security	700		
Staff Wages (Sales)	220 000		
Staff Wages (Admin)	50 000		
Stationery/Printing/Postage	2000		
Subscriptions	500		
Telephone & Fax	2000		
Training	500		
Travel/Conferences	500		
Uniforms	2000		
Total Expenses	485 400		
NET PROFIT	74 600		
[Before Depreciation, Interest, Taxes & Shareholders Salaries]			
Depreciation	50 000		
Interest	40 000		
Shareholders Salaries	50 600		
Total Business Expenses	**626 000**		
NET PROFIT BEFORE TAX	**(66 000)**		

Exercise

* Using this information, identify where the problems are occurring in the existing business.
* List up to 10 steps that are achievable over the next 12 months to correct the poor performance.
* Identify the 12-month outcomes from your steps—in terms of cost savings, cash flow improvements, and profit results.
* Use the template below as a guide to present your recommendations.

	List each problem area that you can identify	Describe the remedial action that is required for each problem	Report the overall expected financial benefits form each action (Improvement minus cost of improvement)
1			
2			
3			
4			
5			
6			
7			
8			
9			
10			

Turn to page 336 for a sample solution.

Feedback on self-development exercises

Self-development exercise A

Achieving success in a small business is much easier for some people than for others. The objective of this exercise is to help you to reach your own conclusions about self-employment as a career alternative for you. It is important to remember that questionnaires like this are always subject to some degree of uncertainty. If you feel strongly that this one has incorrectly assessed some aspect of your personality then you are probably right. Nevertheless, it should help you to recognise some things about yourself that you may not have previously known. The characteristics assessed are listed here.

Extroverted or introverted?

Count the number of 'a' boxes you ticked in the column beginning with question 1 on the answer sheet. A score of 7–10 indicates that you have an *extroverted* personality. A score of 0–3 indicates that you have an *introverted* personality. A score of 4–6 indicates no clear tendency between extroversion and introversion.

Success in organising and operating a small business is highly correlated with an individual's tendency toward extroversion. Extroverted individuals are sociable, active, occasionally impulsive, and enjoy working with people. They draw their energy from others and their charm and charisma helps them to gain support from customers, staff and suppliers. Introverted individuals are territorial, reflective, hesitant, and prefer to work in solitude. They find it difficult to develop the kind of interpersonal relationships that attract customers, motivate staff and encourage suppliers to look after them.

Rationalist or humanist?

Count the number of 'b' boxes you ticked in the column beginning with question 2 on the answer sheet. A score of 7–10 indicates that you have a *rationalist* approach. A score of 0–3 indicates that you have a *humanist* approach. A score of 4–6 indicates no clear tendency toward one approach or the other.

In order to achieve success in a business of your own you need to be able to make rational decisions. Rational decision-makers generally make logical decisions based on the facts alone, and ignore the feelings of other people. Humanists usually consider people first when they make decisions. They are very sensitive about other people's feelings, and they tend to approach business decisions with a great deal of compassion. The analytical, logical and somewhat impersonal rationalist has been shown to be associated with survival and success in small business. Unfortunately, the sensitive and compassionate humanist does not tend to perform as well.

Flexibility

Count the number of 'a' boxes you ticked in the column beginning with question 3 on the answer sheet. A score of 7–10 indicates that you are *flexible*. A score of 0–3 indicates that you are *inflexible*. A score of 4–6 indicates no clear tendency one way or the other.

Flexible individuals accept change as natural. They may have many projects under way at the same time. Sometimes they even appear to be indecisive because they like to keep their options open. Inflexible individuals like a planned, predetermined way of life. They have a tendency to resist change and they like to finish one project before beginning the next. Having made a decision, inflexible individuals are not likely to change their minds.

Successful small business operators are flexible. This flexibility is related to the ability to deal with risk spontaneously and indicates a special tolerance for ambiguous and uncertain situations. Flexibility is not the indecision that it may appear to be—it actually consists of a series of revised decisions that reflect new information as it appears.

Creativity

Count the number of 'b' boxes you ticked in the column beginning with question 4 on the answer sheet. A score of 7–10 indicates that you have a *high capacity for creativity*. A score of 0–3 indicates that you have a *low capacity for creativity*. A score of 4–6 indicates that you have average creativity.

Success in a small business is directly related to an individual's capacity for creativity. Creative individuals are idea generators while non-creative individuals tend to use the ideas of others. If you are creative then your inventiveness and intuition will enable you to visualise how you will react in new situations. Your creative intuition also plays an important role in reducing risk by compensating for a lack of information. If you are not creative, you will suffer from a competitive disadvantage that will probably reflect itself in the performance of your business.

Ability to plan

Count the number of 'a' boxes you ticked in the column beginning with question 5 on the answer sheet. A score of 7–10 indicates that you are an *effective planner*. A score of 0–3 indicates that you are an *ineffective planner*. A score of 4–6 indicates that you are an average planner.

A number of research studies have shown that successful small business operators have the ability to set realistic goals and plan how they are going to achieve them. If you are an effective planner you will be at ease with formulating and implementing an overall plan for your business. If you are an ineffective planner you may have a problem not only with the establishment of your business but also with its ongoing operation.

Initiative

Count the number of 'a' boxes you ticked in the column beginning with question 6 on the answer sheet. A score of 7–10 indicates that you have a *high degree of initiative*. A score of 0–3 indicates that you have a *low degree of initiative*. A score of 4–6 indicates average initiative.

Many individuals who intend to become self-employed simply never end up in business. They include the procrastinators, those who lack self-confidence, and others who see too many hurdles to overcome. For these individuals the missing ingredient is initiative. There is considerable agreement among researchers that successful small-business operators actively seek and take the initiative. They willingly put themselves in situations where they are personally responsible for success or failure. Successful small business operators are doers: they are goal-oriented and action-oriented. They are very conscious about how they use their time and they are appalled by wasted time.

Independence

Successful small business operators have been shown to have a strong sense of independence. This sense of independence, however, stems from two needs: one is the need to achieve autonomy in one's life, while the other is the need to achieve security and stability. Count the number of 'b' boxes you ticked in the column beginning with question 7 on the answer sheet. A score of 7–10 indicates that your sense of independence is based upon the need for *autonomy*. A score of 0–3 indicates that your sense of independence is based upon the need for *stability and security*. A score of 4–6 indicates that your sense of independence is balanced between these two needs.

Autonomy is important to individuals who do not wish to be bound by the constraints of large organisations. They have an over-riding need to do things in their own way, at their own pace, and according to their own standards. Therefore they tend to be pulled towards work situations in which they can satisfy their need for autonomy. Security and stability are important to individuals who want their future to be certain. Not every small business operator wants or needs unlimited growth. If they can achieve the security and stability they seek, then these individuals are content. People are different and want different things out of life, so it is important to recognise these differences and to take them into account when contemplating the type of business that is best for you.

Sense of purpose

What is your purpose for becoming self-employed? Are you drawn by the challenge of starting and managing your own business? Or will self-employment enable you to achieve a certain lifestyle? Count the 'b' boxes you ticked in the column beginning with question 8 on the answer sheet. A score of 7–10 indicates that your purpose for going into business is based upon the need for *challenge*. A score of 0–3 indicates that your purpose for going into business is based upon the need for an integrated *lifestyle*. A score of 4–6 indicates a balanced purpose between challenge and lifestyle.

Some individuals look upon self-employment in terms of the pure challenge of organising and operating their own business. They define success in terms of overcoming obstacles, solving problems and winning against competition. The type of business they choose and the way they run it provides an ongoing opportunity for challenges. Other individuals look upon self-employment as a way to integrate and balance their family, career and personal development. This is not independence—it is the need for a balanced way of life in which career decisions do not have to dominate. It places a premium on things like where to live, the amount of time spent working, and the whole family-versus-business relationship.

Emphasis

What emphasis will you place on your role as a small business operator? Do you see yourself as a general manager or are you more inclined to pursue a particular technical or functional specialty? Count the number of 'a' boxes you ticked in the column beginning with question 9 on the answer sheet. A score of 7–10 indicates an emphasis on *general management*. A score of 0–3 indicates an emphasis on a *technical or functional specialty*. A score of 4–6 indicates an equal emphasis on both.

Some individuals want a business in which their overall managerial efforts are what matters. They want to exercise their capacity to identify and solve problems, to influence and control other people, and to be stimulated by crises. A general manager needs staff to actually operate their business, so they seek somewhat larger operations that can support the necessary payroll. Other individuals have strong talents in a particular functional or technical specialisation. They build their sense of identity around the content of their work and see themselves as a specialist. These individuals find the work itself intrinsically meaningful and satisfying. They look forward to their own business in terms of that specialisation. They tend to shun management responsibilities and usually prefer a smaller operation with fewer staff.

Determination

Determination is much more than initiative. It is demonstrated by a well thought-out, assertive action plan driven by a deep desire to succeed in your own business. Count the number of 'a' boxes you ticked in the column beginning with question 10 on the answer sheet. A score of 7–10 indicates strong determination. A score of 0–3 indicates weak determination. A score of 4–6 indicates average determination.

Determination generally makes the difference between actually starting a business and just talking about it. Being goal-oriented is not enough—what you also need is the determination to make it happen. Successful small business operators tend to believe strongly in themselves and their ability to achieve the goals they set. They believe that events in their life are mainly self-determined and that they have a major influence on their personal destiny. They possess an intense level of commitment to overcoming hurdles, solving problems and completing the job.

Self-development exercise B

	Jan	Feb	Mar	Apr	May	Jun	Jul	Aug	Sep	Oct	Nov	Dec
Kilometres												
2-tonne truck	8500	8500	8500	0	8500	8500	12 500	12 500	12 500	12 500	12 500	12 500
6-tonne truck	3000	3000	3000	3000	3000	3000	0	4300	4300	4300	4300	4300
Receipts												
2-tonne truck	19 550	19 550	19 550	0	19 550	19 550	28 750	28 750	28 750	28 750	28 750	28 750
6-tonne truck	12 000	12 000	12 000	12 000	12 000	12 000	0	17 200	17 200	17 200	17 200	17 200
Total	31 550	31 550	31 550	12 000	31 550	31 550	28 750	45 950	45 950	45 950	45 950	45 950
Disbursements												
Variable cost 2TT	1190	1190	1190	0	1190	1190	1750	1750	1750	1750	1750	1750
Variable cost 6TT	1320	1320	1320	1320	1320	1320	0	1892	1892	1892	1892	1892
Lease payments	5200	5200	5200	5200	5200	5200	5200	5200	5200	5200	5200	5200
Fixed costs	19 800	19 800	19 800	19 800	19 800	19 800	19 800	19 800	19 800	19 800	19 800	19 800
Overhauls				5830								
GST				200			4425					
Provisional tax			13 500				13 500				13 500	
Total	27 510	27 510	41 010	32 350	27 510	27 510	44 675	28 642	28 642	28 642	42 642	28 642
Beginning cash balance	835	4875	8915	(545)	(20 895)	(16 855)	(12 815)	(28 740)	(11 432)	5876	23 184	26 492
Net cash flow	4040	4040	(9460)	(20 350)	4040	4040	(15 925)	17 308	17 308	17 308	3308	17 308
Ending cash balance	4875	8915	(545)	(20 895)	(16 855)	(12 815)	(28 740)	(11 432)	5876	23 184	26 492	43 800

It is clear that you will not generate enough cash in March to pay the bills that come due. April has a serious cash flow shortage and you could be out of business after the fourth month. The positive cash flow in May and June improves the position slightly but in July a further cash crisis will occur increasing the overdraft to $28 740. Steady positive cash flows beginning in August will repay the overdraft and you will finish the year with a $43 800 bank balance. Now you can go to your bank and show them how much finance you will need, when you will need it and when you will be able to pay it back. Without cash flow budgeting, you may not be able to anticipate your needs until it is too late.

Self-development exercise C

Check your total score with these results.

Greater than 80

Your preparation is highly advanced and you are ready to export. At this point you can use the services of New Zealand Trade and Enterprise to help you take the first steps into exporting and to develop your network of contacts in the export market.

Between 60 and 80

Your preparation is advanced. You may need some further help in developing a full export strategy and this service is available from New Zealand Trade and Enterprise. NZTE can help with market research, visits to trade fairs, introductions to buyers, agents or distributors. They may even help you find joint venture partners or offshore investors.

Between 35 and 59

Your company is on the right track but needs further preparation before exporting is recommended. Your weaknesses are identified by the scores in each section and you need to develop a plan to lift your business into the export-ready category by improving your weak areas. 'The Guide to Exporting' publication available from NZTE will give you directions on how to improve your position.

Less than 35

You are under-prepared to export at this stage. There are a number of things that you need to work on before you are ready for the export challenge:

- Firstly, you need to establish a stronger domestic position for your business, preferably with national distribution.
- You need to develop products and services that are suitable for export markets but are not too dissimilar from what you already produce.
- You need to be in a strong financial position with enough financial resources available for export marketing and product development.
- Your knowledge of the management and operational issues involved in exporting needs to be further developed. You may want to talk to other exporters, your local branch of Export NZ, freight forwarders, your accountant or your bank to find out more about exporting.

Self-development exercise D

The following list covers a plan for Puhoi Building Supplies followed by a forecast of the overall effects.

The main problem areas	Remedial action that is required for each problem	Budgeted financial effects
Cash flow		
1 Debtor Turns	Improve the collection of debts—reduce the days-debtors from 77 to 60 days	93 000 (cash in)
2 Fixed Asset Turns	Lease or hire low-utilised assets and sell off redundant equipment	50 000 (cash in)
Profitability		
1 Occupancy Cost	Negotiate a new lease contract, and/or sublet some of the yard/building space to reduce the occupancy cost to 5 per cent of sales	25 000 (cost reduction)
2 Staff Cost	Review work/job descriptions and examine potentials for training and redeployment (into sales-related areas?) or redundancy	3500 (extra training cost)
3 Gross Margin	Target an increase in gross margin by 3 points—check pricing/invoicing accuracy—check for slippage—negotiate better purchase prices—change the stock mix—encourage DIY customers—promote high-margin lines	76 000 (profit increase)
4 Interest Cost	Apply the free cash gained from the cash flow actions above, to lower the highest cost debt (first the overdraft @ 12 per cent, then the term loan @ 9 per cent)	6000 (from OD) 8370 (from term loan)
Marketing		
1 Low Average Invoice Value	Build relationships with trade customers to increase their spend with PBS	Increase in revenue
2 Stock Mix	Change the stock mix to attract and build the DIY sector—this will improve gross margin, cash flow and total sales	Increase in revenue, margin and cash flow

	The main problem areas	Remedial action that is required for each problem	Budgeted financial effects
3	Branding	Negotiate entry into one of the major-brand trading groups (e.g Placemakers, Mitre 10, Benchmark, ITM). This will improve stock purchase costs and gross margin, market share and revenue, and internal transaction processes and reporting	Increase in revenue, margin and cash flow
4	Market Share/ Revenue	Target a 10 per cent increase in sales from the results of the three actions listed above to give $250 000 of new sales at the higher margin	62 500 (profit increase)

If we apply these changes to the current financial reports and allow the owner-manager a proper salary, the actions above will produce the following forecast of financial performance and financial position after the next 12 months. The affected areas have been highlighted.

PBS Annual Accounts (12-month forecast after remedial actions)

PROFIT/LOSS ACCOUNT		BALANCE SHEET	
SALES (20% cash)	**2 750 000**		
Opening Stock	420 000	Owner's Equity	300 000
Purchases	2 051 500		
Closing Stock	420 000	Current Assets (stock)	420 000
Cost of Sales	2 051 500	(debtors)	327 000
		Fixed Assets	300 000
GROSS PROFIT	**698 500**	Intangible Assets	100 000
Less Expenses		**Total Assets**	**1 147 000**
Acc Levy	2500		
Accounting	3500	Current Liabilities	
Advertising	7000	Creditors	540 000
Bank Charges	2000	Bank OD	0
Cleaning & Rubbish	4000	Total	540 000
Electricity	8000		
Entertainment	0	Term Liabilities	307 000
Fringe Benefit Tax	0		
General	2000	**Total Liabilities**	**847 000**
Hire Purchase & Lease	0		
Insurance	6000	**Net Assets**	**300 000**
Licences & Registration	700		
Legal & Consultancy	800		
Marketing Fee	7200		
Motor Vehicle Expenses	1500		
Occupancy Costs	125 000		
Packaging	2000		
Repairs & Maintenance	10 000		
Security	700		
Staff Wages (Sales)	220 000		
Staff Wages (Admin)	50 000		
Stationery/Printing/Postage	2000		
Subscriptions	500		
Telephone & Fax	2000		
Training	4000		
Travel/Conferences	500		
Uniforms	2000		
Total Expenses	**463 900**		
NET PROFIT	**234 600**		
[Before Depn, Int, Tax & Shareholders Salaries]			
Depreciation	50 000		
Interest	25 630		
Shareholders Salaries	100 000		
Total Business Expenses	**639 530**		
NET PROFIT BEFORE TAX	**58 970**		

Index